"*Love & Vodka* is a warm, funny tale of an American who follows his heart to Ukraine. There he discovers a world where men are meant to be strong, drink copious amounts of vodka and resuscitate cars seemingly beyond repair. Will he or won't he win his girl? Read on to find out in this zany tour of Ukraine through the eyes of a young Michigander."

  — Susan Viets, author, *Picnic at the Iron Curtain*

"Imagine a world where people think, act, and respond differently to the way you've always known—and then let R.J. Fox take you there with this book. Not enough has been written about everyday life in the former Soviet Union, and it's captured beautifully here."

  — Tony Hawks, bestselling author of *Round Ireland with a Fridge* and *Playing the Moldovans at Tennis*

"For all of us who wish we were more adventurous in travel and in love, R.J. Fox is the perfect guide to Ukraine and the heart. *Love & Vodka* is funny, moving, and full of surprises."

  — Laura Kasischke, author, *The Life Before Her Eyes* and *Space, in Chains*

"Sharply observed and wickedly funny. When romance goes Ukrainian."

  — Jack Barker, editor *TravelMag: The Independent Spirit*

"*Love & Vodka* is an old-fashioned love story told with uncommon wit and unabashed warmth. R.J. Fox guides his readers through the dangers of cold showers, straight liquor, and unfamiliar customs, to sweet new romance under gentle Ukrainian rain."

  — Ana Maria Spagna, author, *Test Ride on the Sunnyland Bus*

"An utterly charming romp of a novel, rich with humor and culture shock—and at its heart, a solid gold love story. Don't miss it!"

  — Liz Crowe, author of the award-winning *Stewart Realty* series

"*Love & Vodka* is an easy ride to this foreign land. The kind of travelogue you want to take to bed or the beach or the metro … one to be read when you have the time to truly savor a travel experience. It's a blend of love story, light history lessons and a close look at Ukraine through the eyes of a young, American man."

  — Adriana Páramo, author, *Looking for Esperanza*

LOVE & VODKA

ABOUT THE AUTHOR

R.J. FOX is the award-winning writer of several short stories, plays, poems, and fifteen feature length screenplays. Two of his screenplays have been optioned to Hollywood. His work has been published in numerous journals and magazines.

He is also the writer/director/editor of several award-winning short films. His stage directing debut led to an Audience Choice Award at the Canton One-Acts Festival in Canton, MI.

Fox graduated from the University of Michigan with a B.A. in English and a minor in Communications and received a Masters of Arts in Teaching from Wayne State University in Detroit, MI.

In addition to moonlighting as a writer, independent filmmaker, and saxophonist, Fox teaches English and video production in the Ann Arbor Public Schools, where he uses his own dreams of writing and filmmaking to inspire his students to follow their own dreams. He has also worked in public relations at Ford Motor Company and as a newspaper reporter.

He resides in Ann Arbor, Michigan.

Visit www.foxplots.com or follow him on Twitter @foxwriter7.

To Anne Gautreau

ACKNOWLEDGMENTS

I would like to thank the following: Anne Gautreau (who knew I was writer before I did, sparking a dream I refused to let die), Jon and Laurie Wilson (for taking a chance on me when nobody else would), Ellen (for reminding me who I was and for your continued support and understanding), my two beautiful children, my parents, my sisters, my Grandpa Fox and Grandma Kolleth, my Godmother Jo-Jo, Matthew and Mandy Meyer, Mike Hendin, Steve Holowicki, E.J. Holowicki, Greg Marcks, Lev Golinkin, Maria Karimova, Maxim Dyukov, Michael Ivanitskiy, Levon Mesprov, Yelena Zilberman, Katerina Rekowski, Kyle Wilson, Davy Rothbart, Jeff Kass, Susan Viets, Tony Hawks, Laura Kasischke, Liz Crowe, Ana Maria Spagna, Adriana Páramo, Don Brown, Gary France, John McKeighan, Svetlana Dembitskaya, Alexander Alexandrov, Mary Ann Schmedlen, Alison Eberts, Duncan Long, Jack Barker/*Travel Mag UK*, Michelle Young/*Untapped Cities*, *Yareah Magazine*, *Cold Noon*, *Airplane Reading*, in*Travel Magazine*, *The Commonline Journal*, *Hack Writers*, *Riverteeth*, Ann Arbor Area Writer's Group, Starbucks, the Plymouth Coffee Bean, Moby, Ukraine, love, vodka, my students, every person who told me not to give up, every person who told me to give up (my fuel), every rejection letter (more fuel) and finally, every person who ever asked about my writing or read my writing over the years; you'll never know how much it means to me. And, last but not least, to the real-life Katya and her family—thank you ... and I'm sorry.

Note regarding the spelling of "Dnipropetrovsk" vs. "Dnepropetrovsk"

After Ukrainian independence in 1991, and in a conscious move to reclaim Ukrainian culture, language, sovereignty and identity, the Ukrainian government renamed the city from the Russian spelling "Dnepropetrovsk" to the Ukrainian spelling "Dnipropetrovsk." Throughout the book, I use the Ukrainian spelling "Dnipropetrovsk" in preference to the Russian spelling. Following a law passed in 2015 in Ukraine to eliminate all place names honoring the Soviet past, a new name for the city will be determined.

CONTENTS

CALIFORNIA DREAMIN'

Traveling alone is something everyone should do at least once in his or her lifetime. It allows you to really focus in on every moment, free from distraction, creating a deeply spiritual experience that cannot be replicated when traveling with companions. Cliché as it may sound, you really get to know yourself.

Traveling by myself on the first leg of my trip to Hollywood had been exhilarating. However, as I reached the midway point, I no longer relished my lone-wolf status. As I wandered the grounds of the Universal Studios Hollywood theme park, I found myself in a deepening melancholy mood. I quickly realized that an amusement park was not the ideal venue for a solo expedition—especially with all the time spent waiting in line.

Contributing to my mood was a flood of memories from a family vacation taken during my senior year of high school to Orlando, Florida. One of the highlights of that trip was a visit to Universal Studios. It had been the perfect family vacation in every sense of the word. Reflecting back on those sun-soaked days—surrounded by my entire family—provided stark contrast to my present circumstances: alone in the damp, chilly, half-empty movie-themed park, chasing pipe dreams like tumbleweed though empty backlot streets—a symbol of my elusive Hollywood dream.

As I made my way around the park, I found myself desperately wishing I had someone with whom I could share this experience.

And the next thing I knew—I did.

I first spotted her in line for the *Terminator* ride. She was standing a few feet in front of me in the "waiting room" of the theater. My first view of her became one of those moments where time stands still—one that you keep on permanent display on life's memory mantel. She was beautiful in a classic, "Euro" sort of way: blue jeans; blue jean jacket; red shirt; little butterfly hair clips; tap, tap, tapping her foot to the techno beat of the cheesy introductory *Skynet* video as we awaited entrance into the main auditorium.

She appeared to be alone, too, and I wondered to myself: *What are the odds two people would be walking through an amusement park alone? She must be here with someone who is perhaps not a fan of Austrian cyborgs, therefore sitting out this particular attraction.*

After the introductory video finished, the doors to the auditorium opened. The crowd surged in and I promptly lost sight of her. After I settled into my seat, I peered around the theater hoping to locate her. I spotted her in the front row. For a brief moment, I considered catching up with her after the show, but instantly realized that I would never act upon this impulse. I knew myself well enough to know that simply approaching a female stranger was not in my repertoire.

As the show ended, I stood up to make sure I didn't lose sight of her. But as the large crowd filed out, I lost her almost immediately—assumingly forever—as I had so many girls before her.

I tried to erase my memory of her as I typically do with any lost opportunity (real or perceived), and continued exploring the park, despite my escalating boredom. But no matter how much I tried, I couldn't stop thinking about this most beautiful stranger. I spent the next several hours hoping that we would somehow cross paths again by some magical twist of fate, but as the day wore on, I realized it was not meant to be and decided it was time to head back to my hotel—but not before stopping to grab a bag of Peanut M&M's from a vending machine.

As I turned around, there she was, heading toward the entrance of the *E.T.* Ride—also munching on Peanut M&M's. I had no intention of riding this ride, remembering how lame it was when I rode it with my family in Florida. But now, I had no choice but to experience it again.

Without hesitation, I made a mad dash toward the line. I had no game plan whatsoever, but that didn't matter. I was on autopilot, which for me, probably meant that I should have prepared for a crash landing. As I approached the front of the line, I watched her climb onto one of the bicycles. The attendant turned to me and asked: "Just one?"

"Yes, just one," I replied.

The attendant proceeded to direct me to the bicycle right next to her.

And there we were. There was no turning back.

The great bicycle chase was about to begin.

"So … have you been on this before?" I awkwardly blurted out.

"No. But I love *E.T.*," she replied. *At least she's not ignoring me,* I thought. I detected an accent; eastern European perhaps?

"What about you?" she asked.

"Oh, I've been on it before," I said. "I hated it."

"So why are you on it again?" she asked, throwing me for a loop.

Because I'm following you! I almost said, before scrambling to think of something less stalker-esque.

"Uh … I thought I'd give it a second chance," I replied.

Phew.

"I'm sure it won't be as fun as the *Terminator* ride," she said. For a moment, I wondered whether she might have recognized me, but she seemed to give no indication.

"You liked that one?" I asked.

"I *loved* it! I went on it, like, six times! *Terminator's* my favorite movie. That ride is so amazing!"

"As amazing as this?" I joked.

"But I thought you didn't like it?" she replied, puzzled.

"No, no, I'm joking. This ride is horrible," I said.

She looked a little confused and laughed nervously, adding "It's not so bad. *E.T.* is so cute."

"But he looks like a dog turd," I replied.

"Turd?! What is *turd*?"

Oh boy. That is a question one never thinks they will have to answer. I hesitantly blurted out, "poop!"

"Oh, like a shit?"

"Yeah, like a shit!" I said. We both laughed uncomfortably, continuing our seemingly insignificant chit-chat until the ride came to an end.

One of the "highlights" of the *E.T.* ride is that the animatronic *E.T.* says a personal "goodbye" to each and every passing guest in the ride's final stretch. However, as far as that little alien asshole was concerned, I might as well have not existed. My name was not mentioned at all.

"Hey! That little turd didn't say my name!" I said in mock dismay.

She laughed. "Didn't you record your name?"

"What do you mean?" I asked.

"In the line at the start. There was a microphone. You were supposed to tell your name."

"Oh man, I must have accidentally passed it," I replied. *Rushed past it, more like; while pursuing you.*

As we disembarked, I assumed we would go our separate ways. It was fun while it lasted. And more importantly, a major stepping-stone in my social development. I had initiated a conversation with a female.

Things were looking up.

I gestured for her to walk ahead of me as we proceeded toward the exit to the ride, unable to think of anything worthwhile to say amid the unavoidable awkwardness. Standing outside the *E.T.* ride, under a light mist, it soon became clear that neither of us was in a big rush to go our separate ways. I stared down at the damp ground sheepishly, before summoning up the courage to break the silence:

"So … if you don't mind my asking," I began. "Where are you from?"

"Ukraine," she replied.

"Oh, the Ukraine? Wow," I said, innocently.

"No … just Ukraine," she replied.

"Huh?"

"Just Ukraine. There's no 'the.'"

"Uh? Oh. Sorry about that," I said, embarrassed.

"No, don't be sorry. It's an American thing to call it 'The Ukraine.' I don't know why, but I think people assume it was just a region or something in Russia during the Soviet Union—not its own country. It would be like calling Germany 'The Germany.'"

I laughed, adding, "Well, then again we are *the* United States."

She laughed. I interpreted that as a cue for me to ask her if she wanted to join me for another ride.

"I would love to," she said, looking at her watch, "but my friend is probably waiting for me."

"*Boy*friend?" I asked, with uncharacteristic bluntness.

"No. Family friend," she replied.

"Could I at least walk you to the gate?" I asked.

"I wouldn't forgive if you if you didn't," she said, with an inviting smile.

We headed up the long escalator to the park's main level and continued our conversation.

"By the way, I'm Bobby," I said, offering my hand.

"Katya," she said, shaking it.

"Nice to meet you, Katya," I said enthusiastically.

"Nice to meet you too, Bobby," she replied.

"So … do you live here in California?" she asked.

"No, Detroit," I said, expecting the usual half-grimace/half-sympathy expression most people give when I tell them where I'm from. Instead, her face lit up and she appeared genuinely impressed.

"Do you know Henry Ford?" she asked.

"Henry Ford? No, he died a long time ago," I replied.

"I'm joking!" she laughed. "I know he's dead. I read a book about Henry Ford when I was little and have been interested in Detroit ever since."

I smiled sheepishly, adding "I'm actually from Dearborn—a suburb of Detroit and ..."

"Henry Ford's birthplace," Katya interjected.

"Yes!" I said, impressed with her knowledge.

"So ... what brings you to California?" I asked. "Are you an actress?"

"No. But maybe I should be ... then I can co-star with Arnold Schwarzenegger," she said with a smile, before explaining how she was an exchange student from Ukraine, staying in Mississippi, but visiting family friends in California.

"So why are you here alone?" I asked.

"Oh, they've been here so many times, they decided just to drop me off. But I kind of like traveling alone, though."

"Me too!" I said. "But to be honest, I was starting to get sick of myself, wishing I had someone to talk to."

"And here we are," she replied.

"Yes. Here we are," I said.

"So, why are you here?" she asked.

I explained my reasons for being in Los Angeles—that I had come to attend a couple of screenwriting and film workshops and meet with industry contacts in hot pursuit of my Hollywood dream.

Her face lit up as she listened in rapt attention.

I had never met someone who was so impressed with the fact that I was trying to be a screenwriter. She responded in a way that suggested that I *was* a screenwriter—not a *wannabe*. For a writer, this kind of attention is priceless.

"So, are you going to miss the U.S. when you leave?" I asked.

"As much as I miss my family and friends back in Ukraine," she said, "I'm definitely going to be sad to leave. But I also know that I'll be back someday. I don't know how and when, but I'll be back. I do know that this trip has changed my outlook on my country in many ways."

"How so?" I asked.

"How much further Ukraine still needs to go," she replied.

"How do you mean? It can't be that bad," I said, cluelessly giving her country the benefit of the doubt.

"By Ukrainian standards, I'm actually pretty optimistic," she explained. "There are few options. In life. In work. In love. In Ukraine, men are either jerks, criminals, or mama's boys ... or most of the time, all three."

"Wow. Sounds like a great place!" I said, sarcastically.

"How is this so?" she asked, puzzled.

I think the sarcasm was lost on her. As I would come to learn, sarcasm does not exist in Ukrainian humor. In fact, *humor*—at least how I understand it—doesn't really exist in Ukrainian humor. Or, shall I say, it's simply a different type of humor that doesn't exactly translate very well. From what I eventually gathered, Ukrainians pretty much say the same thing about American humor.

"It can't really be that bad, can it?" I asked, naively.

"Perhaps you should come visit sometime and see for yourself?" she replied. It felt like both an invite and a threat.

"You never know," I said, even though the former Soviet Union was not exactly high on my list of future travel plans.

Before we knew it, we had reached the exit gates. The light mist had turned into a steady drizzle. Somehow, we had managed to float from one end of the park to the other, with no recollection of getting from point A to point B—the magical hallmark of any great conversation.

It was at that point that I realized the depth of our connection, despite not fully understanding it.

"So ... I guess this is it," she said in a regretful tone.

"Where were you earlier in the day?" I asked.

"Where were you?!" she replied.

We stood in the rain, prolonging the inevitable notion that two strangers who—for a brief moment, *weren't*—were about to become strangers again. Strangers who randomly stumbled upon one another's paths before once again going their separate ways. We encounter so many strangers in life who bear no impact—yet we both sensed that this particular chance meeting meant ... *everything*.

She opened her handbag and pulled out a small notepad and pen.

"Here, give me your e-mail address," she said, thrusting the pen and notepad toward me.

I eagerly obliged.

As I scribbled down my e-mail address, I couldn't help but notice the unusual, hand-carved wooden pen in the shape of a crucifix.

"Cool pen," I said.

"Yeah. A friend of mine from Africa gave it to me." she said "He told me it's a reminder that no matter how far away we may be, we all sleep under the same sky."

I handed the pen and notepad back to her. She scribbled her e-mail address onto a separate page of her notepad, tore the page out, and handed it to me. Just at that moment, a car horn sounded. She looked over toward the car and waved.

"I have to get going," she said.

A sudden sense of melancholy rose up inside me.

I offered her my hand.

"It was great meeting you, Katya," I said.

She shook it. "You too, Bobby."

I managed a half-smile.

She slowly pulled away, despite the obvious and sudden magnetism that was keeping us together.

She walked through the turnstile and over to the waiting car. Before climbing into the car she turned, smiled, and waved.

And then, just like that, she was gone.

And I was once again alone.

PART I

1

A UKRAINE ODYSSEY

Following our fateful Hollywood encounter, Katya and I kept in touch by e-mail, initially writing to each other every other week. In June—three months after we met—Katya left Mississippi and returned to Ukraine. Meanwhile—after months of soul-searching—I decided to extend my college career by going back to obtain a teaching certificate.

We continued e-mailing. Weekly. Then daily. Then several times a day. E-mails became instant messages. And before long, Katya had eagerly read all of my scripts, showing more interest in my writing than anyone ever had in my life.

Next thing we knew, we were in love—despite not really knowing what to do with it, considering the vast geographical distance that separated us. We knew for certain that we had to see one another again. We just had to figure out how.

The new year arrived, shrouded in that rose-colored, euphoric blanket known as being in love: a magical blanket that makes you feel as though all was right with the world, that the grass was greener, the sky was bluer, and everything else was just … better.

Next thing I knew, I was standing at the counter of a local jeweler—choosing an engagement ring. Next—following the approval of Katya, and more importantly, her parents—I booked a flight to Ukraine for mid-August. All the while, I kept this little secret completely to myself—mostly out of fear that if I told my friends or family about it, I would realize *how crazy I was*—either by simply hearing it spoken aloud, or by their reactions. Then again, I thought, perhaps telling someone about it would somehow make it feel more real—or force me to realize how completely insane I was.

Since I was still living at home, I figured I should probably inform my parents of my imminent trip to the former Soviet Union. I began by showing them a photograph of Katya, assuming that they would be so taken in by her natural beauty, they would surely understand my feelings.

"This is my pen pal," I began nonchalantly—neglecting of course to mention that I was madly in love—with a girl I had met for about one hour at an amusement park in Los Angeles, who lived half way around the world.

"She's from Ukraine," I said, awaiting the inevitable response.

"The Ukraine? What?!" my father exclaimed, as though I were referring to an alien galaxy.

"It's just Ukraine, dad," I explained. 'There's no, 'the.'"

My mom's response was more understated. "The Ukraine? Wow. Where's that?" She paused for a moment before adding "She's beautiful." I was quite sure that in my mom's mind, this translated into the fact that I would have no chance with a girl who looked like that.

"Oh, and guess what? *I'm in love with her!*" I blurted out, to my parents'—and to my own—surprise. "I met her in March when I was in L.A., at Universal Studios. We've been in touch by e-mail ever since. I'm sorry I didn't tell you earlier, but ..."

"Is she in love with you?" my mom asked, somewhat taken aback.

"Yes ... yes, she is," I replied in a tone I thought was convincing.

They weren't convinced.

"Wow," my mom said again. I watched her face as she stared at the photo of Katya, trying to process my out-of-the-blue bombshell.

"Bobby ... you have to be careful," my mom finally said, before adding "are you going to see each other again?"

My mom had provided me with a perfect segue to inform them that I was actually *going* to Ukraine. I chose to leave out one "minor detail"—that I was also taking an engagement ring.

"What?! Are you nuts?!" my dad said, laughing incredulously.

The thing was—he was right. *I was nuts.* Who in their right mind would do what I was doing? *What was I thinking?*

As irrational as my decision seemed, I knew in my own mind that I *was* doing the right thing. That I *was* thinking. After all, what did I have to lose, other than $1,300 for my plane ticket? Even the clerk at the jewelers told me that I could return the ring if Katya said no.

At the very least, I would gain the experience of going to a part of the world I would otherwise not have considered traveling to. Writers need to see the world, right? More importantly, if we were truly in love, then something had to give. So by that rationale, I had more to lose by not going. If I didn't go, I knew that I would spend the rest of my life wondering *what if?*

Once my trip was announced, there was one thing I knew for certain: life in general suddenly felt a whole lot better. I felt calmer, more confident … and painfully aware of how *slowly* time can move. Never had I wanted a summer to pass more quickly—and never did a summer drag on so long. Of course, I knew that once the time came for us to be together, I would be begging for the days to last forever.

No matter what I was doing, I couldn't help but feel Katya's presence. I missed her—mostly at night, when the mind is most liberated from distraction and most vulnerable to the senses. Fortunately, there was always the moon. It was comforting to think that for a few hours, we shared the possibility that we could both be looking at the same thing at the same time, despite the vast gap of earth and sea separating us.

2

DEPARTURE

Despite time's stubborn resistance, August 18—the date that had been hovering over my head since the moment I booked my trip to Ukraine—was almost here.

A few days prior to my departure, I had managed to secure a long-term substitute teacher position, teaching English at my alma-mater—Edsel Ford High School in Dearborn, Michigan, starting immediately after my return in early September. I was somewhat reluctant to take this on, considering the full load of college classes I would be taking in the fall. However, this was simply too good of an opportunity to pass up. And besides, at that point it felt so far off, considering the adventure that awaited me.

Travelers to Ukraine were required by the U.S. government to receive a series of immunizations and inoculations against influenza, chicken pox, polio, measles, mumps, rubella, diphtheria, pertussis, tetanus, tuberculosis, hepatitis A, hepatitis B, rabies, and possible zombie attacks. I was about to become either super immune or quite possibly half dead.

The night before my departure—following weeks, days, hours, minutes, and seconds of what felt like endless waiting—an unexpected wave of melancholy washed over me. Perhaps it was the result of the cocktail of immunizations running through my body. Or, perhaps it was the realization that one chapter of my life was coming to an end. As much as I looked forward to the next chapter, I knew that I was saying goodbye to a piece of myself that would never be the same. I was at the starting gate of what would most likely become the most memorable experience of my life—and yet all I could think of was the finish line. It is a problem I have always had. Rather than living in the moment, I tend to think about how every moment eventually comes to an end.

The next morning, thankfully, the sadness was gone, replaced with nervous excitement. With my "secret" nestled securely in my pocket, I was ready to begin my journey. No doubts crossed my mind. There was no turning back. There was only the future.

My parents—still clueless of my plan to propose to a girl that they had never met and that I only had been with physically for less than an hour—accompanied me to the airport and waited with me at the gate.

As we headed through security, I encountered my first setback. "Empty your pockets," the security agent commanded.

I scrambled to devise a plan, because I knew that once my little secret was set free from its incubated state of naivety, I would be called to reason—or worse, committed. I discreetly removed the ring case from my pocket and whispered to the agent: "Please don't let them see this," nodding in my parents' general direction. To my pleasant surprise, the guard complied. She gave it a quick inspection, shielding it out of view of my parents, before tactfully handing it back to me, adding, with an unexpected smile, "Good luck."

Crisis averted.

Shortly after arriving at the gate, we saw a couple in their mid-twenties. They were both crying and holding onto each other's hands tightly, not wanting to ever let go, but knowing that the time to let go was looming. It was quite clear that they were about to say goodbye for a long period of time. He looked American. She looked European. *Ukrainian? I felt compelled to ask them what their story was. Who was leaving? How long were they going to be apart? Would their love continue to grow during their separation? Or did they know deep down that this was the end of the road?* Only time would tell, even though I wouldn't be a witness to their outcome. Only mine. Ours.

Boarding time. The couple cried even harder, embracing one another as though doing so could stop time. They kissed, drowning in each other's tears until there was nothing left but goodbye. As it turned out, it was the girl who was leaving. Just before she entered the walkway, she turned and blew him one final kiss goodbye—her face ravaged by tears. And then she was gone.

To this day, I often think about that couple and wonder if they are still in love. And if so, I wonder if they are together or separated by distance.

And then it was my turn to board.

"Please ... be careful," my mom pleaded for the umpteenth time.

"I will mom, don't worry," I said.

"And don't let anyone take advantage of you."

"She's not like that, mom," I reassured her.

"Bobby, you never know," she replied.

"But *I* know," I said confidently.

"I still think you're nuts," my dad said. I wished that deep down he was rooting me on—but I knew he wasn't. All I could manage in response was a half-hearted smile.

"Be careful," my mom repeated like a broken record.

"I will, mom" I said, smiling, trying my best not to appear irritated.

She began to cry.

I fought with all my might to hold back my own tears. I hugged her tightly, adding "I'll be fine, mom … I'll be fine."

And with that, I walked over to the check-in clerk, checked in, turned and waved to my parents, then headed down the walkway which led to the plane—aware that I was on the precipice of something extraordinary. There aren't too many times in life that you actually recognize a turning point as it happens. Never in my life had I felt more *free*.

As soon as I settled into my seat, I fished for the ring to make sure it was still tucked away safely in my pocket. As the plane began to taxi, I took out my journal and wrote: "I am currently taxiing toward the most important trip of my life. *Cherish this trip. Cherish every second of it.*"

As the flight—and the soon-to-be-shortened night—went on, the nagging need to constantly check for the ring intensified. In the rare moments I fell asleep, I would suddenly wake up, paranoid that somebody had stolen it while I was sleeping. I felt like Gollum guarding his *precious*. I cannot sleep on planes as it is. It's even worse when I'm suffering paranoid delusions that somebody is going to pickpocket me as I sleep. No matter how long the flight, no matter how tired I was, I remained in a semi-conscious, zombie-like state until the plane touched down.

Upon my arrival in Frankfurt, Germany—with several hours to spare before my connecting flight to Dnipropetrovsk, Ukraine—I called Katya.

It was great to hear her voice—a voice I realized that I had barely heard, despite belonging to the person I was about to propose to. I couldn't help but think that this was the closest we had been geographically since the day we had met in L.A. All that was separating us now was a three-hour flight.

With ample time to kill, I decided to rest against a column in front of an old-fashioned shuffling flipboard displaying gate information. Shuffle after shuffle, I waited for my destination to show up, like somebody desperately watching lottery drawings.

Over an hour later, the word—"DNIPROPETROVSK"—appeared, barely fitting on the board.

If only I knew how to pronounce it.

3

DESTINATION: DNIPROPETROVSK

I headed toward my assigned gate, stopping for a bouquet of flowers along the way. When I arrived at the gate marked "Dnipropetrovsk," I immediately noticed that everyone in the crowded waiting area appeared sullen; no smiles, no laughter. Not a word of English was spoken. Not a word of German, either, for that matter. The atmosphere felt intimidating and I felt as though I stuck out like a sore thumb.

I managed to find a seat between two middle-aged men who either apparently had never heard of deodorant, or simply ran out a long time ago. They both glared at me as though I had just announced that I had slept with their mothers.

I took the ring case out of my pocket and examined it for the hundredth time. From the corner of my eye, I felt someone ... *something* staring at me from across the aisle. I looked up. It was an old Ukrainian "babushka woman." Carrying a cage. A cage containing a chicken. This image begged the requisite questions: *Why a chicken? Did she come to Germany just to get this chicken? Was it for her? Was it a present? A pet? A future dinner? Both??* As I continued staring at her chicken, I realized she was staring at me. More specifically, *glaring* at me. *Was I being cursed?* But what had I done? Is staring at someone's chicken a crime in Ukraine? Unable to come up with the answers I so desperately craved, I simply stared down at the ring. But I could feel the woman's glare intensify. *But why? Do old Ukrainian babushka women hate rings? Hate Americans? Hate Americans who carry rings?* I figured that her glare would subside, that she would return to minding her own business. But each time I looked up, there she was, glaring, as if to say *come on, just try it, I can take you down any day*. I put the ring case back into my pocket. She continued to glare. Thankfully my imminent curse was curtailed by a loud announcement. It was time to board.

I headed through the tunnel, assuming that it would lead to a plane. But it simply led to a stairwell. The stairwell led to a shuttle. The shuttle finally led to another terminal, where our Dniproavia plane awaited.

Should I be worried? I convinced myself that at the very least, if it was an airline with a habit of crashing, then surely I would have heard of it.

Our plane was one of those small propeller planes that looked like its best days of service were during the Cold War. We boarded through the rear. The sound from the propellers was deafening.

I struggled to find my seat. A flight attendant—demonstrating no ability to speak English—looked at my ticket, then led me down the crowded aisle. I couldn't help but notice the tattered upholstery and torn, dirty curtains. Not to mention the blistering heat that magnified the smell of body odor.

Upon reaching my seat, I glanced through a complimentary Ukrainian newspaper, pleasantly surprised by full-color nude photos, along with the occasional fully-clothed, dour-faced diplomat.

A woman to my left held a crying baby—a problem which was remedied by her swiftly whipping out a supple breast upon which the baby could feed.

As the plane began to taxi, the passenger to my right did the sign of the cross repeatedly. This action intensified upon take off.

A man across the aisle covered his head with a newspaper. Another man took a swig of vodka from a bottle. I simply clutched my broken armrests for dear life and closed my eyes, joining my neighbor in intense prayer.

I knew that I could finally relax once my fellow passengers began to pull out their baskets of food and bottles of vodka, filling the cabin with the nauseating stench of pickled herring and smoked fish—the scents of which were compounded by the dirty diaper that was being changed next to me. I had no choice but to lift up my shirt to cover my nose. And of course, *I* was looked upon as the weirdo … as the freak. *Weak American,* their stares seemed to be saying.

I reclined back in my seat, only to be immediately kicked at from behind. Something, presumably nasty, was spoken by the bearded face that slithered in from behind me. I interpreted this to mean *pull up your fucking seat now, asshole!* I took his friendly advice and did just that. I then took out my Russian-English phrase book in a vain attempt to translate what I had just been told. All I gathered was how much the Cyrillic alphabet resembled drawings of tables and chairs.

A stewardess with a purplish bee-hive, make-up plastered on her face in the manner of a circus clown, and a deep smoker's cough, came by with a refreshment cart. She handed me what bore some vague resemblance to beef stew, a rock-hard bread roll, and a can of what appeared to be apple juice. I tried to pull down my tray, but it was broken. So I balanced the items on my lap and dug into the mystery *stew/goo*—trying to ignore the little voice telling me that I was making a big mistake.

After the stewardess had collected my stew tray and empty can, by some divine miracle, I felt myself slowly dozing off to sleep, until I was interrupted—*by the sound of a drill*. Startled, I looked around the cabin. It didn't take long for me to focus in on a wild-haired mechanic with several missing teeth who bore an uncanny resemblance to Doc Brown from *Back to the Future,* drilling into the ceiling of the plane.

I didn't sleep another wink.

Two hours later, the plane began its descent. I looked out of the window—half-expecting to see a Ukrainian gremlin on the wing—at the sparse countryside, finding it hard to believe that we were approaching a city of more than one million people.

The stewardess passed out what I gathered to be a customs form, but it was in Russian so I couldn't be sure. I raised my hand and blurted out down the aisle: "Excuse me!" Based on the reaction of every passenger, I might as well have threatened to blow the whole plane to smithereens, so apparently startling was my foreign tongue to their ears.

The stewardess approached, all but asking me to quiet down. I showed her my customs form: "English?" I asked.

"Da, English. Minute." She hastily took the form from me. Moments later, she returned with an English one. I couldn't help but feel a slight tinge of shame for not learning at least a few basic Russian phrases in the months leading up to my trip.

Finally, the plane touched down in Dnipropetrovsk. Unscathed.

The passengers exploded into wild applause. I was taken aback. *Aren't we supposed to land safely? Was this a major feat for a Ukrainian flight?*

I had a feeling we weren't in Michigan anymore.

4

WELCOME TO DNIPROPETROVSK

I disembarked onto the tarmac at the Dnipropetrovsk International Airport (which was roughly the size of the average, small county airport in the U.S.) and was greeted by the sight of a foreboding single, small, grey, Soviet-era terminal.

Inside the stuffy, dingy building, I followed the herd toward passport control. It was here where I learned my first lesson in Ukrainian queues—as in: they don't exist. The concept of forming a line was pretty much reduced to a survival of the fittest free-for-all. Perhaps years of Soviet control is to blame for this. I was later told that I wouldn't survive in Ukraine if I had to live there, where the weak are truly eaten. I take this as both an insult and a compliment.

After I allowed several people to push their way past me, frustration set in and I started standing my ground by inching a step closer toward the customs booth. As I waited, two Ukrainian men in front of me argued with an official in Russian before being rather forcefully arrested.

With my turn approaching, anxiety crept in. The grim-faced officials with their Soviet-looking, olive-colored uniforms didn't help matters. As threatening as their stern demeanor appeared, I would soon discover that this expression was status quo for just about every Ukrainian when out in public. In private, it's a different story all together—warm and hospitable would best describe it.

After what felt like ages, it was finally my turn.

As I approached the booth, I nervously dropped my passport, clumsily picking it up off the dirty, grey floor before handing it to the official, who hovered over me like a judge presiding over court. He proceeded to stare at it for what seemed like a full minute, flipping through the pages, *feeling* the pages, as though inspecting it for authenticity, and periodically looking up at me with complete and utter suspicion.

This is how people disappear, never to be heard from again, I thought to myself.

Hold your composure. You have nothing to hide ... but neither did many of those jailed under Stalin.

As the customs official continued thumbing through my passport, I suddenly grew paranoid that he was somehow reading my thoughts, therefore making me feel like I was doing something wrong, which in turn, would give him reason to think I actually was. I was certain that I was about to become victim of the thought police. It didn't help that I had recently finished reading *1984*.

He looked at me again. *Yep, he's on to me,* I thought, clutching onto the ring case in my pocket for comfort.

And that's when he called over another official. *They're closing in on me! Just like those other guys who were arrested.*

The second official flipped through my passport, just as his cohort had, then stared at me, likely confirming the suspicions already placed upon me as he nodded to his comrade.

In a stern, official tone, he asked me something in Russian:

"I'm sorry, but I don't speak Russian," I said.

He repeated himself, in broken English: "What is purpose to visiting Ukraine?"

"I'm visiting a friend," I replied nervously, beginning to feel guilty for no rational reason.

"Tell me your friend's name," he said, sternly.

I gave them Katya's name.

As both officials proceeded to stare at me, sweat began to drip down my forehead. It felt as though they were trying to burn through me.

The first official muttered something to me in either Russian or English. I couldn't understand either way.

Dumbfounded, I asked him to please repeat himself. So he did. And I still didn't understand. Nor did I the third time.

Frustrated, he finally, reluctantly, stamped my passport, handing it back to me in a manner that suggested disappointment for not being able to place me under arrest, before adding:

"Welcome to Ukraine."

And with that, I was on my way to the next obstacle on the obstacle course known as Ukraine: luggage claim. How difficult could that be? I approached the squeaky luggage carousel, which was distinguished by a truly unique feature. Unlike every other luggage carousel I have ever encountered, which typically allows luggage to continue to go around and around until claimed, this particular carousel failed to provide that convenient luxury. In fact, "carousel" would not be the proper term to describe it. It was simply a conveyor belt that rudely dumped your luggage at the end of the line, forming a heaping pile of luggage on the floor, which in turn caused a feeding frenzy of passengers swarming the pile like vultures on a carcass, searching for their belongings.

I was beginning to find it increasingly difficult to believe Katya was waiting on the other side of this chaos. Despite my growing impatience, I decided to avoid the feeding frenzy and wait for the crowd to thin out a bit. As I was waiting, I noticed something rather peculiar about the luggage itself. Almost every suitcase was wrapped tightly with cellophane and packaging tape, covering every square inch. Despite my initial confusion, it didn't take me long to realize why. Most of the bags that had not been wrapped like mummies were opened with personal belongings hanging out. So naturally, I assumed this would be the condition I found my luggage in. And with that thought, I continued to obsessively, compulsively check my pocket for the ring—relieved that I hadn't packed it in my suitcase.

As luggage and loose miscellaneous personal items continued to cascade into the stockpile below, I began to panic. *Where is my suitcase?* I took comfort in the fact that new luggage continued to come through the portal, but it was clearly winding down. And then it came to a stop. I figured/hoped/prayed that it was somewhere in the five-foot pile that had formed at the end of the line. Meanwhile, two people began to fight over the same suitcase, before realizing who its rightful owner was (as it turned out, it was neither of them). As the pile grew smaller, so did the crowd swarming around it. And then, there were none. And my luggage was still nowhere to be seen.

Desperate, I poked my head through the portal. Nothing. I had no choice but to seek help. I scanned the room and noticed what I assumed to be an information booth. Just as I turned to leave, I heard the conveyor belt hum and buzz, struggling to ramp up before finally starting again. I stared at the portal. Nothing. I waited and waited until lo and behold, there it was. My suitcase! Fully zipped, too! Hallelujah! Without a doubt, a good omen. I grabbed it and headed on to the next stop on my road to Katya: luggage inspection.

After my suitcase had passed through the X-ray machine, I was ordered to open it up. Once again, I was overcome with that irrational paranoia airports create when you begin thinking that maybe you *are* doing something illegal. Being in an airport in the former Soviet Union only amplified this feeling. As the inspector proceeded to remove every item from my suitcase, I was reminded of how painfully difficult it was to fit everything in there to begin with. And now, I was being granted the opportunity to do it all over again.

While digging through my toiletries bag, the inspector pulled out my prescription allergy medication and held it up to me as though he just found a brick of cocaine.

"What's it?" the inspector said in a gruff, accusatory tone, in broken-English.

"Allergy pills," I said.

The inspector was clearly confused.

"Allergies. Al-err-gees," I said, still not getting my message across.

The inspector quickly grew frustrated with our inability to communicate. This wasn't good. He opened the bottle, sniffing the contents before dumping a couple of pills into his hand to examine them.

I decided to try a different tactic, mimicking several sneezes, and pretending to blow my nose.

The inspector nodded in understanding and dumped the pills back into the bottle. It worked! Twenty minutes later, everything was jammed back into my suitcase, but zipping it shut was another matter altogether. No matter what I did, I couldn't get it to close. I re-arranged some of the items, but this did little to help. Just as I began looking around for some cellophane, another inspector came to my aid by sitting on my suitcase— no doubt an important part of his job description.

Now, all that separated Katya and me was an opaque sliding door.

I imagined that once the door was open, we would run toward each other across an empty arrivals lounge (in slow motion) and hug tightly, with romantic music playing in the background and babushka women throwing rose petals in our path.

In reality, once I passed through the door, I was greeted by a heaving mob awaiting their loved ones, holding enormous bouquets of flowers, instantly putting my meager bouquet to shame. Just as Ukrainians don't like waiting in line, nor do they like moving out of the way of somebody trying to get through. And as if that wasn't enough, hustling taxi drivers— eager for business—tugged and grabbed at both me and my luggage in a desperate attempt to take me to destinations unknown. I had no choice but to plow my way through, protecting my bouquet at all costs, desperately hoping that Katya's first glimpse of me wouldn't be this savage struggle I was enduring.

In the months leading up to our reunion, I had imagined countless ways this would play out. Battling aggressive, odor-plagued taxi drivers had never been part of the equation. All of a sudden I started to feel nervous. Now that the moment had finally arrived, how would we react when we saw each other? *Would we run toward each other with open arms? Would we slowly approach? Would we shake hands? Would we hug? Would it feel awkward or natural? Would we even recognize each other at all, now that we were together in the real world, rather than the digital one? Just how should two people react who are madly in love yet existing in the complete absence of physical proximity? Would it even feel real? Is it even possible that this could be real?*

I was finally about to get my answer, as I spotted Katya: an angelic vision in green. We recognized each other instantly; it was as though we had just seen each other yesterday. Our eyes locked; without hesitation, I ran toward her. We hugged. And it felt as though we had hugged countless times before. We embraced each other tightly. No words were needed.

As I later described in my journal: *We hugged and it was so surreal, so unbelievably unreal.*

While we embraced, I noticed for the first time, however, how incredibly tall she was and how incredibly short she made me feel, despite my being of average height.

"So, how was your flight?" she said through an enormous, beautiful smile, breaking the silence.

"I survived," I said, taken aback by how natural being with her felt.

"This is my dad," she said, motioning toward the tall, authoritarian-looking gentleman standing by her side. *How did I not even notice him? Was I that blinded by love?* Yes, I was *that* blinded by love.

Katya's father was an imposing man with a Lurch-like demeanor. He wore a permanent scowl on his weather-beaten face, which seemed to suggest that somebody had just pissed him off. Certainly not the kind of person you would want to cross or meet in a dark alley on a dark night — or at an airport passport control checkpoint.

"Pleased to meet you," I said, offering my hand. He looked me straight in the eye and shook my hand firmly with a vice-like grip.

"Sergei Andreovich. *Dobro pozhalovat' v Ukrainu*," ("Welcome to Ukraine") he said, continuing to study me for flaws with his steely gaze.

It is important to point out that in Ukrainian culture, the normal way to greet your guest is by using your first and middle name. Furthermore, middle names in Ukraine are patronymics — in other words, derived from the father's first name. Males tack on the ending "-vich" or "-ovich"; females tack on "-avna, "-ovna," or "-ivna." Therefore, Katya's middle name is Sergeiovna. If a male was named after his father and the father's name was, say, Andrei, he would introduce himself as Andrei Andreovich.

Katya translated, as she would do throughout my visit, since neither of her parents—like the majority of people I encountered in Ukraine, particularly the older generations—spoke English.

Speaking through Katya as a translator was something to which I quickly grew accustomed. Before long, it didn't feel like I was being translated at all. It certainly helped that Katya was a remarkably skilled translator. In fact, this was her field of study at Kharkiv National University, one of the oldest universities in Eastern Europe, located about 140 miles north of Dnipropetrovsk.

"Did you get any sleep?" Katya asked.

"Not much," I said. "I can't sleep on planes."

"You must be tired," she said.

"No, I've never felt more awake," I said, smiling.

Sergei reached for my suitcase.

"Thanks, but I got it," I said. But Sergei insisted.

As they led me out of the terminal toward the parking lot, I put Katya's hand into mine—surprised at how utterly natural and right it felt. *But would her dad mind? Does he know?* If he noticed, he didn't seem put off by it. And she certainly didn't, either. As I later learned, it was common for friends to hold hands, which is what he probably assumed.

We got to Sergei's car—an old, white, rusted-out Zhiguli/Lada. Sergei opened the trunk. I attempted to help him lift my overloaded suitcase into the trunk, but he once again refused my services. He actually seemed annoyed that I would even bother. I decided instead to get into the car. Katya sat in the back seat with me. Fortunately, Sergei didn't appear to take any issue with this.

The drive from the airport to the family's downtown Dnipropetrovsk apartment took about twenty minutes. Along the way, I was bombarded with reminders that I was in another world. The Cyrillic lettering was perhaps the most obvious reminder. I also noticed the lack of street signs and—more shocking—lane markers, a detail that was made more jarring by the free-for-all approach drivers took to the road. Drivers essentially had no choice but to jostle for position and forge their own lanes whenever and wherever they pleased. I couldn't help but find this to be a striking parallel to Ukrainians' apparent disdain for forming civilized lines. It certainly didn't help that most roads were in poor condition, forcing drivers to swerve around potholes and sinkholes.

A few other observations about Ukrainian traffic: most of the cars were older, smaller cars from the Soviet era and mostly driven by men. I noticed the occasional SUV—usually a hallmark of the new Ukrainian rich. Almost as prevalent as old clunkers hogging the road were *marshrutkas*— or route vans—usually driven by angry bald men with seemingly little to no patience.

Three-quarters of the drive consisted of countryside, with practically nothing to suggest that we were approaching a big city. It was only after we were just outside the city limits that billboards started to emerge.

Unlike the sprawling suburbs of big American cities, the main cities in Ukraine are surrounded by farmland and quaint roadside villages. City limits are taken a lot more literally. It is much like the desert surrounding Las Vegas. And like the desert, Dnipropetrovsk's terrain is mostly flat, unlike other, hillier, or even mountainous areas of the country like Yalta, or Kiev.

And then, just like that, we were in the city.

It was at that point that I remembered: *I still didn't know how to pronounce "Dnipropetrovsk."* Not only was the word long—it had way too many consonant clusters bumping together; it could really use an extra vowel or two.

Trying my best not to appear a complete idiot, I casually said to Katya, "By the way... just how do you pronounce your city?"

"Dnipropetrovsk," Katya began. "Knee-prop-e-trovsk."

I made an attempt. Not even close. Katya repeated it again, more slowly the second time. "Knee...prop...e...trovsk."

Once again, not even close.

I caught a glimpse of Sergei smirking in the rearview mirror.

"You'll get it," Katya said, encouragingly. "Everyone does."

I wasn't so sure.

Dnipropetrovsk is Ukraine's third largest city (behind Kiev and Kharkiv). An industrial city of around one million people, located on the banks of the mighty Dnieper River, its name derives from a combination of Dnieper and Bolshevik revolutionary, Grigory Petrovsky. It is also the birthplace of such notable figures as Olympic Gold Medal figure skater

Oksana Baiul and *Peter and the Wolf* composer Sergei Prokofiev.

In the 1950s, Dnipropetrovsk became the center of Soviet nuclear missile, arms, and rocket building—the very weapons of mass destruction that had been aimed at the U.S. during the Cold War. The city certainly would have been a prime target of the U.S. if war between the two superpowers had ever erupted.

In 1959 Dnipropetrovsk was officially "closed" to all foreign visitors. This goes a long way in explaining the general distrust Ukrainians—especially the older generations—have toward foreigners.

The city was finally opened to foreign visitors in 1987 during *Perestroika* ("restructuring")—a political reform within the Soviet Union closely linked to Gorbachev's *glasnost* ("openness") policy, which many believe ultimately led to the demise of the Soviet Union.

Aside from the fact that both cities begin with the letter 'D', the parallels between Dnipropetrovsk and Detroit are striking. Not only were both cities manufacturing and industrial giants that have suffered economically over the past few decades, but both contributed greatly to the military-industrial complex of their respective nation. Just as Detroit was nicknamed the "Arsenal of Democracy" during World War II for manufacturing tanks, trucks, guns, and planes, Dnipropetrovsk very well could have been referred to as the "Arsenal of Socialism."

Today, Dnipropetrovsk is a bustling city, still facing the same economic problems that define modern Ukraine. Like most of eastern Ukraine, Dnipropetrovsk has been living in Russia's shadow since the collapse of the Soviet Union in 1991. As a result, the language, culture and customs are aligned with Russia, unlike the more independent-minded western Ukraine, whose primary language is Ukrainian. Mostly Russian is spoken in eastern Ukraine, including Dnipropetrovsk.

When we first entered the city, I was struck by the endless rows of Stalinist-era apartment buildings. *How does one not get lost here?* Not that the U.S. isn't marked by "sameness," especially in the suburbs, which are represented by any combination of Best Buy, Target, Applebee's, McDonald's, Arby's, Walgreen's, Wal-Mart, and Lowe's.

Within a few minutes of entering the city, we passed a McDonald's— the glowing, golden arches of capitalism (and a welcome relief when one grows tired or distrustful of native cuisine). With the marked exception of McDonald's, there were remnants of the former Soviet Union everywhere, including the enormous, abandoned Yuzhmash missile plant that sprawled several blocks, completely enclosed by a tall, brick wall.

"Once upon a time, beyond those walls were missiles that would have crushed your country," Sergei proudly proclaimed.

"Well, I'm glad it didn't come to that!" I replied nervously, directing my attention to the large, rusted, above-ground water and gas pipes running along the road like an enormous Habitrail from the depths of hell—a visible and symbolic *scar* of the Soviet Union and all of its inefficiencies.

Much of the architecture of modern-day Dnipropetrovsk was built during the reconstruction period after World War II, including the Central Railway Station, which we passed by. Following the war, the station was stripped of its Russian-revival ornamentation and redesigned in the style of Stalinist Social Realism. Rather than restoring war-damaged buildings to their previously ornate glory, many were completely demolished and replaced by drab, non-descript Soviet-style blocks.

Much of the city's center consisted of pre-revolutionary buildings, featuring a mix of Stalinist and constructivist architecture, whereas the residential districts consisted primarily of low-rise apartment houses of the Krushchev era (*Khrushchyovkas*), which later evolved into the construction of high-rise prefabricated apartment blocks, similar to the white-gray bricked apartment building (facing the Dnieper River) where Katya and her family resided. These post-modern western-style, high-rise apartment buildings had begun to transform Dnipropetrovsk's skyline, although the ghosts of the Soviet Union were still ubiquitous.

We drove past a statue of Lenin, which I embarrassingly mistook for Joseph Stalin. Sergei laughed, explaining that all the statues and streets named after Stalin had been removed and renamed.

"Why?" I innocently asked.

"Because Lenin didn't murder millions of his own citizens," Katya said. "Although, according to many of the older generations, nor did Stalin," in reference to the affection and denial many older Ukrainians had in regard to their former, iron-fisted ruler. The Soviet government's forced collectivization of agriculture during this period is considered to have created a man-made famine, now referred to as *Holodomor* ("death by hunger"). Rural Ukrainians were hit especially hard, where the government's policies effectively created full-blown genocide. This happened in a country nicknamed the "Bread Basket of Europe," where millions of Ukrainians were literally deprived of the very food they had grown and cultivated with their own hands.

After my crash course in Ukrainian history, we finally arrived at the family apartment building and parked in the courtyard, which contained several pieces of rusted playground equipment that one could easily assume were abandoned if it wasn't for the fact that several children were playing on them. A group of boys were kicking around a soccer ball. Twisting through the playground were several of the hideous above ground pipes, marring any potential for anything resembling a scenic view. Two overflowing, foul-smelling, rusty garbage dumpsters butted up against the playground didn't help matters, nor did the stray mutts and cats that roamed freely around the yard like they owned the place.

We got out of the car and Sergei once again insisted on carrying my luggage. As we headed toward the building, I noticed three old babushka women sitting on a bench near the entranceway. They glared at me, just like the woman at the airport (perhaps one of them was the woman from the airport?!). Trying not to appear intimidated, I smiled politely and carried on.

Sergei dragged my luggage up the three crumbling, concrete steps that led to the entrance of the building.

I attempted to give him a hand, but again he refused.

"Is there another entrance?" I asked.

"No. Why?" Katya asked.

"Well, what would somebody do who is in a wheelchair?"

"They don't leave the apartment," she replied matter-of-factly.

"Can't they build a ramp?" I asked.

"For just a small handful of people?" she replied.

This was Ukrainian logic *and* compassion at its finest. Apparently, the Ukrainians with Disabilities Act had yet to be signed into law.

Sergei proceeded to punch in a code on a keypad that unlocked the heavy, metallic door, coated in the faded remnants of various stickers that had been posted over the decades.

I struggled to pull the door open for Katya and Sergei, revealing a dark and foreboding stairwell accented by peeling green paint.

As we headed up the stairs, I asked if perhaps we should take the elevator, considering the weight of my luggage.

"Nobody's legs are broken," Sergei said in reply. Judging by the look of the elevator, there was probably more than one reason not to take it. Fortunately, we only had to go up one flight until we reached the apartment. As we stood on the dimly-lit landing, Katya "rang" the doorbell—if you could call it a *ring*. This sounded more like a rusty chainsaw trying to slice a bell in half. The industrial din echoed throughout the bowels of the musty stairwell.

Moments later, soft footsteps were heard, followed by the rattling of what sounded like a warden's iron ring of keys opening a door. Then a second door. And then finally, the door that we stood in front of, revealing a cozy, warm interior, contrasting with the drab stairwell. We were immediately greeted by the delicious aroma of Ukrainian cuisine.

Framed by the golden warmth of the apartment was Katya's mother Elena who greeted me with a warm hug. Elena was wearing an apron—an accessory I would later rarely see her without. She was a stoic, pear-shaped woman who exuded patience, strength, and grace, despite a face that suggested constant weariness and hardship. Unlike Sergei's stern, authoritarian demeanor, Elena was a calm foil with a soft voice, typically reserved for when spoken to or when she had a profound observation to make. She was a woman of few words, but of a confident, refined, and sophisticated presence. Consummate housewife on one level, Elena was also a pediatrician who worked at a local kindergarten.

We entered the cedar-paneled apartment, adorned with Turkish rugs, on both the hardwood floor and walls.

"*Dobro pozhalovat domoj*" ("Welcome to our home"), she said in a warm, welcoming tone in Russian (translated by Katya). "*Pajalusta snemeetya oboov*" ("Please remove your shoes").

I obliged, realizing that Katya and Sergei had already removed theirs.

"There are some guest slippers for you to wear," Elena said, pointing to a pair of worn, but comfy-looking slippers. I put them on just as a tall (taller than Katya), slender woman with short, badly-dyed blonde hair and a perpetual pout appeared. She seemed to pout even as she smiled.

"This is my sister, Nastya," Katya said.

I offered my hand, but Sergei quickly intercepted, pulling me away from the door. I was confused.

"It's bad luck to shake hands over a threshold," Katya proceeded to explain. "But you're safe now." As I was soon to discover, superstitions are as embedded into the culture of Ukraine as vodka.

Following my initial confusion, I proceeded to shake Nastya's hand. "Nice to be meeting you," she said in broken English. Like Katya, Nastya also took English lessons, but never quite mastered the language as well as her little sister. This is attributed to the fact that Nastya is ten years older than Katya and only started taking lessons at the same time as Katya. Also, Nastya had not spent a year in the U.S. like Katya.

For reasons I never fully understood, I barely saw Nastya after that first night. She was either at the clinic where she worked as an ophthalmologist, or with her boyfriend, Dimitri.

Dimitri came by one evening to boastfully show off his fake dog poop and BB gun, which he jokingly pointed at me, proclaiming "Capitalist swine!" before giving me an old-fashioned noogie. Fortunately, that was the first and last time I would see Dimitri on that trip.

"Are you hungry?" Elena asked.

"Oh ... I don't want to trouble you," I said.

"I'd only be troubled if you didn't eat," Elena replied.

Judging by the satisfying aroma filling my nostrils, I knew that Elena had already gone through the trouble of preparing a meal.

Elena asked Katya to take me to my room at the end of the short hallway. The modest, but comfortable apartment consisted of three bedrooms, a living/dining room, an office, a shower, and a toilet (the shower and toilet were separate rooms, neither of them much larger than a closet).

"This is your cage," Katya said as we entered her room. I immediately noticed the lack of an essential piece of furniture: a bed. Then again, a bed would barely fit in a room so small. Where a bed should have been was a small, flaming red couch, which battled for real estate with an old, clunky computer that resembled a patched-together hybrid of a Commodore 64 and an Apple IIe.

"You don't have a bed?" I asked.

Katya pointed to the red couch.

"It turns into a bed," she said.

"So what's with the rugs on the wall?" I asked.

"Well, a little known secret about Ukrainian people is that we have the ability to walk on walls. Especially while drinking vodka."

I wasn't sure how to respond.

"Wait. What?" I asked.

"I'm just joking!" Katya replied. "It's for insulation, since the heat in this building is *a suck*."

"You mean *sucks*?" I said, trying not to laugh.

"Yes. It sucks. Sometimes, the heat doesn't work at all. We're all at the mercy of the building landlord. If one person in the building doesn't pay, we all must suffer."

"How can that happen?" I asked innocently.

"It's Ukraine," Katya simply replied.

I quickly learned how this phrase applied to so many different aspects of Ukrainian life.

I glanced over at a glass display case which contained several dolls and toys from Katya's childhood. Directly next to it was an open, screenless window, overlooking the park and dumpsters below. The modern convenience known as screens apparently had not yet been introduced to Ukraine.

While passing by the room, Sergei noticed me staring out of the window. Concerned, he said something in Russian.

"What's your dad saying?" I asked.

"He said you shouldn't be looking out the window," Katya replied.

"Why?" I asked.

"Somebody could throw something at your eyes."

"Seriously?!" I said.

"Well, it does happen sometimes."

I decided to appease Ukrainian paranoia on this first of what would become many occasions. This was the same paranoia that had Sergei convinced that his phone line was tapped. Then again, I'm sure that any Ukrainian who lived in the former Soviet Union would be somewhat suspicious.

I redirected my attention to Katya's desk, where I noticed several photographs that were neatly displayed underneath a sheet of glass, including a photo I had sent her taken of me from a post-college trip to Germany the year before, raising a glass of beer for a toast. Katya blushed when she noticed that I spotted the photo. The remaining photos featured various family members, including her grandfather in his World War II military uniform and a black and white photograph of a little girl pulling a sled.

"Is this your mom?" I asked.

She looked. "No, it's me!" Katya replied.

"Then why does this photo look like it was taken in 1955?"

"Color photographs were still a luxury back in the 1980's. They were a luxury for most of the 90's, too!"

Katya proceeded to show me the small closet where my pillows and blankets were stored.

"So where are you going to sleep?" I asked.

"In the living room," Katya replied.

"I don't want to steal your bedroom," I said feeling guilty.

"I don't mind," Katya replied.

We stared at one another in silence.

"So ... am I what you remembered me to be?" Katya asked.

"Yes. Exactly," I replied. "What about me?"

"Yeah ... I think so," Katya said. "I just can't believe you're here in my room!"

"Seems kind of surreal," I said.

"Do you have any idea how many times I dreamed about you being here, Bobby?" Katya asked.

"In your bedroom?" I replied.

Embarrassed, Katya clarified: "Well, not in my bedroom exactly. Just here. In Ukraine. I just never thought the day would actually come."

"I told you I was coming," I said, smiling.

"I know. But I thought for sure you would change your mind. Or something bad would happen. Like a plane crash. Can I have another hug, please?"

I hugged her, tighter than before, smelling her perfume and freshly-washed hair.

"Okay, good. Just making sure I wasn't going to wake up again," Katya said.

"No, this time, it's for real."

And with that, Katya left me to unpack.

I headed over to the window and looked down, aware that I was putting myself at risk of "having something thrown at my eyes." An elderly man in tattered clothing was digging through a dumpster, occasionally pulling out scraps of food that he eagerly devoured. I couldn't help but wonder whether the delicious aroma of Elena's cooking filling my nostrils was also reaching his.

5

UKRAINIAN SHOWER

Following my long journey from Michigan, and before dinner, I decided that I would freshen up with a relaxing shower. Upon entering the bathroom, my first clue that this might in fact *not* be a relaxing shower was the complete lack of a shower curtain. My second clue—while Katya was demonstrating how to draw water out of the faucet—was discovering that there was no hot water.

"Why isn't there any hot water?" I naively asked.

"It's summer," Katya replied.

While still confused by this logic, I noticed Elena enter the bathroom with a large, iron pot of boiling water, which she placed in the bathtub.

"Is that soup?" I asked.

Laughing, Elena explained: "Not soup. You wash using this."

I looked at Katya, certain that this was a practical joke. But it wasn't.

"You'll survive. Most of you at least," she said, before leaving me to my own devices.

I undressed, turned the shower on, and slowly climbed into the bathtub in the same, cautious manner I would climb into a swimming pool. Only this was worse. This was akin to finding myself in swimming pool in the middle of Antarctica … on the coldest night of the year. The stream of frigid water felt like icicles piercing my backside. *God help me,* I thought, *how would the front feel*? I delayed the inevitable for as long as possible, before turning myself slowly around to face an onslaught of ice daggers piercing my nipples and genitals. It literally took my breath away. *What if I have a heart attack? When I don't show up for dinner, they will come looking for me and find a shriveled, dead American in their tub!* The ice-cold spray caused me to back up into the steaming pot of water. It took a few seconds for my brain to fully register the fact that scalding iron initially feels no different than frigid water. And then the pain hit.

After my entire body had been doused in ice water, I stepped away from the stream and proceeded to slowly dip a washcloth into the pot of boiling water, burning my fingers in the process. I quickly put my hand under the shower—one advantage to having icy-cold water in such close proximity.

I looked up with a plea to the heavens to get me through what should logically have been a simple task. And what did I see, but my own reflection, captured in the mirror running both the length and width of the tub. Never had my package looked so small and shriveled. Not to mention upside down.

I decided to take advantage of the frigid water by spraying some of it into the pot of hot water using the hand-held faucet. When the pot water reached a relatively safe temperature, I quickly washed myself before setting my sights on one last task: my head. I sprayed one quick burst of ice water onto my head—a feeling comparable to jumping head first into a thorn bush—and shampooed my hair.

I knew I had no choice but to endure this icy torture until *most* of the shampoo was rinsed out of my hair, completely oblivious to the fact that I was spraying water all over the floor and walls of the bathroom, further justifying the need for that miraculous invention known as a shower curtain. Getting shampoo in my eyes didn't help matters, either. To alleviate this, I blindly reached for the handheld faucet and blasted my eyes with icy spray until I could see again. Finally, I finished what was both the shortest and longest shower of my life.

As I climbed out of the tub—shivering like a wet Chihuahua—I slipped on a puddle of water, which I quickly sopped up with my dirty clothes.

And that's when I realized that I had forgotten to bring a change of clothes into the bathroom. Fortunately, I was able to escape the bathroom, wrapped in my towel, unseen.

As I got dressed, I tried repeating to myself "Knee…prop…a…trovsk," in a vain attempt to get it right. I continued to fail miserably. Some things were just never meant to be. *I simply couldn't live without my vowels.*

6

THE FIRST SUPPER

Following my bathroom adventure, it dawned on me that I should call home. My parents were probably worried sick about me. Of course, I should have known not even a phone call was easy in Ukraine. Each attempt led me to a Russian-speaking operator, who informed me, with Katya's assistance, that it was not possible to connect at this time. Ten attempts later, I gave up.

I asked if it would be possible to send an e-mail instead. However, there was nothing remotely in the ballpark of convenient about using the Internet at Katya's apartment. This was very disconcerting, especially considering the fact that the family computer was conveniently located in Katya's bedroom. Not only did the family quite possibly possess the slowest computer on earth—and more than likely populated with every virus on earth—but everything in the dial-up process was composed in Cyrillic. Trying to understand dial-up Internet mumbo-jumbo is confusing enough in English. This may as well have been written in Wingdings. The first few attempts at dialing up resulted in busy tones. When we would finally get through, we would be promptly disconnected. Twenty minutes later, we were finally online.

Once we finally established a connection, I was unable to actually get onto the web to check my e-mail and had to resort to a non-web-based e-mail program, which was akin to working in HTML code. By the time we opened up the e-mail program, another five minutes had passed. Typing moved at a very slow pace. First of all, the letters were arranged differently on the keyboard, which took some getting used to. Then there was the lag itself, which had nothing to do with my typing skills. On the contrary, the computer simply couldn't keep up with my typing. There was a 3–5 second lag between striking a key and the letter actually showing up on screen. As a result, ten minutes were spent typing this: "Made it here safely. So far, so good. Miss you and love you. A bit tired. Will write again soon. Love, Bobby." After waiting over ten minutes for the message to send, we lost the connection and had to begin the whole process again. Apparently, there was no 'drafts' folder, either. When we finally got back online, I retyped my message, and sent it off after much excruciating delay. Sending one brief message took fifty minutes! I would have been better off just paying $30 to call home.

Following my disastrous attempts at modern modes of communication, Katya led me to the living room, where a Ukrainian feast awaited. A small TV stood on a stand in the corner. A dining table folded into an end table that fit snugly between the couch and a piano. The couch provided seating on one side of the table (not to mention, it also turned into a bed, once again proving the Ukrainian knack for space economy). Move over IKEA!

At the end of the table was a cage containing Katya's beloved, completely blind parakeet, Fernando. Fernando's party trick—which can possibly be blamed on his blindness—was his obsession with humping people's toes.

Awaiting us was a large spread of traditional Ukrainian dishes, which reminded me a great deal of the more familiar Polish cuisine: *borscht* (beet soup), *Kotlety* (a cross between meatballs and hamburgers), black bread (*chernyy khleb*)—rye bread that I mistook for chocolate-flavored, *Kartoplia* (boiled potatoes with no shortage of butter and dill), an assortment of salads, including *Olivye* (a type of potato salad, with peas), *Vinigret* (another type of potato salad, with beets), *Kvasheni ovochi* (a mix of pickled vegetables), pickled herring, and last, but not least, an endless supply of vodka—the primary staple of any Ukrainian meal.

Katya and I were seated on the couch side of the table. At first glance, the couch appeared comfortable, but in reality, it was far from it. It wasn't the couch itself, which was rather stiff, but rather, its low height and overall proximity to the table. This put an enormous strain on my back. I couldn't help but feel like a child in desperate need of a booster seat. No matter how I shifted my position, I could never get comfortable. Not wanting to come across as a weakling, I didn't make an issue of it. I simply chose to eat uncomfortably for the duration of my trip. When my back began to ache too much, I would sit all the way back on the couch for a few moments until I had finished chewing. I learned to take full advantage of this back-and-forth strategy by taking a big bite of the slightly stale, dry bread, which afforded me more time to rest my back before I needed to reach for my plate again.

Seated with us at the table was Katya's Babushka, her grandmother on her mother's side. To describe Babushka succinctly, she was a brawnier version of the apple-offering witch from Snow White ... only less pleasant. Her once strong, stocky frame had been diminished through illness, but her inner strength overshadowed everything. From the moment we met, Babushka didn't take too kindly to me. Being that I was a foreigner didn't help matters. She stared at me with suspicion as though I were a spy sent to report on her every move.

As Babushka watched me fill up my plate with what I carefully considered to be helpings that were neither too little, nor too large, she shook her head, saying something in Russian that I was pretty sure translated into "asshole."

"What did she say?" I asked.

"Let's eat," Katya interpreted.

I wasn't convinced.

Katya advised me not to take anything she said to heart. It was "her illness talking." But I couldn't help but feel judged; despised; inferior.

Sergei lined up the glasses and poured out hearty shots of vodka. Considering my low tolerance to alcohol—especially straight shots—I initially considered politely refusing it. But in another effort not to appear weak or ungrateful, I decided to "give it a shot." This was my first mistake.

I noticed that everyone had a shot glass except for Elena. "Your mom doesn't drink?" I asked.

"Somebody has to stay sane," Elena replied after Katya's translation.

I sniffed my drink, as though I expected it to smell like something other than alcohol. Sergei stood up, regally holding his glass aloft. His presence, even his most jovial moments, filled the room with shadows, demanding complete attention.

Everyone else followed suit by raising their glasses, with me being the last to join in.

"This might take a while," Katya sighed.

Sergei began his toast, with Katya translating:

"Today, we celebrate the arrival of a visitor from the United States—our former enemy—into our home. Fifteen years ago, this occasion wouldn't have been possible. But if there's one thing life promises more than anything, it is change. Bobby, if you need anything at all, please let me know and your wish will be our command."

"Thank you," I said gratefully.

"Say 'Spasibo,'" Katya said.

"Placebo?" I asked, confused.

"Spasibo! Thank you."

"*Pozhaluysta*," Sergei replied.

"My dad says 'You're welcome,'" said Katya.

Sergei continued his toast in Russian as Katya rolled her eyes, signaling with her hands for her father to hurry up, seemingly already tired of having to translate, or, rather, knowing from past experience how long-winded he could be.

"Bobby, I wish you a great trip, great health, great memories and a great learning experience."

"Sergei! Let the poor boy eat," Elena retorted.

Sergei gave in, offering his glass for me to clink.

"*Za vashe zdorovie*," he said ("to your health").

Everyone joined in, then downed their shot.

I held the glass up to my mouth. I wasn't quite ready.

In an instant, however, all eyes turned toward me. I had no choice. With the pressure building, I lifted the glass up to my mouth, downing less than half the shot, trying to remain calm and collected, but making a face like a baby taking medicine. Babushka rolled her eyes in disgust, helping herself to another shot as though trying to show me up. My eyes immediately watered as the vodka burned my throat, then my chest. My face turned as red as the borscht in my bowl.

Babushka glared, presumably putting a curse on me. Sergei tried his best to hide what I was pretty convinced was disapproval for the shame I had caused, as I sat back down, wiping the tears away from my eyes.

"Are you okay?" Katya asked, concerned.

"Yeah, I'm fine," I said, barely able to get the words out.

Katya poured me a glass of mineral water. I raised it to my mouth, choking on the effervescence. At this point, I was struggling to down even a glass of water.

"I'm just not used to drinking it straight," I said.

"Cock?" Sergei asked, staring directly into my eyes.

I froze. Perhaps, I heard it wrong. I *hoped* I had heard it wrong.

"Why did your dad just look into my eyes and say 'cock'?" I asked.

"Not 'cock,'" Katya said, laughing. "'Kak'. It's Russian for 'why.'"

"Oh!" I said. Now it made sense. Sergei was equally confused by my odd reaction to his innocent question. I finally answered "Well, in the U.S., most people mix their vodka with something else. Like juice."

"Like for child?" Sergei asked.

I thought it was a joke. *It wasn't.*

"Well … the more practice you get, the better you become," Sergei added.

"At what … being an alcoholic?!"

"A Ukrainian!" Katya said. "Can you handle it?"

"Bobby, you don't have to finish it," said a concerned Elena.

"No, that's okay," I replied "I have to finish what I started."

Feeling the full weight of Ukrainian expectation and honor firmly on my shoulders, I grabbed the remainder of my shot … and took a baby sip. Then another. And another. And finally it was all gone. My first shot! Everyone—with the exception of Babushka who simply rolled her eyes—applauded as though I were a toddler who had just used the toilet for the first time. I took a bow. With everyone else's attention directed at me, I noticed Babushka eagerly helping herself to yet another shot, for good measure.

Sergei promptly held the bottle up to my glass, simultaneously flicking his neck with his forefinger, adding, "Bobby, *chut-chut*?"

"Papa, no," said Katya.

"What's a chut-chut?" I asked.

"He's asking if you want more," Katya replied.

Wanting to redeem myself and restore what was left of my manhood on the heels of my shower, I flicked my neck in return, proudly proclaiming, "chut-chut!"

I then lifted up my shot glass for Sergei to pour more vodka into it, but he rather forcefully demanded that I put the glass down.

"You're supposed to keep the glass down when pouring a shot," Katya explained. "And you're also not supposed to pour a shot for just yourself. It indicates you're an alcoholic," Katya explained to me.

"That's too many rules for something involving alcohol," I replied.

"It's our culture," Katya further explained.

Smiling with pride, Sergei poured two more shots. Not wanting to be left out, Babushka thrust her shot glass in front of her son-in-law.

"Papa!" begged Katya, who turned to me and pleaded: "Bobby, please don't."

Boastfully, I replied, "When in Rome …," defiantly flicking my neck.

"This isn't Rome. This is Ukraine," reminded Katya.

"One more can't hurt," I said.

"Don't do it, Bobby. You're not Ukrainian!"

As wise as it would have been to follow Katya's advice, I knew there was no turning back. I may have already won Katya over, but I knew my greater mission was to win over her parents—especially her father, who held the keys to my possible future with his daughter. So rather than helping my cause by demonstrating the ability to stand by my convictions—I gave in, staring into my shot glass as though preparing to dive off the edge of a cliff.

"I'm warning you," Katya said. "This stuff has a way of taking over you when you least expect it. And trust me, you don't want to know what my father would do to sober you up."

I looked at Katya, then at Sergei, who raised his glass in my honor, proclaiming, "To Bobby!"

Realizing there was no turning back, I raised my glass to his, before managing to down at least two-thirds of the shot this time around. Once the burning subsided and my tears were dried, I polished off the remainder of my shot, a mini-buzz already taking hold of me.

"I'm going to need a new liver if this keeps up," I said.

"I'm not translating that," Katya said, one of many times she felt the need to censor me—a key advantage when translation is necessary, albeit against the code of translator ethics.

Sergei then said something excitedly to Katya and turned toward me, nodding and smiling, gesturing toward the now half-empty vodka bottle. Katya turned to me and in an exasperated tone, said "he says perhaps you would like to give a toast'?"

"Sergei Andreovich, compared to your toasts, it would only be a disappointment," I said, hoping to dodge a bullet.

"Well, a man must first know how to drink a toast before he gives a toast," Sergei joked in reply. *Bullet dodged.*

"Bobby! Eat!" commanded Elena. "We're not expecting any more guests."

As I began to eat, I could feel Babushka's eyes watching over me. She bluntly declared in Russian and with great disgust: "Too skinny." She then slammed another shot for good measure. Surely this had to be an illusion, or some sort of parlor trick.

The thing was, she was right. I had lost a lot of weight in the months leading up to my trip as a result of the combination of my hefty class load and the anticipation of this trip.

Although I was already full, I filled my plate back up with seconds, carefully avoiding the pickled herring at all costs.

Elena offered me what looked like a giant cube of fatty bacon.

"It looks like a big chunk of fat," I said.

"That's why it's called "fatback" or salo," Katya said.

That sounds healthy, I thought to myself.

"Eat!" Elena said. "Tastes good!"

I reluctantly gave in, then reached for another helping of potatoes for good measure.

Katya pointed to a plate of what looked like sliced pieces of ham.

"What is it?" I asked hesitantly.

"Cow tongue," Katya replied.

"Oh ... no thanks."

"I'm joking, Bobby. It's ham."

I grabbed a slice with my fork and immediately took a bite.

"Good?"

I nodded.

"Moo!" Katya said with a sly grin.

"Are you serious?!" I exclaimed, my mouth still full of the sinewy meat.

"You said you like it, right?"

I spit it out into my napkin. Babushka rolled her eyes.

"You eat steak, don't you?" Katya asked.

"Yeah."

"You have no problem eating cow's butt?"

Katya had me there.

She reached over with her fork and stabbed a slice of tongue before dipping it into the salt bowl, flipping it this way and that until it was completely covered in salt. Unlike a relatively sanitary salt shaker, Katya's family preferred a communal salt dipping dish, similar to a large sugar bowl. Double and triple dipping was apparently no cause for concern. And, apparently, neither was high blood pressure.

Sergei offered me more vodka. This time, I politely refused, to the relief of both Katya and Elena. I took a bite of bread and leaned back against the couch to relieve my aching back.

After presenting the family with the gifts that I brought from Michigan and sharing family photos, it was time for dessert, adding at least another hour to our total couch time. In Ukrainian culture, meals are not intended to be eaten quickly. They are to be savored. And at the centerpiece of every dessert is tea. An average Ukrainian consumes five cups of tea a day.

As Sergei poured honey into his tea, he looked me squarely in the eyes and proudly—and loudly—proclaimed, in broken English:

"Bobby, *I love honey!*"

I nodded, smiling awkwardly, trying to make sense of what he was telling me. I turned to Katya, "Did he just say he loves honey?"

"Sure! He might not know English very well, but he definitely knows how to say his favorite treat," Katya replied.

"Honey is his favorite treat?" I asked.

"*I love honey, Bobby! Sometimes! Yesterday! Today and tomorrow! I love honey! I love the United States! I love Ukraine!*" confirmed Sergei in a heavy Russian accent.

"My dad just demonstrated the full extent of his English vocabulary," Katya said, laughing.

"Very good!" I said, as Sergei popped an entire lemon wedge into his mouth, which he proceeded to suck dry before swallowing it whole. Nothing about the process seemed to faze him.

"Did he just eat a lemon?" I asked Katya.

Katya responded by eating her own lemon wedge just as Sergei had. I couldn't believe what I was witnessing.

"We have a saying in Ukraine. Only when you eat a lemon do you appreciate what sugar is," Katya said. "Try one."

"Oh, no thanks," I said, adding "So how do I say 'I love honey' in Russian?" I asked.

"*Ya lyublyu*—I love—*myod*–honey. *Ya lyublyu myod*," Katya explained.

I decided to give it a shot, totally butchering it. "*Ya lyublyu myod! Ya lyublyu Ukraine! Ya lyublyu Dnipropetrovsk!*"

Everyone burst out laughing at my Russian hatchet job, particularly the way I pronounced—or rather *mispronounced*—Dnipropetrovsk.

Katya corrected me. "Knee-prop-e-trovsk, remember? Knee…prop…e…trovsk!"

I repeated it after her, improving slightly. Katya kept coaching me through it, along with Sergei and Elena's assistance. Sergei moved his hands like a conductor— "*Knee…prop…e…trovsk! Knee…prop…e…trovsk!*" —until I proudly exclaimed, in a strong Russian accent, "Dnipropetrovsk!"

Sergei, Elena, and Katya burst out in applause. Babushka gave me what I quickly surmised to be her patented glare.

"There you go!" said Katya. "Easy! Now you have truly arrived!"

"*Molodetz*, Bobby!" Sergei proclaimed ("Well done!").

"Dnipropetrovsk! Dnipropetrovsk!" I chanted over and over again like a delirious fool.

Sergei grabbed my shot glass. I was ready to oblige, but both Katya and Elena convinced him otherwise. He gave in, handing me the bottle.

"What's going on?" I asked.

"Remember what I was saying? You're not supposed to pour a shot for just yourself."

Oh, yeah!" I said, not bothering to ask why this rule didn't apply to Babushka. I proceeded to pour a shot for Sergei, accidentally overfilling his glass and spilling vodka onto the plate of lemon wedges.

"I'm so sorry," I said, embarrassed.

"Not a problem," Sergei replied. "Now even better!" he said, grabbing a lemon wedge and shoving it into his mouth.

This round of shots was followed by one more. And then we finally ate dessert. We ate until we couldn't eat anymore.

Following dinner, Katya and I retreated back to my room and sat on the couch—with the door left open so we could be under constant supervision by Sergei and Elena.

"I don't think your grandma likes me very much," I said, concerned about the mystery travesty that I must have committed.

"She's just not used to foreigners … and she's also very sick," Katya replied.

"With what?"

"She has a tumor in her stomach."

"Cancer?"

"We try not to use that word here," Katya said sullenly. "The doctors won't treat her. She's too old. They don't want to waste their time."

"That's horrible," I said, genuinely appalled.

"We're all convinced that the vodka is the only thing keeping her alive. Ironically, you know what she said to me about you?"

"What's that?" I asked, dreading the answer.

"She said you look sickly, and that I need a strong man. Not somebody who looks like he's going to die soon."

Unsure of how to respond, the only thing I could do was to quickly change the subject.

"Your dad sure takes his vodka very seriously," I said.

"Find me a Ukrainian man who doesn't," Katya said in return.

And she had a point.

Ukraine takes vodka *very* seriously. To call vodka—or *horilka* as it is known in Ukraine—the national drink of Ukraine may be somewhat of an understatement. It is more a way of life. *A religion.* In fact, many Ukrainians are actually suspicious of those who *don't* drink!

The word *horilka* is derived from the Russian *gorzalka*, which in turn, came from the Polish word *gorzec*, meaning to burn. Or, as Ukrainians are apt to say: "A good, warmed vodka makes a carnation bloom inside your stomach." Some Ukrainian vodkas are made with honey, milk, and, as I would find out ... hot peppers! Nobody can doubt Ukraine's love for the distilled drink in all its myriad forms ... especially in its *purest* form: straight.

"I hope you don't think my dad's an alcoholic," said Katya. "He only drinks for special occasions, you know."

"What makes you think I would get that impression?" I said, teasingly with a wry smile.

I thought it would be obvious that I was joking. But judging by Katya's reaction, I realized that this wasn't obvious, remembering that sarcasm is not a hallmark of Ukrainian humor. Ukrainian jokes are essentially stories—more often than not involving vodka—usually containing a twist that is flat, dry and lacking that one key element of any joke: *a punch line.*

"Seriously, though ... your dad is great. And so is your mom. They have made me feel very welcome. Your grandma on the other hand ..."

"She means well," Katya explained, still not cracking a smile at my lame attempts at humor.

In an effort to create a diversion, I reached into my suitcase and pulled out a white teddy bear I had brought for Katya.

"Thank you, Bobby! He's so cute," Katya said, hugging him tightly.

I grabbed the opportunity to lean over toward Katya and hug her.

And then—for the first time—we kissed.

SPOKOINOI NOCHI

After the dishes had been washed, dried and put away, we joined Sergei and Elena for a walk along the banks of the Dnieper River. We passed by several riverfront cafes, all blaring a mish-mash of annoyingly infectious Russian pop. Across the river, on the much more industrial left (northern) bank, I could see an endless row of factories, spewing out plumes of green and purple smoke. In recent years, this once industrial wasteland has seen a rise in residential areas between the smokestacks.

On the far more populated right (southern) bank, young couples made out, smoking cigarettes, and swigging beer and vodka. Empty bottles littered the concrete landscape. The lack of any public garbage cans didn't help matters, although I doubt it would have made any difference. The number of smokers in Ukraine in general was shocking enough to me; but even more staggering was the number of teenagers (and pre-teens) openly smoking and drinking in public. Technically, the legal drinking *and* smoking age in Ukraine is eighteen. However—like so many laws in Ukraine—this law appeared to be somewhat arbitrary and, as far as I could tell, was not enforced. According to the World Health Organization, Ukraine leads the world in alcohol consumption among youth. To further put things in perspective, champagne was served at Katya's high school prom.

One thing I couldn't help but notice (no matter how in love) was the plethora of tall, slender women in short skirts. To sum it up, Ukrainian casual is American slut. The type of clothing American women wear to clubs are the norm for business and social life in Ukraine. In contrast, Ukrainian men bring mesh tank tops, jump suits, and sandals with socks to the table.

Furthermore, the ratio of women to men walking down any given street was at least 2:1. There is a likely explanation for this: most women in Ukraine do not drive. As a result, they rely on public transportation. And walk. A lot. This probably goes a long way in explaining the great shape Ukrainian women are in as a whole. No wonder why Katya felt so insecure when she returned from Mississippi following a year of Southern cooking. Sadly for the women of Ukraine, God did not bless their male counterparts with equally good looks, which is one of many reasons so many Ukrainian women seek greener pastures elsewhere.

Sergei and Elena walked ahead of us, hand-in-hand. After a few minutes, they informed us that they were heading back. Katya asked if we could stay out for a little while.

"Don't stay too late," Elena warned Katya before heading back. We nestled upon the railing along the river, watching the hordes of people milling about and engaging one another in a never-ending stream of conversation as night descended upon Dnipropetrovsk.

Suddenly, something caught Katya's attention. "Look!" she said, pointing straight ahead.

It was a little kitten, taking an evening stroll along the riverfront.

"Here, kitty," Katya said. The kitten approached us, purring. Katya picked it up by the scruff of its neck.

"Oh my God, you're going to kill it!" I exclaimed.

"No," said Katya. "This is how kittens are picked up by their mommies. She's happy. Listen."

The kitten was purring like a little engine as we both petted it. Katya set the kitten free into the night.

"We better head back," Katya said. "It's almost curfew."

"What time's curfew?" I asked.

"Dark," Katya replied.

"Are you serious?!" I asked.

"My parents are very paranoid. They think once it gets dark, everyone on the street is a murderer, a rapist, a robber, or a victim."

On the surface, this particular area of Dnipropetrovsk appeared relatively safe. I certainly never felt like my life was in danger in any way. However, Katya's parents had a point: the U.S. Embassy rates the crime threat in Ukraine as "high." After all, Ukraine is a country that has been mired in escalating economic and political turmoil, so it is only natural for crime to rear its ugly head from time to time. Katya had told me about gangs of drunks who would roam around simply looking for fights.

And with that in mind, we headed home, the thin sliver of a moon floating above our heads, shining brightly behind a swirl of factory smoke.

When we returned to the apartment, Katya showed me how to transform the couch into a bed—a task which seemed much more difficult than warranted.

Katya then showed me a photograph of herself. I recognized the location instantly. "This was taken at Universal Studios, a couple of hours before we met," she said.

I fished around in my Eddie Bauer backpack and pulled out a photo of my own. "This photo of me was also taken a couple of hours before we met, by a Japanese tourist," I said.

We both smiled.

I then noticed the wooden crucifix pen Katya had handed to me at Universal Studios when we exchanged e-mail addresses. I stared at it as though it were the seventh wonder of the world.

"Where would we be without this pen?" I asked.

"We would have found another one," Katya said, smiling, before adding, "I'll never forget that day. I thought you were so cute."

I had never thought of myself as someone anyone would find "cute."

"You did?!" I exclaimed, genuinely shocked.

"Yes, of course!" she replied, smiling.

"Well, I'm glad we both felt that way about each other," I said—still not fully believing her.

I then reached into my backpack and handed her a draft of my latest screenplay—an animated fable about a runaway housecat. Katya looked at the cover, where I had handwritten: "For Katya, my muse."

"So … I am your muse?" she asked.

"Of course," I said.

"Sounds like a lot of responsibility," Katya replied.

"It is," I replied with a sly smile.

Unaware of what to say to each other next, we sat there in silence. I noticed that Katya was blushing.

And then suddenly—and completely without warning—a rush of emotion overcame me and I felt myself begin to well up. I tried my best to cover it up, but it was no use.

"Are you crying?" Katya asked.

"No … not at all," I replied.

"Yes, you are. Why are you crying?" Katya asked.

"I'm just so happy, " I replied. "I don't want this to end."

"You hardly even drank," Katya said.

"No, it's not that at all," I said.

And then—to my surprise—Katya said, "What kind of man cries?" This caught me totally off guard.

"What do you mean, what kind of man cries?" I asked, wiping my eyes.

"A man shouldn't cry in front of a woman," Katya said matter-of-factly.

"Why not?" I asked.

"A man should always appear confident."

"A man who doesn't cry is a man in denial," I remarked. "I think everyone needs at least one person in their life that they can openly cry front of. No questions asked. Same goes for farting!"

"Gross! My dad never cries. But he definitely farts!"

"How do you know that he never cries?" I asked.

"Well ... if he does, he never shows it."

"My question is, what kind of man is ashamed to cry?"

"Yeah, well it just wasn't the way I raised."

I guess the "sensitive man" had not yet arrived in Ukraine. Or, as was the more likely scenario, he had already been kicked out.

"Let me guess ... women are expected to know their place, too."

"I suppose you have a point," Katya said. "I shouldn't be so judgmental. To be honest, I actually find the fact you cry kind of sweet."

We endured another awkward silence, before I leaned over toward Katya and began kissing her. Just as our kissing started to become passionate, Katya gently broke away.

"I ... um ... better get to bed," she said, adding "I'm so happy you're here, Bobby."

And just as I had written so many times before, but never had the opportunity to verbally express, I uttered "I love you, Katya."

"Ya lyuyblyu tebya, tozhe," Katya replied back in Russian.

And with that, she walked out, closing the door behind her.

I stared at the closed door, trying to grasp the full magnitude of the past twenty-four hours. *Surely, this was a dream. It had to be.* But it wasn't.

I proceeded to remove the ring box from my backpack, secure in the realization that considering how well things were going, I was one giant step closer toward my goal. I knew now that it was not a matter of *if*; it was a matter of *when*. I had initially planned on popping the question at the end of my trip. That way, if Katya said no, I could spare us both a lot of awkwardness before returning home, putting it all behind me. But the downside to putting it off would be having to deal with the anticipation and uncertainty throughout the duration of my trip. I decided I was simply too jetlagged to continue this internal debate and stuffed the box back into my backpack before shutting off the light and climbing into bed.

Even though I had been awake for almost thirty hours, I didn't feel the least bit tired. Despite this, I figured that once my head hit the pillow, I would fall asleep in no time. However, the pillow turned out to be part of the problem. First of all, it was by far the largest pillow I ever laid my head on and way too big for my little head. Its goose-down softness—normally a good thing—caused my head to sink so deep into its center that the ends folded over my face, making it feel as though a goose was attempting to suffocate me. The only way to prevent this was to lay my head on the very edge of the pillow, which wasn't exactly comfortable, either.

Making matters worse were the rumblings in my stomach. Something I had eaten didn't agree with me. It had to be the mysterious *stew/goo* from the plane. My concerns about possible food poisoning were compounded by the stifling 90-degree heat (Ukraine's summers are as stiflingly hot as its winters are numbingly cold), despite an open window. My general discomfort was made worse by the mosquitoes that were buzzing around my head, routinely sucking blood from my body. I wrapped the sheets around me, but the mosquitoes continued to buzz around my forehead. The sheets also made the heat even more unbearable. Suddenly, I found myself in a heat/mosquito catch-22: keep the window open for at least a small breeze, and get eaten alive by mosquitoes; or, shut the window and suffocate. Initially, I thought the first option was the lesser of two evils, but the mosquitoes were quickly growing in number, so I got up to close the window. This proved to be yet another challenge due to the warped wooden frame. After a fair amount of twisting and pulling I finally managed to close the window.

With the exception of the insomnia I had experienced the summer before I started college, I have always been a sound sleeper, usually falling asleep within seconds. But on this particular night, I stayed awake waiting for the sandman; apparently he had not received the memo that I was out of town. Or maybe he was simply passed out in a Ukrainian gutter?!

As the night dragged on, I grew concerned that the next day would be wasted in a zombie-like state. Of course, thinking about this only made it more difficult to fall asleep.

I stared up at the glow-in-the-dark stars on the ceiling above my head, remembering all those times back home when I stared at the moon and the stars in the night sky, which always made me feel closer to Katya, despite the vast distance that separated us.

Aside from my general restlessness, the rumblings in my stomach continued to worsen. I lay there listening to my stomach doing its best impression of a bubbling swamp.

And then—suddenly—I felt the need to get to the bathroom ... *immediately!*

I climbed out of bed and opened the door—which let out a loud aching, melancholy creak—before tiptoeing out into the hallway.

I crept over to the bathroom, struggling to find the light switch before remembering that the toilet was actually in the room next door. Once there I struggled again to find the light switch. I closed the door—which thankfully didn't creak—and sat myself down on the toilet, snug tightly between the walls like a doll in a box.

At this point, my stomach was really starting to ache. After some stresses and strains, and a few heave-ho's—and completely without warning—I let out an almighty *rip*—one that rattled the walls of the bathroom.

No, no ... please. Not on my first night here. Goddamn that airline food.

I sat there in silence, shocked and embarrassed.

Nervous to try again—but knowing that I had no other choice—I went for the final push. Finally, after a long, arduous, and nerve-wracking battle, I managed to strike gold.

Could they hear me? I'm sure they can. They must be able to.

I attempted to flush the toilet—a task that consisted of pulling a little lever centered at the top of the toilet *up*, which was counter-intuitive after a lifetime of being trained to push down.

But ... *there was no flush.*

I panicked, staring down at my floating "twozies." I tried to flush again, but to no avail. Realizing there was nothing I could do, short of waking someone up, I stepped back into the bathroom to wash my hands. I first tried the sink. *No water.* I tried the tub. *Nothing.*

I stepped back into the hall, pausing briefly to consider waking Katya. I decided, however, that with my luck, Katya's parents would catch me trying to enter her room, assuming I was up to no good. And that's when I remembered the small bottle of hand sanitizer I carried in my backpack. My OCD finally paid off.

I quietly returned to my room and, creaky door notwithstanding, sanitized my hands and laid back down to look at the stars above my head, which had now lost most of their glow.

As I lay there wishing that there was something I could have done about the embarrassing toilet situation, I slowly began to accept the fact that sleep was not on the cards. At least my stomach felt better.

I glanced over toward the computer, wanting nothing more than to go online and read news from back home. But I knew it was no use. Even if I knew how to get online and was able to establish a connection, it would take up to ten minutes to load up a single webpage. As I continued staring at the computer, it felt as though it were taunting me.

As dawn began to break, I heard what sounded like a cat in heat echoing in the distance. As the sound drew closer, it began to sound more human, perhaps a perverse hybrid of cat and human female. As it drew closer, the "moan" became more audible. "*Mooolooookooo!! ... Mooolooookooo!!*" repeated the voice over and over again. I knew that word from somewhere. And then it suddenly hit me: *A Clockwork Orange!* The Korova Milk Bar in the movie *A Clockwork Orange* sold *Moloko Vellocet* ("drug milk," which would help you to prepare for a spot of the old "ultra-violence"). Of course! She's peddling milk!

After a few minutes, the milkmaid's voice began to fade off into the distance, drowning in the cacophony of dawn in this big, vodka-soaked city.

8

SURVIVOR: UKRAINE

Two sleepless hours later, I could hear footsteps. Someone was up and about. I heard a door open. This was followed by the sound of the toilet flushing. *"Please don't let it be Katya!"* I thought, picturing the "comrades" that I left behind in the night now being whisked away.

Whoever it was disappeared down the hallway. Several minutes later, I heard Katya's voice. Trying my best to shake off my embarrassment, I ventured out of my room. Katya greeted me in the hallway.

"Good morning!" she said cheerfully. "How did you sleep?"

"Great," I said, not really sure why I was lying.

Fortunately, my stomachache was now completely gone.

"Liar," Katya said. "How did you sleep *really*?"

"I didn't," I admitted.

Katya smiled, shaking her head.

"By the way, I couldn't flush the toilet last night," I said. "I wasn't doing something right."

"No, it wasn't you. We shut the water off at night," Katya said.

"Why?" I asked.

"So it doesn't flood."

"Does that happen?" I asked.

"Sometimes."

And with that, we headed into the living room for breakfast, where another huge feast awaited—mostly leftovers from the night before.

"Wow! This is breakfast?" I asked.

"Ukrainian-style," Katya replied.

Ukrainian-style breakfast was certainly no bowl full of Cheerios. Bacon and hash browns are one thing. But mashed potatoes?

Two hours later, after the last drop of tea was poured, I decided once again, against my better judgment, to check my e-mail.

After wasting another forty-five minutes trying to establish a connection, I gave up. Katya told me if the problem persisted, she would eventually take me to an Internet café. Taking into account how often Katya e-mailed me and how much of a struggle this was, I now realized the full extent of her love for me. Anyone who endures that much torture to send a simple e-mail had to be in love. Or a sadist.

After momentarily giving up my personal e-mail battle, we set out with Sergei, who had agreed to drive us to downtown Dnipropetrovsk. As we approached Sergei's car, I spotted a middle-aged couple with a small child digging through the dumpster.

I asked Katya if the city had a homeless problem.

"They're *bomzhee* … I think you would say *bums*," Katya replied. "But they're probably not homeless. They're just looking for something to eat. We never saw this until a couple of years ago."

Katya went on to explain that many of those who were now homeless had previously been living in government-issued homes from the Soviet Union. She went on to explain that many of them were unemployed alcoholics, simply left behind by a system that no longer cared. Or at least stopped pretending to care. Once the wall came down, the people who lived between the cracks were suddenly left to fend for themselves. The problem is, they didn't know where to go. They had nowhere to go.

We got into the car and Sergei drove wildly past endless rows of apartment buildings, flashy storefronts and snack kiosks like a newly-licensed New York City cab driver. I held onto the "oh, shit" bar for dear life with one hand and Katya with the other. Katya, meanwhile, remained calm. She was clearly used to it; this was oddly comforting — similar to the way I felt on the Dniproavia flight upon realizing how at ease all the other passengers were.

I noticed several of the apartment buildings had what appeared to be tin foil over many of the windows.

"What's with the foil?" I asked.

"Keeps apartments cool in the summer," Katya said in reply.

"Does it work?"

"They wouldn't do it if it didn't," Katya said in a traditional Ukrainian, no-nonsense demeanor.

As we passed a jogger, Sergei pointed and proclaimed, "My brother!"

"Wow … is that your uncle?" I naively asked.

"No!" said Katya, laughing. "My dad calls every runner his *brother*. He likes to run."

We stopped at a market and bought chocolate bars and lemon-vodka—a more authentic Russian equivalent to *Smirnoff Ice*. I assumed that we would drink them later, but when Katya opened hers up in the car, I quickly learned that unless you are driving, it is legal to drink alcohol inside a moving vehicle. I also learned that a seatbelt latch makes a great bottle opener! And from what I observed, seatbelts are used more often in Ukraine for opening bottles than for their intended use.

Once we had reached the center of Dnipropetrovsk, Katya asked Sergei to drop us off so we could take a walk on our own. Sergei drove away and Katya took me by the arm. This felt awkward to me—as though we were walking down the aisle. In Ukraine, however, linking arms is more customary than holding hands.

"What about our drinks?" I asked, wondering where we might be able to find some brown bags.

"What about them?" Katya replied. "We can still drink them."

"On the street?!" I exclaimed, equally shocked and amazed.

"Sure. Why not?" Katya said, looking confused. "You don't do this in Michigan? People did this in Mississippi."

"No way! Not at all," I replied, "It's illegal—in *all* of America—even Mississippi!"

"Really? That is so *stupid!*" Katya replied.

"Couldn't agree more," I said.

I was about to get my first true test of surviving the streets of Ukraine. For starters, the demeanor of the general public: describing it as "rude" would be a gross understatement. If *Survivor* truly wanted to test the endurance of its contestants, it should send them to Ukraine and force them to figure out things on their own, free of translators and "modern conveniences" that earn us the reputation of *spoiled Americans*—conveniences such as air conditioning, window screens, hot water ... and good, old-fashioned *kindness*.

The judgmental stares I had been experiencing since the airport in Frankfurt were not imagined.

"Maybe I'm just paranoid ... but I feel like I'm being judged everywhere I go," I said.

"You probably are," Katya replied calmly.

"Because I'm an American?"

"That ... but also because you are *dark*."

"Dark?" I said, confused.

I never thought of myself as *dark*. By American standards, I am certainly white, despite my olive-skin tone from my mom's Sicilian side. But back home, I certainly don't appear "ethnic," even at the height of summer. However, from the pale-skinned perspective of Ukrainians, I was *ethnic*—which meant I was "different." And "different" in Ukraine isn't exactly embraced. For the first time in my life, I truly felt like a *minority*. By no means am I suggesting that I understand what it's like to be a minority in the true sense of the word. What I am suggesting, however, is that for the first time in my life, I was aware of my skin color. I felt different from everyone else. *Alienated*. And only when experiencing such a thing, can one truly begin to empathize.

Truth be told, I didn't see a single "minority" during my entire trip. From what I could tell, diversity and Ukraine were like oil and vinegar: they didn't mix. Diversity was simply not embraced in any shape or form. This quickly became evident to me when I began snapping photos ... with a *camera* ... an apparatus that had become a symbol of Soviet distrust. Ukrainians were suspicious of cameras—especially cameras pointed in their general direction, which probably explains why Ukrainians rarely smiled in photographs. This fact was compounded in Dnipropetrovsk by the fact that the city had remained "closed" for so long under Soviet rule. Once I became aware of the history, I understood that the Dnipropetrovsk's citizens' general "coolness" toward strangers wasn't really personal—*at least, not fully.*

We approached an unusual circular building with a tent-like metallic roof.

"What's that?" I asked.

"That's the circus," Katya said. Upon closer inspection, each tip of the "tent," contained a intricate weather-vane in the form of a circus animal.

"When I was little," Katya said, "this was my favorite place in the world. I used to love the clowns."

"No way," I countered. "I can't stand clowns."

"Why?" asked Katya.

"All you have to do is look at a picture of me being held by a clown at a parade when I was two years old. The look of fear on my face ... I haven't recovered since."

"But they're meant to make you laugh," Katya said.

"That's what they want you to think," I said. "But they're all evil!"

Katya admitted that the clowns—like most everything else in the former Soviet Union—were no longer the same.

"In recent years, clowns have been known to pickpocket people," she said. "So I see your point."

Suddenly, Katya threw a protective arm out in front of me.

My first thought was that I was about to be stabbed by a clown, but then I realized that I was mere inches away from falling down a manhole. And judging by the pitch darkness—a very deep hole.

"You have to be careful," Katya said.

"Why isn't there a cover?" I asked.

"Bums steal them and sell them for scrap," Katya explained.

"Why don't they get replaced?"

"They do. But then they get stolen again."

Katya went on to tell me about a family friend whose daughter fell into an uncovered manhole late at night. She wasn't found until the next morning. She survived, but had serious injuries that required surgery. Imagine having to live with that memory for the rest of your life? And who knew what would be down there with you?

I let this experience serve as a warning to be on the lookout every step of the way, keeping one eye ahead and one eye down. In fact, that's probably the best piece of advice I can offer to anyone traveling to Ukraine.

Our next stop was a crowded, open-air market, where stray, mangy mutts hunted for scraps and grimy kittens rubbed against the nearest legs they could find.

Endless kiosks were run by sullen-faced vendors, selling just about everything one would expect to find at a Wal-Mart. However, unlike Wal-Mart, the clothing, perfumes, CDs and DVDs they were selling were all pirated. DVDs of movies *currently in theaters* (and some not even out yet) could be bought on a "five-movies-in-one DVD" for $3.00. Some of these DVDs actually looked very professional. Most of them didn't. These kiosks were not black market, behind-the-counter operations. This was taking place right in the open. Katya explained how the U.S. government had started to crack down on Ukraine, which holds the flag of being one of the world leaders in media piracy. Judging from what I was witnessing with my own eyes, one thing was clear: *the crackdown wasn't working.*

As we continued our way through the congested market, the smell of smoke filled my nostrils. We turned a corner, only to discover a heaping pile of trash burning in the middle of the street. Hordes of people walked past it without any regard to its existence. To them, it was status quo—just one more obstacle, among many, blocking their path. I stood transfixed as the flames grew higher and higher. Several minutes later, a fire truck arrived and extinguished the flames.

As we rounded another corner, an old man with a Santa Claus beard played an accordion while his dog sat by his side, repeatedly vomiting and then proceeding to eat its own vomit. Contenders for the next season of *Ukraine's Got Talent* perhaps? But these aforementioned items weren't a match for the most shocking thing about the market. This honor was reserved for the stacks of meat and fish on display underneath the blistering sun with no refrigeration—enjoyed first by swarms of flies and other unidentifiable bugs before being purchased for human consumption. Suddenly, the previous night's stomach issues made sense.

"Aren't people worried about getting sick?" I asked with great concern.

"That's what vodka is for," Katya said, "Vodka kills the bacteria."

We stopped to purchase some beer and a tasteless, pretzel-like snack called *booblik*—notable for its name alone.

One thing that stood out to me were the perpetually dour expressions on people's faces as they dragged their heavy shopping bags through the market. Even those who carried no bags looked sad. I reminded myself that in private, Ukrainians were warm and hospitable; in public, they didn't tend to show that same warmth. I certainly wasn't going to be hearing the phrase "have a nice day" any time soon!

"Do Ukrainians always look this gloomy?" I asked.

"What do you expect from a country whose national anthem begins with 'Ukraine is not yet dead'?" Katya replied matter-of-factly.

She had a point. At least the anthem later redeems itself with the line "Luck will still smile upon us on us brother-Ukrainians."

Katya continued: "We live in a country where everyday life is unpredictable. We have to adapt to so many things. Rules, laws, governments, economic conditions. Nothing stays the same. No guarantees. It's not easy. It's not like America. Anyway … one thing I noticed when I lived in Mississippi is that Americans smile too much. Maybe that is fake? Maybe we are just more *real* here in Ukraine?"

The only faces perhaps more gloomy than the customers were those of the overworked vendors.

"Do these vendors work out here even in winter?" I asked.

"Of course," Katya replied. "They have no choice. Many have college degrees. Some are probably doctors. But since there's no guarantee of a paycheck from their regular job, this is how they must feed their family."

"Doctors?" I said in surprise.

"Let me put it this way; if it wasn't for my dad, my mom couldn't survive on her salary alone. And that's also why my sister still lives at home. And they are both doctors."

"I can't imagine," I said. "That's just not right."

"Well ... it's not a matter of what's wrong and what's right," Katya continued. "In Ukraine, either you are poor or you are poorer. And if you're rich, you're only rich through corruption. There's no in between. No dreams. That's why I never take anything I have for granted, because even though my family doesn't have much, we have much more than many others here."

A young boy—no more than ten-years-old—approached us, begging for money. His face was caked with dirt, his clothes ratted and torn.

I reached into my pocket and gave him some loose change, most of which were U.S. coins. The boy smiled briefly and said "Spasibo" before approaching the next passer-by. This man shoved the boy aside as though he were one of the stray dogs roaming the market. I found this shocking— but Katya didn't bat an eyelid. I felt naive, over-privileged, sad, hopeless ... *helpless*. It was a different world.

As we continued to make our way through the market, Katya— completely out of the blue—remarked: "How did you find me?"

"You gave me your address," I said, confused.

"No! I mean ... look at all these people. It's just ..."

"Fate?" I asked.

"Or random coincidence of two people being in the right place at the right time?" Katya replied.

"No. I don't think so," I said. "I've never been the kind of guy who could just walk up to a female stranger and strike up a conversation. But somehow ... with you ... *I had no choice*."

I heard music coming from a nearby stall.

"What's that song?" I asked Katya.

It turned out to be "Not Going to Catch Us" by Russian pop group t.A.T.u. This became our de facto theme song throughout the trip. t.A.T.u. were two, hot, barely legal pseudo-lesbians who had caused a great deal of controversy by going against the grain of mainstream Ukrainian thinking—that there are simply "no gays in Russia or Ukraine." They further appealed to their audience by performing in nothing but bras and panties. A few years later, they released an English-language album in U.S., spawning a one-hit wonder with their song, "All the Things She Said." The first time I heard it on the radio in the US, my initial thought was that, by some divine miracle, I was somehow understanding Russian!

As the song concluded, an old babushka woman approached, cup in hand, pointing at us with her long, boney finger: "Take care of one another," she said, in Russian. "No matter what happens in life, take care of one another."

"She wants money," Katya said. "Don't give her any."

I reached into my pocket anyway, and put whatever remaining change I had into her cup. The woman thanked me and left.

"I hate gypsies," Katya said.

"She was a gypsy?"

"Yeah. You couldn't tell?"

Having never met a gypsy, it was not a categorization my brain was trained to assign to people. But I suppose if someone had asked me to describe a gypsy, she would definitely fit the bill.

"They're just so sneaky. And if you cross them, they give you the evil eye."

"Evil eye? Like a curse?" I said, bewildered.

"Yes. Exactly. That's what they're known for."

"Then it's a good thing I gave her money. I can't afford to be cursed."

"They like to take money with one hand and stab you in the back with the other. That's why I prefer not to even look at them," Katya said. "In fact, you'd better give me your wallet. I'll put it away in my purse."

"Why?" I asked.

"Pickpockets. They target westerners, especially Americans."

"How would they know I'm American?"

"They're watching you," Katya said. "Most Ukrainians don't give spare change to beggars and gypsies."

Katya's reply was quickly confirmed by the fact that seemingly every beggar in Dnipropetrovsk began to narrow in on us, as though the Robin Hoodskov they had been waiting for had finally arrived.

I reluctantly handed over my wallet, which Katya buried deeply into her purse.

"What about purse snatchers?" I asked.

"Yeah, that's a problem, too." Katya replied.

Despite this logic, I decided to just go along with her plan and say nothing.

"First my heart ... and now my wallet," I sighed.

"... and next, your soul," Katya said, laughing demonically.

We headed over toward the CD vendor who had been playing the t.A.T.u. song. Since Katya only owned two or three CDs, I decided to help her amp up her collection. Katya chose close to a dozen pirated CDs from Russian and Ukrainian artists, including *t.A.T.u*, *Detsl*—a dreadlocked rapper and Eminem-wannabe, *Alsou*—a Tatarian-Muslim pop diva (who was helped to fame by her father—a very-well-connected oil executive and Russian oligarch), *Zemfira*—a sexually ambiguous Black Sabbath-, Nazareth- and Queen-inspired rocker who shrieked like a tone deaf Janis Joplin, some miscellaneous compilation CDs, and some U.S. artists such as Christina Aguilera and Katya's personal favorite—Britney Spears. The highlight of her selections, however, was a popular Ukrainian folk singer named Verka Serduchka—a drag act (real name, Andriy Danylko) who performed as a flamboyant, middle-aged, rural female train steward (or, from time to time, as a female ballerina). He/she was like the Ukrainian precursor to Lady Gaga in terms of stage presence and persona—years ahead of Gaga. In addition to his successful recording career, Verka Serduchka toured frequently and made numerous appearances on Ukrainian variety shows. Of course, despite his flamboyant stage presence and personality, Katya insisted that he couldn't be gay, since "there were no gays in Ukraine."

We made our bargain of a purchase—a dozen CDs for about 25 *grivnas* (the rough equivalent of five American dollars). The grivna—originally the currency of the medieval state, Kievan Rus—has been the national currency of Ukraine since 1996, replacing the *karbovanets*, which had been subject to hyperinflation in the early 1990s following the collapse of the Soviet Union.

We headed toward what appeared to be a large mob gathering on a street corner. Despite my apprehension, the "mob" turned out to be passengers waiting impatiently for the next electric trolley to arrive. Katya pushed her way through the crowd, dragging me along. The looks on people's faces could have easily been translated as "Check out this idiotic, dark foreigner ... and where is his leash?"

"Isn't this pissing people off?" I asked.

"What do you mean?" Katya asked.

"Cutting in line like this?"

"*There is no line.* Survival of the fittest," she said, "You have to be aggressive, or you'll get eaten alive."

We stopped in the middle of the mob, when Katya grew tired of dragging me through the throngs like a child—something Ukraine had a habit of constantly making me feel like. As we waited, we were pushed and shoved aside by stinky, sticky men who apparently were never introduced to that wonderful product known as deodorant. I held onto Katya tightly, shamefully aware that I was probably coming across as scared shitless.

Finally, the trolley arrived. As soon as it was spotted heading our way, the crowd started to surge toward it, as though it was the last train out of hell. It was completely packed, stopping to let a few people out. A few people fought their way in as though their lives—and their souls—depended on it. The rest of us had to be backed away, literally—by a conductor with a stick—forcing us to wait for the next train.

The next train was also packed, but this time, more people got out. Thanks to Katya's determination, we managed to get on board this time, somehow finding a tiny piece of real estate to stand on amidst the hordes of passengers, shoving and muscling their way in. The entire train was packed from top to bottom, side to side, with bodies contorted every which way as though we were all part of the world's largest game of *Twister*. The trolley was so packed, there was no need to hold onto anything for support. It was like being stuck inside a package full of styrofoam peanuts.

I nervously began to whistle, until Katya whispered:

"Bobby. Stop. It's impolite to whistle in public."

"Sorry," I blurted out, drawing the ire of every passenger within earshot. To distract me, Katya demanded: "Kiss me," drawing even more glares.

"Oh, and that isn't impolite?" I asked with a sly grin.

"No, not in Ukraine."

I kissed her, as a man's butt bumped and grinded me from behind.

To the casual observer, it would be easy to conclude that there was absolutely no way that another human being—not even an infant—could possibly fit into this trolley. Yet at every stop, there were more passengers entering than exiting. *This is how people suffocate to death*, I thought in a growing panic. And at each stop, hordes of people ran toward the trolley, as though it were carrying the body of Lenin himself.

Like the spin of the needle in *Twister*, each stop meant a painful repositioning of the body, as people left the train or got on. *Right foot blue. Left foot yellow.* Only in this particular version of the game, nobody followed the rules. Because there were no rules. This was complete and utter chaos. *This was Ukraine.*

Throughout it all, the frail ticket seller was bounced around like a pinball, desperately trying to collect money, but lucky to charge less than half the passengers. Even those who attempted to pass their money over to her from the opposite side of the train would have it end up in the pockets of less noble countrymen.

As a new swarm of people forced themselves on board—despite the demands of the conductor to back off—I was pushed into a babushka woman's lap, affording me a unique view of the patented glare. Due to the clustered, entanglement of arms separating us from one another, Katya was unable to come to my aid. I was left to fend for myself. Fortunately, the babushka had surprising strength when it came to pushing dark foreigners off of her ancient, musty lap—just as an argument ensued by two men fighting for the same precious spot. The door of the train kept attempting to close, but a rather hefty woman's butt was preventing it from doing so. After getting banged in the butt five or six times, she finally found the energy to heft herself forward, giving the door just enough clearance to close. The train heaved away slowly from the stop, and on to the next.

At this point, a large man's smelly armpit was now hovering over my face, his sweaty hairs all but touching the tip of my nose whenever the trolley bounced. I looked away, only to be treated to the sight of a hairy-legged middle-aged woman with a giant mole on her nose, applying lipstick.

Throughout it all, I remained mute, fearful of blowing my cover if I dared speak English, even though I knew that they knew that I was not one of them. I concluded they would most likely throw me out the door, which might not have been the worst thing in the world, considering the circumstances.

When we reached our stop, Katya pushed her way toward me and aggressively pulled me by the hand through the sea of people like a little brother, swimming up current as new passengers arrived, with no regard to anyone trying to get off.

The trolley actually started moving before we got off, with the door biting me on the butt. One hearty tug from Katya did the trick, as I nearly fell to the broken concrete below. No longer constrained by my fear to speak, I proclaimed with exasperation: "You-have-got-to-be-kidding-me!" Katya shrugged, wondering why I was making such a big deal out of nothing.

On the one hand, I would have much preferred to have walked. But on the other hand, had we done so, I never would have had this truly unforgettable—if not emotionally scarring—experience.

We exited onto the tree-lined *Prospekt Karla Marksa* (Karl Marx Avenue)—Dnipropetrovsk's central avenue, mostly featuring Stalinist Social Realism architecture. As we made our way down the avenue, we noticed a crowd gathered on a main corner. The scene that greeted us quickly put the trolley ride "adventure" into perspective. As we drew closer, I could see a motorcycle helmet lying in middle of the road. Fifty feet further down the road lay a crumpled motorcycle and close by, the lifeless body of a young man—perhaps no more than eighteen or nineteen years old. He was lying face down on the concrete, his broken right arm twisted unnaturally behind his back. A steady stream of blood flowed from his head toward the curb. Rescue personnel were standing over his body, but it was clear there was no hope. A feeling of dread filled my stomach and I remember thinking that somewhere, a mother was totally unaware that her baby was gone forever.

As we stared in disbelief at the horrific scene, I noticed something almost equally shocking. Most of the crowd had already dispersed. Everybody else was a mere passer-by, doing exactly that—*passing by* without taking a second glance. It was one thing not to notice. But of those who did notice, the vast majority didn't seem to react with any emotional response. They merely continued walking, too consumed with the trials and tribulations of daily Ukrainian life or unwilling to "become involved"; too consumed possibly with concerns about whether they would be able to put enough food on the table for their family; or simply too absorbed or imprisoned by the hustle and bustle of life in the big city. *Life just carried on.* The image of that young man lying dead in the street will remain burned into my memory.

Struggling to put this horrific sight behind us, we continued down the avenue in silence. A few blocks later, despite my feelings toward the seemingly uncaring passers-by—*and despite myself*—I could feel myself being drawn toward the dazzling lights of a very kitschy casino. I pleaded with Katya to go in. I had no intention to gamble, but I just had to see what a Ukrainian casino looked like. However, my plan was foiled at the door when we were refused admission—on the account of the fact that I was wearing shorts.

"What if I had been planning on dropping several grand in there?" I said, incredulous.

"Doesn't matter," Katya replied. "You have to be dressed up."

We decided to cross the street and head toward a nearby artists' market. I was determined to get what I so eloquently described as "one of those Russian dolls-inside-a-doll thingamajigs."

"Of course," Katya responded. "They're called *Matrioshka*."

"I want one," I said, acting like a little kid in a candy store.

"Okay," Katya said. "But whatever you do, don't speak."

"Why not?" I asked.

"Because … if they hear you speaking English, they'll charge you more," Katya replied, once again reminding me of the red, white, and blue target I was wearing on my back.

We headed into the market. Tables were filled with handmade crafts for sale, including a huge assortment of wooden Matrioshka "nesting" dolls, artwork and wooden trinkets featuring traditional Ukrainian designs. The artists looked weary. Some of them smelled of booze.

Unable to speak, I simply had to point to the ones I liked—making me look less like a *foreigner* and more like a *mute*.

After I made my selection, Katya handled the negotiating and payment. In Ukraine, *everything* is negotiable.

We then headed down the street and through the columned entrance of Globa Park—Dnipropetrovsk's Central Park—a large expanse of land featuring rickety carnival rides, cafes, discos, an arcade, a children's train, and, in the center, a large, dirty pond complete with rusted, Soviet-era paddleboats.

As we strolled through the park, I observed two drunks passed out on a bench. One of the men held a nearly-empty bottle of vodka in his hand; the other had a balloon on a string wrapped around his wrist. A violinist played a sad, somewhat fitting, Tchaikovsky melody under a small-foot bridge. We made our way toward an amusement arcade where Katya went on to beat me in a game of air hockey.

While passing through the Soviet-era rides, Katya asked if I would like to go on any of them. Upon close inspection, it became clear that these rides had in all likelihood not been maintained since the wall came crumbling down.

"Are they safe?" I asked hesitantly.

"Of course they're safe," Katya replied, adding "they've been here for years."

I felt paradoxically both alarmed and comforted by her response. Looking over my options, I decided that the bumper cars were probably the safest bet. Other than my seat-belt jamming up, I survived.

After that, and at Katya's urging, I decided to set my fears aside in favor of romanticism and give the Ferris wheel—or *koleso obozreniya* (observation wheel)—a spin. The romantic mood was soon interrupted, however, by the loud, incessant grinding of the wheel's moving parts, caused by what I presumed to be old age and rust. The Ferris wheel is—quite possibly for good reason—nicknamed "the Devil's Wheel" in Russian.

As we slowly made our way to the top, the wheel stopped abruptly every five seconds or so to let more passengers on-board—each time causing our carriage to shudder violently. I began to wonder whether this was how it was all going to end. My fear must have been obvious—especially when we reached the top. There was a loud clunk, which caused our carriage to swing back and forth. The wheel then came to an unnaturally long halt.

"Are you okay?" Katya asked when she saw the look of terror on my face. "You look like you just saw a ghost."

"Is this normal?" I asked. "All this stopping and starting?"

"Yes. Of course," Katya replied. "They're just letting more people on. It's no big deal."

"Well … it just seems like we should be moving by now," I replied, gripping the handrail tighter and tighter.

"It's fine. Just enjoy the view," she said, as I felt my dual phobia of heights and claustrophobia begin to kick in. If this was "the Devil's Wheel," then I was most definitely in hell.

"Look!" Katya suddenly exclaimed. "You can see my apartment from here," she said, pointing. I looked over toward an entire landscape of similar looking Soviet-style apartment blocks. Any of them could have been hers. I pretended to recognize the one she was pointing at and smiled, adding an unconvincing "Oh … yeah." I was more concerned as to whether we would make it off the ride alive. I tried again to convince myself that if Katya wasn't fazed by this deathtrap masquerading as a carnival ride, then I shouldn't be fazed. That *kind of* worked.

"Kiss me," Katya demanded, reminding me that this was supposed to be a *romantic* ride. I leaned over, very slowly and carefully, and kissed her.

And then, as though on cue, the Ferris wheel—after a few fits and starts—began once again to splutter into action. When we reached the bottom, the attendant unlocked the handrail and motioned for us to exit.

"That's it?!" I exclaimed—relieved on the one hand, but, on the other hand, feeling completely ripped off.

"We went all the way around," Katya responded matter-of-factly.

"Yeah! Once! And that shouldn't have even counted because they were loading up all the cars."

"We could go on it again," Katya suggested.

"Oh … no … that's okay. I'm fine," I said. *There aren't enough grivnas in all of Ukraine to pay me to go on that thing again!*

In fact, to avoid any possibility of having to endure another ride, I quickly suggested that we get an ice cream from a nearby vendor.

"I'll have that one," I said, pointing to an ice cream cone of some sort.

"I want to see you order, Bobby," Katya demanded.

"Why?"

"I want to see you take charge."

"How?" I asked.

"It's easy."

"Uh … Okay."

I could tell I wasn't going to win this argument.

"I'm all for taking charge," I said, "but not when I can't speak the language."

"There are other ways to communicate. I'll have a fruit bar."

"I'm not ready to take that leap of faith yet," I said.

"It's just ice cream," Katya replied, laughing.

"Maybe if I were drunk," I said.

"This isn't rocket science," Katya replied.

I stood my ground and stared at her in silence.

Katya finally gave in. "Okay … watch, listen, and learn."

Katya caught the vendor's attention, speaking in English, while pointing to each item, making it clear as to exactly what she wanted.

After handing her the ice cream, the vendor specified the amount in Russian. Katya then handed her ten grivnas, shrugging her shoulders in a manner that suggested she needed help. The vendor took the required amount, before giving Katya back her change. And lo and behold … she did it. As it turned out, an ice cream cone in Ukraine is more expensive than a CD.

"You are amazing," I said to her, as she counted her change.

"I'm surprised she didn't rip me off."

"What if she did?" I asked.

"I wouldn't have let her get away with it. I would have had to go back to my Russian roots to get my money back."

"But if it were me, how would I know?"

"It's a chance you would have had to take," Katya replied. "You just have to accept that they are going to use you."

"Did I mention you are amazing?"

"Yeah, but I like to hear you say it," Katya said, smiling.

"You *are* amazing."

After I kissed her, she looked down at her hand, which was covered with melted ice cream.

"Look at what you did, Bobby!" she exclaimed.

I proceeded to lick it off.

"Gross!" Katya proclaimed.

"How is that gross?" I asked.

"In Ukraine, we don't lick in public!"

"Oh, okay … I see," I said, remembering all the couples we saw making out the night before. I decided to leave well enough alone.

We then headed over to a curb overlooking a paddle-boat lake. Shortly after sitting down, a babushka approached us, waving her boney finger:

"What are you doing?!" the babushka started in on us. "You will catch a cold from sitting on cold concrete like that!"

Katya laughed, translating as the woman continued to yell.

"Just ignore her, she's talking nonsense" Katya said. "She'll go away." But this babushka was persistent. We finally got up just so we could shake her.

Babushka: 1. Bobby & Katya: 0.

Katya proposed taking a ride on the paddle boats. This seemed like a safe enough proposition to me. We approached the attendant on the paddle-boat dock. All I could make out of the conversation was the attendant responding with a curt "nyet."

"They're not open," Katya explained.

"How come?" I asked naively.

"Well, I think they might be open. I'm thinking that he said that they're not because he doesn't want to work."

"Isn't there somebody we can talk to?"

"Who?!" Katya said—definitively closing the door to that possibility.

We wondered over to a bench overlooking the pond.

"When I was little, I used to love coming here to feed the ducks," Katya said. "There used to be a lot more of them."

"What happened to them?"

"Bums took them."

"What do you mean 'took them'? Took them where?"

"To eat."

"What?! On the way home from selling the manhole covers as scrap?"

"Probably, yes," Katya said. "And speaking of food, we better head back before my parents worry. It's almost time to kushat."

"Who shat?!"

"*Kushat!* Eat!"

As we walked back past the Ferris wheel, we heard shouting and saw a small crowd of gawkers. It appeared that the wheel was stuck. As I looked at the passengers in the top car, I recognized them as a family that had been standing in line behind us. It had been over an hour since we had left the ride. Since we had to head back for dinner, we never found out how long they ended up having to stay up there. Katya explained to me that it happened all the time. Despite this knowledge, that hadn't stopped her from taking me on it. At least next time, I would be better prepared to say "nyet."

As we continued our way out of the park, I begged Katya to take another mode of transportation back home. We approached a taxi, idling in the middle of the street, only to discover the driver was asleep … or, possibly, dead. Katya tapped on the window, and the driver didn't budge, giving more credence to the latter theory. She knocked again. This time, he woke up, but angrily waved us away before falling back asleep.

Katya suggested we take the Metro, convincing me everything would be fine. Unlike the crumbling trolley system, the Metro was in generally good condition, having just opened six years prior. The problem was, it wouldn't take us very far. Dnipropetrovsk's Metro only consisted of one line with six stations. Additional stations had been under construction, but were abandoned when the city ran out of funds to complete the project;

two of the abandoned stations were right in the heart of the city.

While heading toward our platform, we passed a flower vendor.

"Wait here a second," I said to Katya, heading off toward the vendor. The vendor, a rather rotund lady in a headscarf and a heavy, wool coat "greeted" me with a look that suggested a mixture of indifference, annoyance, and disgust. Unperturbed, I began to look through the frail offerings of long-stemmed roses. It took a while, but I finally found one that was passable. As I reached into the bucket to pull it out, the vendor slapped my arm, saying something to me in Russian that was probably along the lines of "get your dirty, fucking hands off my roses, asshole!"

I explained, "Nyet Russkiy." The vendor made the universal gesture for money by rubbing the tips of three fingers together. I reached into my pocket, forgetting that I was not in possession of my wallet.

"One moment," I said to the vendor, who rolled her eyes. I headed back to Katya.

"You don't have to buy me flowers," Katya said.

"I know. But I *want* to," I said, as she handed me my wallet. I rushed back to the vendor and handed her ten grivnas.

"Nyet," the vendor said, shaking her head. I handed her another ten. Satisfied, she gave me back a couple of coins. I knew I was being ripped-off, but I was already beginning to acclimate myself to Ukrainian resignation.

I reached for the rose and once again, the vendor yelled at me. I turned to look at Katya, who was now laughing. As I turned back around, I watched as the vendor grabbed a different flower—one that was clearly on life support and clearly the worst in the batch. I decided that I wasn't going to argue with her. She handed the rose to me in a manner that suggested I was causing her a major inconvenience by simply doing business with her, and that I needed to *leave. Now.*

I trudged over to Katya, and handed her the limp, dying flower.

"Thank you Bobby," she said, kissing me on the cheek.

"I'm sorry it's dead," I added.

"I didn't even notice." Katya replied. "How much was it?"

"About twenty grivnas, I think," I replied.

"Oh, yeah!" said Katya angrily. "She robbed you. I'll be right back."

Katya turned to head back towards the vendor. However, I stopped her from going any further.

"It's okay," I said. "She needs that money more than I do."

Katya reluctantly agreed.

We boarded our train. The ride back miraculously passed without incident—presumably only because I kept my promise not to speak any English.

We got off the train, ascended back to street level, and made our way back to Katya's apartment building, winding our way through street after street of similar looking buildings.

"I don't know how you get around here," I said. "Everything looks the same."

"It's easy," Katya replied. "Some buildings are uglier than others."

That night, I lay there staring at the stars above my bed, replaying the day's events in my mind. It all still felt like a crazy dream. But there was one thing about which I was *sure*. I reached over to my backpack and took out the ring box. I decided then and there: *tomorrow would be the day.*

But first, I had to make it through another restless night.

9

A DAY AT THE BEACH

As I sat on the couch in my room, waging an internal debate as to whether I should carry the ring in my pocket or in my backpack, the door creaked open and Katya entered—leaving me no choice but to quickly shove the box behind my backpack.

"Ready?" Katya asked.

"Yep," I said, trying to remain calm and collected, but failing miserably.

"Are you okay, Bobby?" Katya asked, sensing my nervousness. I assured her that I was and gave her a comforting hug.

"Okay, let me grab my purse," Katya said. As she left the room, I slipped the ring box into my backpack.

In the few minutes before we left, I obsessively-compulsively double- and triple-checked to make sure that the ring was safe—as though it could somehow find a way to slip through the canvas fabric.

We were off to Monastyrsky Island, located on the Dnieper River. During the ninth century, Byzantine monks formed a monastery at this location, which was destroyed by Mongol-Tatars in the thirteenth century. The island is now home to Shevchenko Park (named after the famous Ukrainian poet, Taras Shevchenko) and consists of a beach, rides, cafes, a zoo, an aquarium—and a smattering of broken beer and vodka bottles.

The pedestrian bridge leading to the island was a hassle-free ten-minute walk from Katya's apartment, along the Dnieper. No harrowing trams, trolleys, or route vans were necessary this time. By the same token, I couldn't use a mode of public transportation as a cover for the distressed look on my face.

"Are you sure nothing's wrong?" Katya asked.

"Yeah. I'm fine," I assured her with a forced smile.

As we stepped onto the bridge, I noticed several padlocks and various other lock-type mechanisms attached to the rails of the bridge. Katya informed me it was a tradition for young lovers to fasten locks ("locks of love") on the bridge and then throw the keys down into the river below in a symbolic effort to secure their love forever.

"Sounds like a prison sentence," I said.

"No! It's romantic!" Katya said, laughing.

"Too bad we didn't bring a lock with us," Katya said.

"Next time," I replied.

Little did she know that I was carrying a "lock" of my own, waiting to be tied onto her finger in the very near future.

"You look stressed," Katya said.

"No ... I feel great," I said.

"Are you sure? You seem ... distracted."

"Just thinking."

"About what?"

"A secret," I said smiling.

"What secret??!" Katya asked, her eyebrows narrowing.

"Well, if I told you ... then it wouldn't be a secret anymore!"

"Not fair," Katya protested.

"I promise you'll know soon enough," I assured her.

Halfway across the bridge, we came upon a group of teenage boys decked out in tight Speedos, taking turns to swig from a vodka bottle. They were laughing and joking, and leaning over the side of the bridge shouting down to someone in the river. I went over to the side of the bridge and looked down, just as one of their comrades surfaced above the water some fifty feet below.

He was greeted with applause from his friends. He shouted up toward the group and motioned for the rest of his buddies to join him. One by one, they did. It was shocking to see—maybe more so due to the Speedos they were wearing, than the height from which they were jumping.

When we arrived on the island, we were greeted by an enormous statue of Taras Shevchenko (1814–1861), considered to be Ukraine's greatest poet and the foundation of modern Ukrainian literature with a profound influence on the modern Ukrainian language. This is a relevant sample of his work (translated by John Weir):

Don't Wed

Don't wed a wealthy woman, friend,
She'll drive you from the house.
Don't wed a poor one either, friend,

Dull care will be your spouse.
Get hitched to carefree Cossack life
And share a Cossack fate:
If it be rags, let it be rags,
What comes, that's what you take.
Then you'll have nobody to nag
Or try to cheer you up,
To fuss and fret and question you
What ails you and what's up.
When two misfortune share, they say,
It's easier to weep.
Not so: it's easier to cry
When no-one's there to see.

As we ventured onto the island, Katya told me that, according to urban legend, it was somehow mysteriously surrounded by powerful energy fields, creating entrances to parallel worlds.

"Oh, you mean radioactivity?" I joked.

"Probably so," Katya said. "Or, perhaps too much vodka."

We both laughed. Katya then led me past St. Nicholay Church, a small, white Ukrainian Christian Orthodox church, crowned with a golden dome, on the river's edge. I asked if we could go in. Katya initially hesitated because she didn't have anything to wear over her hair, which is custom for women entering a church in Ukraine. She decided to chance it, so we entered, past the judgmental glare of the church caretaker watering a bed of overgrown weeds. The stream of water from his hose caught the golden sunlight just right, creating a mini rainbow.

The first thing I noticed upon entering was an absence of pews. I assumed that this had something to do with the church's diminutive size. However, I later discovered that pews are not traditionally installed in any Orthodox churches. Not even churches are immune from causing discomfort for people in Ukraine. It's no wonder that more than sixty percent of Ukrainians consider themselves non-religious.

Unlike my moderate Catholic upbringing, Katya—despite believing in God—didn't grow up going to church. Sergei and Elena are from an era when religion was banned throughout the Soviet Union. It is for this reason that Santa Claus arrives on New Year's Eve and weddings take place in city halls. Even funerals rarely took place in church. In fact, many of the city's churches were either destroyed during World War II, or destroyed during Stalin's reign of terror in the 1930's.

"Did I ever tell you that my great-grandmother spent twelve years in prison for teaching kids how to cross themselves?" Katya said.

"Seriously?" I said, incredulous.

"It was a crime during our years of communism. But despite this, she never lost her faith. Her son—my grandfather—was jailed, too. Guilt by association. During World War II, while my great-grandfather was fighting against the Nazis in Berlin, they were in jail."

"Your great-grandfather fought in Berlin?" I asked.

"Yes. He helped liberate it," Katya said.

My jaw must have dropped.

"What's wrong?" Katya asked.

"My great-grandfather was captured by the Russians in Berlin, fighting *for* the Nazis," I confessed.

"Did he survive?" Katya asked.

"Actually, yes. He spent twelve years in a Russian prison camp."

"Wow. He was lucky. Very few made it out alive."

"He never talked about it," I said. "About anything he did in the war. Or in prison."

We sat in silence reflecting on this unexpected coincidence, pondering the what-ifs.

Then, out of the blue, Katya asked me: "What do you think heaven's like?"

I thought for a moment before responding: "Well … I like to think heaven is being able to relive your favorite memories over and over again, without the pain, mistakes, and sadness that fall in between. And each time you relive a memory, it feels like it's happening for the first time."

"I like that," Katya said. "What memories would you relive?"

"Every moment of this trip," I said.

"Even this one?"

"Especially this one."

"What about the Ferris wheel?" Katya asked, grinning.

"Yeah, even that one," I said, half in jest.

"I definitely like your vision," Katya said. "And if there is a heaven, I'd like to think that you can also change things for the better that didn't work out the first time."

"Beats sitting on a big, fluffy cloud, that's for sure," I joked.

Just then, like a bat out of hell, the caretaker burst through the church doors, startling us both.

"Where is your head covering, young lady?" the caretaker demanded to know. "Have you no shame in front of God? Shame on you. Shame on you!"

Realizing we had no choice, we left, vanquishing all hope for taking advantage of the perfect setting for a proposal.

"What's his problem?" I asked.

"He's Ukrainian," Katya said, grabbing me by the hand and leading me down dilapidated steps into the wooded area behind the church. We reached the edge of the river and sat down on a giant rock jutting out into the water, the church looming behind us like a stoic guardian.

"I've been coming down here ever since I was a little girl," Katya said. It's where I come to think. You're the first person I've shown it to."

"How did I get the honor?" I asked.

"You must be lucky, I guess."

"I know I'm lucky," I said. "So what do you come here to think about?"

"Anything. Everything. Sometimes nothing ... *You*." She looked away, embarrassed.

"What are you thinking about right now?" I asked.

"The present," Katya said. "Because I never want this to end."

"And what do you see?"

"You. *Us*."

"And how does that make you feel?"

"Happy, secure."

"How do you see yourself ten years from now?" I asked.

"Ten years from now ... hmm. That's a tough one."

"Don't tell me you never thought of it."

"Ten years from now ..." Katya pondered. "Okay. Here it goes. Happily married. Two children. Maybe three. What about you?"

"Oscar-winning screenwriter, happily married, two children. Maybe three."

We smiled at this glimpse of our possible, distant future.

"It's nice to predict the future," Katya began, "but if you think about it too much, the future never comes. Everything happens in the present.

But time moves too quickly for us to realize it, which is why we are always looking at the past. And even if the future does come, it rarely comes the way we imagined it. So that's why I don't like talking about it."

I watched Katya as she sat in quiet contemplation.

This was the perfect opportunity to make my move.

But right at that moment — as though they were reading my thoughts — a group of rowdy teenagers with beer, cigarettes, and vodka crashed our little private party. Sensing danger, Katya hopped off the rock and suggested we head to the beach.

We headed across the island, past more rides — in perhaps worse shape than the ones in Globa Park — past more cafes blaring Russian techno pop and finally arriving at the nearly-empty beach, where vendors hawked corn-on-the-cob, sandwiches and other snacks from heavy, metallic trays hanging over their necks.

Before we hit the sand, we decided to head inside the meager dump of an aquarium. It was difficult to fathom how life of any sort could be sustained in such a place. It smelled of death, so perhaps my suspicions were confirmed. Surprisingly, the variety of aquatic life on display was impressive. The highlight was the "American Turtle," who swam right up to the glass to greet us, appearing to wave (or, perhaps begging for freedom ... or a green card).

"He's waving at us," Katya said. "He must know you're American."

I waved back. The turtle seemingly waved even harder, before swimming away and coming to rest in a faraway corner of his dark tank, presumably to disappear into his shell and cry.

Katya led me out of the aquarium. The sunlight was blinding.

We then found a relatively un-littered spot on the beach, despite the vast amount of cigarette butts, wrappers, and occasional sliver of broken glass protruding out of the sand. A rusty railroad bridge spanned the river, enhancing the picturesque, industrial setting. It was clearly not the most scenic beach in the world, but as far as my impending proposal was concerned, it would have to do. Besides, there was a certain aesthetic to urban grittiness that I found hopelessly romantic. Maybe it had to do with being from Detroit? Or, maybe it had more to do with the sight of Katya in a sexy, blue bikini, revealing more of her snow-white beauty than I had seen up until that moment.

As we lay on our large beach towel beneath the golden sun, kissing, an instrumental version of the "Happy Birthday" song was faintly audible in the distance, growing closer and closer. It had that tinny, slightly out-of-tune quality of ice cream truck music. When the song ended, it started over again. I sat up and looked in the general direction of the sound. In the distance, I spotted the vague outline of what appeared to be a person—perhaps hunchbacked—walking towards us along the shore, with a small, indistinguishable *thing* walking just ahead of him. As they drew closer, I could see that whatever the thing was, it appeared to be on a leash. Was it a child? A dog? *A dog-child?* It was difficult to fathom. Whatever it was, it was wearing pants. Upon closer inspection, I realized it was a *monkey*, being walked by a man playing "Happy Birthday" through a megaphone, desperately trying to lure customers into shelling out 10 grivnas in exchange for a photo with the monkey.

I leaped up, grabbed Katya by the hand and headed toward the monkey, drawing obligatory strange looks from the few scattered beachgoers. *The crazy foreigner was at it again.* But I knew that this was likely to be a once-in-a-lifetime opportunity.

I paid the man and handed him my camera—hoping that he wouldn't suddenly point and say something like "hey ... look over there!" before running off with it. The man then proceeded to position the monkey in my arms, posing me next to Katya. It must have resembled some kind of deranged family portrait.

As the man stepped back to take our photo, he decided he wasn't happy with his monkey's positioning. After he had repositioned the stubborn monkey just so, he took another step back, but this time, the cheeky monkey started playing with—and then pulling—my ear. Suddenly, I didn't feel too keen about the whole idea.

The man gestured wildly and shouted at the monkey—"*Plokhaya obez'yana!*" ("Bad monkey!"), then stepped back to take another photo.

Just before he was able to take the photo, the monkey grabbed *both* of my ears. I screamed in pain. The monkey screamed back. The owner slapped the monkey's paws. But it was no use. As the monkey continued to scream and pull on my ears, the man stepped back to snap a quick photo, before proceeding to grab the monkey away from me. The monkey then demonstrated his dissatisfaction at being berated by peeing on his owner. The man handed my camera back to me and said something in Russian that I gathered to be an apology. He then leaned down and slapped the monkey hard on the back of his head. I watched as they both waddled off, arguing with each other. As we walked back to our towel, I was half-traumatized, half euphoric over the surreal incident that had just transpired.

Following the rogue monkey episode, I had another brush with Mother Nature in the form of a mad bee. After buying corn-on-the-cob (*kukuruza*) from a passing babushka vendor, my enjoyment of said corn was hampered by a pesky bee, perhaps confusing the cob for a honeycomb. Next to my fear of clowns, bees are a pretty close second (being stung by a bee outside of a grocery store at the age of two probably has a lot to do with it, as does my being teased by a clown that very same summer). In an effort to appear brave, I tried my best to remain calm and wait for it to fly away. But I can only feign manliness for so long, especially as the bee kept circling around me, occasionally landing on my corn and fingers.

When I couldn't take it anymore, I darted to my right like a running back dodging oncoming defenders. The bee followed me, so I darted to my left. It followed me again. And by now it was pissed. Meanwhile, Katya kept imploring me to stay still. *But I couldn't.* The bee left me no choice but to make a "beeline" directly toward the water, dropping my half-eaten corn in the sand. Once in the water (and cob-less), I figured I was finally safe. But that insane bee still followed and was now circling my head. It continued to hover above me, even as I fully submerged myself into the water. Fortunately, after a few seconds, it must have decided that it had tortured me enough and flew off to find its next victim.

Still laughing at my expense, Katya decided to join me in the water, which smelled of a putrid mixture of algae, sulfur and other unidentifiable chemical odors. This made sense considering the line of factories across the river.

And then a thought occurred to me.

"This river doesn't happen to flow through Chernobyl, does it?" I said to Katya, with visions of radiation dancing in my head.

"No," replied Katya, giving me temporary relief—before casually adding "but one of its tributaries does."

Located about four hundred miles northwest of Dnipropetrovsk, Chernobyl is famous for the 1986 nuclear power plant explosion that is considered to be the worst nuclear power plant disaster in history. To put this in perspective, *four hundred* times more radioactive material was released at Chernobyl than at Hiroshima. More than one million people are believed to have been affected by radiation from Chernobyl.

Despite Katya's assurances that it was completely safe to swim in a river that received water from a Chernobyl tributary, I considered high-tailing it back to the shore nonetheless; but I stayed put realizing that any potential damage had already been done. As long as I didn't swallow, I figured that any health risks would be kept to a minimum.

Any thoughts of Chernobyl quickly floated away down the river however when Katya swam over to me, flung her arms around me, and started to kiss me passionately. If her plan was to make me forget any potential biohazard danger, then it definitely worked.

After a few minutes, Katya swam back to the shore, but I stayed behind in the water.

"What's wrong?" Katya asked when she realized I wasn't following her.

"I don't think I should get out just yet," I replied, laughing.

"Why? What's wrong?" Katya asked, concerned.

"Well … it's … how can I put it … *a male thing!*"

Katya finally caught on.

"Well, then! I'd better get out of your way," she said, laughing. As she walked back over the sand toward the towel, I tried not to watch her— trying to refocus my attention to my biggest turn-offs list (radioactive waste being one of them) to help cure my "affliction."

And lo and behold, after several minutes, I was once again able to show my front side to the world and rejoin my beautiful mermaid, waiting for me on the towel.

I decided there and then. *It was time.*

"I have something to show you," I said, reaching over to my backpack. "Close your eyes."

Katya covered her eyes and I proceeded to unzip my backpack and remove the ring case. I got down on one knee and opened the case.

"Okay. You can open them now."

Katya opened her eyes. She stared at the ring.

"Katya ... will you marry me?" I asked.

"What is it?" Katya asked, looking genuinely confused—and seemingly somewhat agitated.

"My secret!" I replied. "I was going to ask you at the end of my trip, but I couldn't wait any longer."

"Is this for real, Bobby?" Katya asked.

She still wasn't smiling. *Not exactly the reaction I was hoping for.*

"Remember that secret I told you about?" I reminded her.

"You are *crazy!*" Katya replied.

"Does that mean *yes*?"

"Wow. This feels like a movie or something."

"I know, but it's not. And I need you in my life ... for the rest of my life."

"I don't believe this," Katya said.

"*Does that mean yes?*" I asked again. I was starting to feel nervous.

"I love you Bobby! A lot! And yes I can picture myself with you. But it all seems too good to be true. I need to think; to be sure. Do you have any idea what you're getting into?"

"Of course I do!" I insisted.

"Trust me, in my heart, I want to say *yes* more than anything. But in my mind ... we can't let emotion get in the way of rational thought. I mean ... it's too soon. And my parents. I mean ... this isn't America. It's not Hollywood. I'll need their approval."

"I can talk to them," I said confidently.

"But *you can't* talk to them," Katya replied.

"You can translate," I said.

"Yes ... but it's even more important for my parents to get to know you better. This has nothing to do with how *I* feel."

Katya hugged me, admiring the ring. "Bobby, it's beautiful."

"You had no clue whatsoever?" I asked Katya, smiling.

"Well, I'd be lying if I didn't admit it was in the back of my mind," Katya replied. "But I thought it was just fantasy. Can I try it on?"

"Not until it's official," I said teasingly.

"But what if it doesn't fit?"

"Something tells me it will," I said, putting the ring back into the box and placing it safely back into my backpack, secretly hoping that this would somehow sway her into fully accepting my proposal right then and there. No such luck.

And as we headed off the beach, I struggled to fully grasp whether what had just happened was more success or failure. On one hand, anything less than "yes" was failure. But Katya hadn't said "no." That much was true. But at the same time, a simple "yes" would have made me feel much better about the whole situation.

Katya then grabbed me by the hand and said "Look, Bobby ... as far as you and I are concerned, nothing's changed. In fact, I know it's only going to get better." Despite the fact that my proposal did not exactly go as planned, Katya did have me convinced.

Rather than taking the bridge back, Katya suggested that we head over toward a cable car ride. The cable cars carried riders to a height of more than one-hundred feet above the river, offering incredible views of the city.

After paying the disinterested attendant, we approached the seatless cars—equipped with nothing resembling modern safety standards. Getting into one of the small, fast-moving cars required deft timing and coordination—*two skills that I lack*. I have the same difficulty climbing onto the first step of a down escalator—always fearful that I am going to misjudge my step and fall to my death. Katya easily slipped into the moving car, while I struggled mightily, almost falling out, had it not been for Katya reeling me back in.

I hung on for dear life as we wobbled our way up, high above the Dnieper River. My fear was amplified when we began to drift across land, with the realization that the odds of surviving a malfunction were suddenly much less. It would be just my luck to die in a freak cable car accident, minutes after proposing to the woman of my dreams. I made it my goal right then and there to avoid riding any more elevated Ukrainian amusements, though it was beginning to feel like my destiny.

As we wobbled our way along, Katya kept assuring me that we would be fine. And I wanted to believe her. But one can only cheat death so many times before the law of averages balances out. Katya's attempts at kissing me out of my fear might have worked had it not been for the fact that any shift of weight caused the car to tip more than it should be allowed to. I sold myself once again on the conviction that if it wasn't worrying Katya, then it wasn't going to worry me either. *Easier said than done.*

Five minutes later, we were finally descending toward the station on the other side of the river. Katya prepared for our grand exit.

"Get ready," she instructed. "You have to be *quick*."

I didn't like the sound of that.

"You have to get out as soon as you can."

As the car zeroed in on the runway, Katya popped the door open, practically hanging out of the car as it soared fifty feet above ground. I began to realize that there was nothing to slow the car down. And we were moving at a pretty good clip. Yet somehow, we were expected to exit the moving vehicle.

Upon landing, Katya quickly jumped out and immediately reached for my hand, which allowed me to awkwardly leap out, nearly tripping onto the concrete platform.

Past the judgmental eye of another babushka (I was convinced more than ever that they were all in collusion), I suddenly realized why it had been so important to jump out of the car when we did. As our car entered the turnaround station, I watched as it literally flipped upside down before flipping back around, heading in the opposite direction. And that was no more than twenty feet away from where I stumbled out. Death, or maiming, averted yet again.

Following yet another harrowing Ukrainian experience, we headed over to one of Dnipropetrovsk's greatest landmarks—the Monument of Glory. Perched high above the Dnieper River, the Monument of Glory is a World War II memorial at the foot of Karl Marx Avenue, which, to me, resembled, ironically, the Statue of Liberty.

We sat the base of the monument and took in the scenic view of the river down below. Katya leaned over and kissed me. Before long we were kissing in a way that felt deeper than any other kiss before. The surroundings were fitting, considering that this was a popular site to have marriages blessed.

We then walked alongside the river and headed toward the *Sweet Tooth*—an outdoor café situated on the riverfront. Katya ordered two slices of famous Kiev cake (*Kievsky tort)* and a bottle of champagne (*Sovetskoye Shampanskoye*).

Forty-five minutes later, we were still waiting.

We watched as the waitress served a young couple that had arrived several minutes after us.

"Say hello to Ukrainian service," Katya said.

Over Katya's shoulder, I noticed what appeared to be an unfinished white, yellow, and green skyscraper further down the river. "What are they building there?" I asked.

"They *were* building a hotel," Katya began. "But it wasn't built to code, so they just abandoned it. It's been sitting that way for over ten years."

"The cranes, too?" I said, in reference to the two massive construction cranes that stood alongside the unfinished building—a symbol of inefficient Soviet planning.

"Yep, the cranes, too," Katya replied.

"You mean they just abandoned *everything*?"

"There's really nothing else they can do," Katya replied. "See that railroad bridge?" Katya continued, pointing to a nearby bridge reaching out across the river.

"Yeah?"

"That was also not built to code. Notice how it curves?"

"Yeah???"

"Bridges aren't supposed to curve. They're supposed to be straight. For safety reasons."

"Wonderful," I remarked.

"Everyone's waiting for a train to one day fall into the river," Katya explained. "Of course, there's a greater chance the bridge will collapse first before that ever happens."

She turned her attention to a couple sitting nearby.

"By the way Bobby, you're not the only American in this café."

"What do you mean?" I said, straining my neck to get a better look.

"Let's see, *Jansport* backpack; shorts; tennis shoes; baseball hat."

"You mean Ukrainians don't carry *Jansport* backpacks and wear tennis shoes and baseball caps?" I asked.

"Usually not all three at once. And especially not baseball hats. That's a sure sign that he's American. Of course, the only way to be sure would be to hear him talk."

Katya got up and nonchalantly walked past the couple, then returned.

"Yep … he's American."

"What about his date?"

"Mail order bride," she stated matter-of-factly.

"How do you know?"

"You can just tell … especially by the way she's dressed. And her make-up. Like that of a clown."

"I've heard about those," I said. "But I thought it was more of a stereotype."

"It *is* a stereotype," Katya said. "Because it happens so frequently. Can you believe I've once been approached by a mail order agency?"

"Really?" I said. "What did you tell them?"

"Would you turn down $200?"

"Seriously?!" I asked, shocked.

"No! Of course not," Katya smirked. "I would never be that desperate. And my parents would never approve," she said—indirectly making me nervous about the whole parental approval thing.

"Look at her!" Katya said, glancing back over toward the couple.

Mimicking a thick, Ukrainian accent, Katya continued: "I am poor little Ukrainian girl, looking for love from rich American man to take me to nice American home."

"Love the accent!" I said.

"I don't know what you talk about," Katya continued in an even thicker accent. "This is my natural, how you say, speech. I know my English is not so good. But I study much to improve so I get green card from rich, American man."

"They're probably thinking the same thing about us, you know," I pointed out.

"Probably," Katya replied. "But we're used to it here."

Finally, the waitress arrived with our order. I poured two glasses of champagne and then raised my glass for a lame attempt at a toast.

"To us."

We clinked glasses and sipped, just as our song — "Not Going to Catch Us" — began to play.

After we had finished up our cake and champagne, I paid and put down a tip.

"You don't have to do that," Katya said. "Tips aren't custom here."

"Well, I'm sure she will appreciate it," I said.

"She's going to think you're strange. And she'll probably be offended."

"Well, let her be offended," I said, trying to grapple with the flawed logic. "I'm leaving a tip anyway."

We then stumbled out of the *Sweet Tooth* and passed the Soviet-era "Dnepropetrovsk Hotel." A bunch of scantily clad women were loitering on the steps outside the main entrance.

"Are those what I think they are?" I asked.

"Prostitutes? Yes," Katya replied.

"Are they legal?" I asked.

"You mean in terms of age?"

"Well, that ... but I mean more in terms of prostitution in general."

"No, it's not legal," Katya replied. "But in Ukraine, there's nothing money can't make legal if the price is right."

And with that, we headed back to the apartment, where another Ukrainian feast awaited us.

10

CINEMA UKRAINE

By some divine miracle, Katya's parents granted us permission to see a movie *after dark*. As Sergei dropped us off in front of the *Krasnaya Gvardiya* (Red Guard) Soviet-era movie theater, I felt like I was back in high school. And by Soviet-era, I mean closer on the timeline to Stalin than Gorbachev. Both the exterior and interior of the theater exhibited the drab "colors" one would expect from Stalinist design. The furniture and décor were tattered and torn. At one point, I'm sure that it had some aesthetic value, but now, it appeared as though deathly collapse was imminent.

The movie playing in the nearly empty, single-auditorium theater was *Bridget Jones's Diary*, dubbed into Russian. Fortunately, I had already seen this movie back home, so I didn't have to worry about being completely lost. In an effort to show more independence from Russia, the Ukrainian government mandates that English movies dubbed into Russian are then doubled-dubbed into Ukrainian, even though most Ukrainians speak Russian as their primary language. In fact, some Ukrainians speak no Ukrainian whatsoever. Government officials are also required to speak Ukrainian in public, although many speak broken-Ukrainian since Russian is their "native" language.

Furthermore, unlike the unlicensed, pirated movies sold on the street, theatrical releases are professionally dubbed by different actors for each part. Typically, pirated movies in Ukraine are dubbed over by a single "actor"—who for some reason always sounds gruff and drunk. Furthermore, there is little to no effort to change the inflection from one character to the next, regardless of age or gender.

Another notable detail about Ukrainian movie-going was the fact that we had to choose our seats, much like going to a ballgame or concert. And just like at a ballgame or concert, the cheaper seats were in the back; the "prime seats" in the front. So the opportunity to have to crane your neck all the way back into the row behind you just to see the entire screen was actually more expensive than a seat with far better sight lines. We decided that saving money and being more comfortable was a no-brainer.

We headed over to the concession line and purchased warm beer and a bucket of stale popcorn. The doors to the auditorium were still closed, so I decided to take some photographs. Next thing I knew, a middle-aged woman came running out from a dark corner of the building demanding that I put my camera away at once. Startled, I obliged. Perhaps her concern was that my flash would somehow accelerate the peeling of the paint that was trying its best to cling to the walls and ceiling.

"Don't do that!" Katya warned.

"Why?" I naively asked.

"Because they don't like it," was all she could say in reply.

Suddenly, a bell rang, startling me as it echoed loudly throughout the building.

"Are we late for class?" I joked.

"It means they're seating," Katya replied, unimpressed with my attempt at humor.

And with that, we headed inside the auditorium. Katya began translating for me, but I told her to just enjoy the movie. I enjoyed the challenge of trying to figure out what was being said merely on body language and inflection. And it was amazing how much I was able to understand. Obviously, having already seen the movie in English helped.

After the movie was over, we filed out. Sergei's Taxi Service was waiting for us right outside the door, presumably illegally parked on the sidewalk. On our way home—or at least what I assumed was the way home—we turned onto a narrow road leading up to an exquisite view overlooking both the city and river. It reminded me of one of those views of Los Angeles at night from up in the Hollywood hills.

An endless row of small, "homemade" garages lined the road—one of which was Sergei's. The garage was almost a mile away from the family's apartment building, but then again convenience was not a hallmark of Ukrainian life. There was always the option of parking at the apartment building itself. Doing so, however, would put you at risk of having your car broken into, or stolen. Considering the constant stream of pedestrian traffic heading in and out of the building all hours of the day and night, I found it difficult to fathom how thieves could possibly get away with anything. However, I learned that Ukrainians tend to look the other way when it comes to such matters. Good Samaritans seemed hard to come by—it would be perceived by many as an invasion of privacy. As a result, the preferred alternative was to park in a garage in a seedy-looking alley and risk being beaten by a gang—or bitten by a stray bitch protecting her puppies.

After we had pulled up to the entrance of the garage, Sergei got out of the car and removed an odd, wrench-like tool from his trunk. It turned out that this was the key to a complex, homemade locking mechanism that required the user to crank and twist with all his might to unlock the door—a theft deterrent if I ever saw one. When Sergei finally unlocked the door, he opened it up, got back into the car and drove inside. Inside were tools and various discarded items from the past that you would expect to find in any garage. Several old toys belonging to Katya and Nastya sat forgotten in a corner. A trap door revealed a surprisingly spacious basement for additional storage.

Sergei grabbed his flashlight from his car and we headed out. After he closed the door, he handed the odd-looking locking mechanism to me. I stared at it in the confused manner that I stare at just about any tool.

"My dad wants you to try locking it," Katya said. "He invented this tool," she added proudly.

"Impressive," I said, as Sergei demonstrated how to use it. I began the process of cranking the lock, which I quickly discovered was a much more difficult task than I had expected. Sergei motioned for me to put more muscle into it; this helped me get a few more cranks out of it. When I couldn't get it to turn any more, Sergei grabbed the tool from my hand—clearly disappointed in my lack of strength—and proceeded to get three and a half more solid turns out of it, seemingly with little to no effort.

"*Sila*, Bobby!" ("strength") exclaimed Sergei, flexing his bicep, as if to say "next time, try a little harder."

As we headed down the pothole-marked hill, past dozens of other garages, Sergei walked in-between us, holding on to each of our arms for support. A low growl was heard somewhere in the distance—presumably, a wild, rabid beast ready to pounce at a moment's notice. Fifteen minutes later, we were back at the apartment, unscathed. And all I could think about was the fact that this rather involved process was an everyday part of life for Sergei. Just one more inconvenience amongst an entire lifetime of them. And to think: owning a private garage was actually a privilege.

A few minutes after our return, I heard fireworks exploding in the distance. Katya grabbed me by the hand and we ran over to the balcony where fireworks shot over Monastyrsky Island where I had earlier proposed, projecting starbursts of light over the church. The fireworks were in celebration of Dnipropetrovsk's 250th anniversary, as well as the ten-year anniversary of Ukraine's independence from Mother Russia. But as far as we were concerned, they were for us. And our future.

Lying in bed that night, I once again struggled to sleep, as the events of the day played out in my mind—particularly my proposal.

I had sort of gotten a "yes."

But that "sort of" was what was keeping me awake.

11

NAP NYET

The next morning, Katya and Elena decided to visit the local market, while Sergei headed into work for a couple of hours. I decided to stay behind, as I had a bit of a stomachache and was feeling sleep-deprived. I figured that this would be the perfect opportunity to catch up on all of the sleep I had lost since my arrival.

While seeing her off at the door, Katya informed me: "I'm locking the door from the outside, which means you won't be able to get out."

"What am I? A prisoner?" I asked, a bit alarmed.

"*My* prisoner," Katya said teasingly.

"What if there's a fire?" I replied, not in a teasing mood.

"There's always the window."

"I'd break my leg."

"At least you wouldn't burn," Katya said, demonstrating classic Ukrainian logic and sympathy.

Katya kissed me on the cheek and headed out the door with Elena. I thought that Katya must have been joking about the door being locked, so I checked. It was no joke. There was no way I would be able to get out without a key.

I headed back to my bedroom and looked out of the window just in time to see Katya and Elena cutting across the courtyard. I wolf-whistled. They looked up and waved. Katya blew me a kiss as *bomzhee* scavenged for scraps in the dumpster behind her. I watched Katya and Elena until they were out of sight, before lying down on the couch to take a nap.

But just as I shut my eyes, I heard someone in the next apartment pounding on the wall with a hammer.

Several moments later, the phone rang … and rang … and rang. I assumed that the person on the other end of the line was eventually going to get a clue that nobody was going to pick up. Ten rings or so later, they finally did.

The hammering continued.

Despite the incessant noise, I closed my eyes and tried to relax. And just when I thought I might actually be able to drift off to sleep, I heard a knock at the door (possibly the neighbor asking if we had any more nails). By instinct, I got up and headed toward the door, before remembering that: (a) I was unable to open the door; (b) I couldn't speak Russian; and (c) the person knocking at the door probably couldn't speak English.

I stood there, dumbfounded, in front of the door, staring at the lock, as though I could somehow will it to open. And even if I could, what would I say to the person standing on the other side? Meanwhile, the knocking continued ... *and the phone began to ring again*. And just to add to the mix, I was pretty sure that somewhere, someone was using a drill.

I decided that my only line of defense was to head back to the bedroom, where I climbed back onto the couch, staring helplessly at the ceiling as the hammering continued—now seemingly from *inside* my bedroom. This was followed by the sound of a noisy clunker of an automobile idling outside the window, pumping out Russian hip-hop. After a few minutes, the car drove away, but not before I heard music coming from the window of the apartment above; of all things, a techno remix of "It's Raining Men!" And judging by the rhythmic *thunk-thunk*s on the bedroom ceiling, it seemed that somebody in the apartment was either doing aerobics or making love in time to the song. Having never lived in an apartment, all of these noises—a dissonant cacophony—were of course magnified in my mind.

I closed my eyes and prayed for sleep. And just as I actually began to drift off, I heard the series of outer doors of the apartment being opened.

Moments later, my door opened and there stood Katya.

"I told you you'd survive," she said.

Struggling to open my eyes, I simply smiled, half-heartedly.

12

COMRADE MICKEY

Later that afternoon, my stomachache finally subsided. Following my failed attempt at taking a nap, I attempted one more time—unsuccessfully—to check my e-mail. Sensing my frustration, Katya made good on her promise to take me to an Internet café.

We headed out toward the ironically-named Karl Marx Avenue (*Prospekt Karla Marksa*)—a bustling tree-lined street bursting with capitalism in the heart of downtown Dnipropetrovsk. We passed an endless row of clothing stores, gourmet cafés, appliance stores, and a wide range of high-end specialty shops. Somewhere out there, Comrade Marx was rolling in his grave.

Fortunately, there was no shortage of Internet cafes scattered throughout the city. These became my primary mode of communication with my family back in Michigan. For less than a dollar, I was able to get one half hour of subpar, dial-up Internet service in hot and stuffy conditions, surrounded by a motley crew of Ukrainian teenagers playing shoot-em-up video games and watching porn.

When I opened my e-mail (an improvement over Katya's computer, but not too much), there were *twelve* messages from my mother, worried sick about me and pleading to God for me to write back. Apparently, just as Ukrainian postal mail was frequently stolen, Ukrainian e-mail seemed to be frequently intercepted for no clear reason. My mother had never received my initial e-mail letting her know that I had arrived safely. As far as she knew, I had been kidnapped by a circus of Ukrainian clown rapists. I wrote her back immediately, explaining the Internet situation, and promised her I would try my best to keep in contact, even though there were no guarantees. I am sure this did wonders to ease her fears.

Before my half hour was up, I was ready to leave. We headed back out onto Karl Marx Avenue.

"From the look of all these stores, you wouldn't think this was a poor country," I commented.

"Don't let it fool you," Katya replied. "All of these fancy stores and cafes are just a façade. Most Ukrainians can't afford to eat or shop here. In fact, most Ukrainians never eat out at all. Even McDonald's is reserved for special occasions."

"Then how do all these places stay in business?" I asked.

"Mafia. The corrupt rich. And Americans shopping with their mail-order brides."

"Corrupt rich?"

"Let me clarify," Katya continued. "I'm not saying that all rich people are corrupt, but here in Ukraine, ever since independence, it seems like the only way to become rich is through some form of corruption. That's why some people—especially here in eastern Ukraine—think we were better off with the Soviet Union."

"How?" I naively asked.

"Well … there's rampant corruption. People still live in fear of the government. There is no free press; well, there is, but in name only. Dissidents are still jailed. The only real difference between then and now is that most people would claim to be worse off now than they were during the Soviet Union. And instead of controlled communism, we have wild capitalism in its place."

"So are you saying your dad is corrupt?"

"No. My dad isn't rich. He makes a good living. There's a difference. We don't shop at these stores," Katya explained, gesturing toward the flashy storefronts.

"Then allow this rich American to spoil his mail-order princess," I said.

"Bobby. No! There's no reason to."

"There doesn't have to be a reason. I want to. Is there anything you need?"

When all was said and done, I bought Katya a new purse and a pair of obnoxiously enormous hoop earrings, which were evidently in style, as were mesh shirts for men.

As we continued making our way down the street, Katya introduced me to the Soviet version of a vending machine—a rather rotund babushka woman sitting on a stool in front of a large beverage dispenser swarming with bees. The babushka was wearing a customary vendor apron. After giving her ten *kopiyoks* (equivalent to about two cents in American currency), she handed us two small, chipped glasses. She then dispensed a thick, brown liquid called *kvass* (a fermented beverage made from rye bread) into the glasses for us to drink, paying no attention to the bees that were coating her arm and hands. I kept a safe distance. I wanted nothing more to do with Ukrainian bees. Katya told me that her Babushka spent most of her working life as a kvass vendor, where she cheated customers by diluting the product with water in order to maximize her meager profits.

I took my first sip, hesitantly and let the bitter, viscous fluid trickle onto my tongue. It was tolerable, but by no means anything I would consider tasty or refreshing. It was like a very bitter, heavy root beer.

When we were done drinking, Katya handed the babushka the glasses, which she hastily rinsed off in a bucket of dirty, soap-less water, ready for the next customer.

We approached a toy store whose sign featured the famous, beloved American icons Mickey and Minnie Mouse (clearly Ukrainians have just as much respect for trademark law as they do copyright law). A hapless soul in a tattered imposter Mickey Mouse costume stood out front, waving to passers-by. Even though this was clearly an attempt at being Mickey Mouse, there was something "off" about the costume. It took me a while to put my finger on it before it finally dawned on me. This imposter Mickey had no ears!

"Can we go in?" I asked.

"No! It's for kids. We don't belong there," Katya replied.

"Says who?" I asked.

Katya gave in. Inside, the toy store was not much different than any American toy store—the majority of merchandise consisting of cheap plastic toys made in China.

While Katya walked on ahead of me, I picked up a rather realistic toy snake and snuck up behind her, sneaking the snake up to her face. Katya shrieked. And that's when I first realized that I was being watched ... and followed. First, by store personnel. And then by a security guard, waiting for us—not exactly inconspicuously—at the end of every aisle. I initially tried to ignore it, chalking it up as paranoia, but when I took notice of a second security guard on our trail, I realized we—or more specifically I—were being targeted.

"Are we being followed?" I whispered.

"They're just making sure we don't steal anything," Katya said matter-of-factly.

"You were right. We don't belong here," I replied, turning a corner and bumping right into Imposter Mickey.

13

KGBOᏏᏏy

That evening, we decided to stay in. This provided a great opportunity for me to sample some of the highlights of Ukrainian television. And since I had still not fully caught up on lost sleep, an evening of being a Ukrainian couch *kartoshka* suited me just fine. Like most of the entertainment in Ukraine, the majority of television programming is made in Russia. We started out by watching Katya's favorite childhood cartoon—the widely popular *Nu, pogodi!* (*Just You Wait!*). This is essentially the Russian equivalent of *Tom and Jerry*—only instead of cat vs. mouse, it is wolf vs. bunny. Each episode culminated with the bunny once again outsmarting the wolf. Clinching his fist, the wolf proclaimed at the end of each episode: "*Zayets! Nu, pogodi!*" ("Bunny! Well, just You Wait!"). Roll credits.

Sticking to the theme of children's shows was the Russian *Winnie-the-Pooh* (*Vinni Pukh*), who is nothing like the American *Winnie-the-Pooh*. For starters, he's brown and black and sounds like a gruff alcoholic, as voiced by the beloved comedic actor, Yevgeny Leonov.

This was followed by *Karlson*—an animated series based on a popular Swedish book about a portly, red-headed fellow who flies around with a little propeller attached to his back and who befriends a young boy after flying through his window. To finish off children's hour we watched *Cheburashka*—a bear-like creature (and official mascot of the Russian Olympic team) with enormous ears who arrives in Russia in a crate of oranges from "the tropics." *Cheburashka* befriends Crocodile Gena, who joins him for all sorts of zany adventures.

For the "grown-ups," the program I found most entertaining was the *Jerry Springer*-esque talk show *Okna* ("Windows"). The Ukrainian version of Jerry Springer was the very popular Dmitriy Nagiev, a Bono-like character with slicked-backed hair, permanent sunglasses, and a see-through mesh-shirt. And in true Springer fashion, guests would come on to discuss their problems/air their grievances and dirty laundry, usually resulting in an all-out brawl, much to the delight of the studio audience. The most unbelievable—and memorable—scene I saw on *Okna* was a bride being taken out with a flying kung-fu kick, followed by all out mayhem involving audience members and security guards! Even Dmitriy was unable to avoid the melee and had to be escorted off stage, bleeding, after being clocked in the mouth. *Classic TV*. No translation necessary.

Our TV marathon finished with a cheesy variety show reminiscent of Lawrence Welk, featuring jugglers, fire-eaters, and "singers." If there's one thing I learned about television in Ukraine, it's that they air about as much crap as we do in the U.S. *Crappy but compelling!* Despite not being able to understand a word, it was a fun and memorable evening.

Later that night, once everyone was asleep and dreaming of alcoholic Pooh bears and portly chaps with back-propellers flying through their windows (yet another reason to have screens in your windows!), I decided to take a major gamble. I snuck out of my room into the hallway, making sure that Sergei and Elena's door was closed before approaching Katya's room.

I slowly opened Katya's door and crept in, cautiously approaching Katya, who was asleep. I leaned in and gently planted a kiss on her forehead. She awoke, smiling.

"Bobby! How did you get in here?" she asked.

"I've been trained by the KGB," I replied.

Katya laughed. I climbed into bed next to her.

"Bobby! My parents...," Katya began, starting to panic.

"Don't worry," I said. "They're sleeping."

I kissed her more all over her neck.

"I want you so bad," I said.

"I want you, too. But ... I can't. And..."

Suddenly, I heard Katya's parents' bedroom door open. This was followed by the sound of footsteps. We both froze in terror. To our relief, we realized that the footsteps were heading not toward us, but away, toward the bathroom.

"It's my dad!" Katya said in a panicked whisper. "Did you close your door??!"

"Yes," I said, confidently, clearly remembering doing so ... until doubt and paranoia crept in: *What if I didn't? Or what if I did, but it didn't latch properly causing the door to open? Then my cover would be blown. And I would be forced onto the first flight out of Dnipropetrovsk. Or worse, left alone in the Ukrainian countryside. Or even worse, badly beaten, and left out to perish ... in the Ukrainian countryside.*

We waited in hushed silence. I held my breath, expecting to hear a toilet flush, before remembering that the water was shut off at night. The footsteps returned, growing closer and closer, until they were right in front of our door. And then ... they were gone. *Disaster averted.*

"What if he saw that you weren't in your bed?" Katya asked.

"It was a chance I had to take," I said.

"By risking it all?" Katya replied, clearly annoyed.

"I guess I wasn't thinking," I said, my tail between my legs.

"It's too much Bobby ... too soon," Katya continued.

"I'm sorry," I said, wondering what in the hell I was thinking. "I didn't think it through."

"It's okay, Bobby. But go back to your room. Now."

I opened the door slowly, poking my head out to make sure the coast was clear before creeping back to my room.

The following morning, as I sat on the couch writing in my journal, Katya entered. She sat down next to me. Neither of us said a word for several moments. Katya finally took me by the hand.

"You're not mad at me?" I asked.

"I was just about to ask you that," Katya replied.

"Why would I be mad at you?"

"After last night ... I wasn't sure you'd understand."

"Of course I understand. You were right."

"I never said I didn't like it," Katya explained. "It's just that ... we can't do anything that will give my parents reason not to trust you. And as for me ... I just want to be sure."

"Sure of what?" I asked.

"I don't know. Everything, I guess."

"Don't you trust me?" I asked Katya.

"Of course I do. But paranoia's in my DNA. Besides, it's myself I really don't trust," Katya continued. "Tomorrow, we're going to the dacha for a few days."

"Dacha?" I asked. "Where's that?"

"The dacha is my family's summer cottage," Katya replied. "It will be the perfect opportunity for my parents to get to know you better."

And from that point on, I realized that the remainder of my trip was an audition. And I was determined to win the role—even if it cost me my dignity.

14

BOBBY THE HOOLIGAN

As I was packing for our trip to the dacha, Sergei entered my room and greeted me enthusiastically.

"Bobby! Hello!"

"Privet," I said back in response.

Sergei motioned for me to follow him out of the room and led me to his office, where he showed me his multitude of patents, most of which were related to land-digging equipment—excavators, tractors, etc.

Sergei's interest and fascination with land-digging equipment was formed during his childhood, growing up on a farm in a rural village in northern Ukraine. This background was in complete contrast to Elena, who grew up in the seaside resort town of Berdyansk in southern Ukraine on the Azov Sea.

Sergei's passion led to him filing over seven hundred patents. In addition to being an inventor, Sergei's main source of income came as a professor at the Dnipropetrovsk National University, where he taught mechanical engineering—using protractors and graphing paper, in place of computers and graphing calculators. My visit coincided with Sergei's summer vacation, which consisted of the entire month of August. In addition to teaching and inventing, Katya explained to me how her father took on several "side-jobs" to supplement the household income. Most of these side-jobs were shrouded in secrecy.

Sergei proceeded to show me one of his many model excavators, pointing to a specific part related to one of his patents, before pointing to himself, proudly stating: "Sergei."

He pulled an engineering textbook off the shelf and pointed to the Cyrillic byline, stating his name once again before flipping the book over to point to a photo of himself on the back cover, featuring a serious, determined scowl. He then proceeded to show me another book he had authored, followed by another.

"Very impressive," I said.

"Spasibo," Sergei replied, as Katya entered the room.

"Your father was showing me some of his work," I said.

"He's very proud of his accomplishments," Katya said.

"I can tell ... I mean, he should be," I said, quickly correcting myself.

"Nothing was ever handed to me," Sergei interjected (as Katya translated). "I've always worked hard and with a lot of heart," he continued, beating his chest with his fist. "And like me, I can tell you, Bobby, are a man who follows his heart. And I admire you for that."

"Spasibo!" I said, realizing that I had just passed the first obstacle on my road to acceptance.

Later that afternoon, Sergei took me to my first professional soccer game. Like most Americans, I did not grow up as a soccer fan, but I was eager for the experience of seeing my first European game, between FC Dnipro Dnipropetrovsk and FC Shakhtar Donetsk, two of the top teams in the Ukrainian Premier League.

As it turned out, Sergei was a soccer fanatic—especially when it came to his beloved hometown team. I shared with him my passion for the Detroit Tigers and we both instantly understood our shared allegiance to our respective teams. Katya explained to me how her father was disappointed when he found out his second child was not a boy, therefore crushing his dreams of raising the next Andriy Shevchenko (Ukraine's soccer superstar who played for the rival FC Dynamo Kyiv, before moving on to play for AC Milan in Italy). Unlike in the U.S., there are very few opportunities for young girls to play soccer in Ukraine (or most team sports, for that matter). However, Katya did make her father proud by making the varsity soccer team during her time in Mississippi, despite having no previous experience.

My previous soccer experience, on the other hand, consisted of one season in a recreational league in first grade. There are two things I remember most about my short-lived soccer career—neither of which involved the game itself: the taste of my plastic water bottle and the freshly cut orange slices brought in by somebody's mom that always awaited us when we got off the field. The true highlight of my illustrious soccer career was being known as "the weird little boy who stood in the middle of the field during the game, staring incessantly at his digital, water-proof Casio wristwatch," counting down until the game was over so I could be out of my misery. Obsessive watch-staring was one of countless reasons why I am pretty convinced that I had undiagnosed OCD as a child. This watch-staring habit got so out of hand at school that my teacher actually had to call my parents about it. This led to them taking my watch away. After that, instead of being the weirdo who stood in the middle of the soccer field constantly staring at his watch, I became the weirdo who stood in the middle of the field staring at the skin on his wrist where his watch used to be. Mercifully, my soccer "career" only lasted one season. And here I was, all these years later, about to watch my first professional match.

We arrived at Dnipro's Stadium Meteor and purchased tickets. The modest, outdated, stadium had a seating capacity of close to 25,000. It was about half-full at kick-off. The entire perimeter of the field was undergoing a massive renovation, with deep ditches dug along the sidelines. It appeared as though we had just entered a construction zone as opposed to a functioning sports arena. As if the ditches weren't dangerous enough for the players, there were numerous rusty pipes lying at the side of the field, presumably waiting to be buried in the ditches. For all I knew, this construction may have been going on indefinitely.

Even more striking were the fifty or so uniformed police officers guarding the entire perimeter of the field, presumably ready to fight off any hooligans. Suddenly, I didn't feel so safe. Of course my preconceived notions of soccer fans clouded my judgment. But then again, this wasn't England vs. Germany!

Sergei bought Katya and me a beer. I was a bit surprised that they actually served glass bottles.

"Why aren't you drinking?" I asked Sergei.

"Zero tolerance," Sergei replied in reference to Ukraine's strict drinking and driving limits, which at 0.00% is—perhaps, not ironically—the strictest in the world. Considering how deeply vodka flows through the veins of Ukrainian culture, I was impressed, even if they were perhaps rather irrationally strict about it.

Once the game started, a fan in front us incessantly rattled a noisemaker. Another fan nearby honked an air horn. Looking around, I noticed only a small handful of women. This was most definitely a man's world. In a country where gender roles are clearly defined, this was further proof.

At one point, fans protested what they perceived to be a bad call by shouting profanities and throwing beer bottles and other debris onto the field, validating my concern about glass bottles. This was mob mentality at its finest. A nearby fan kept shouting something at the ref. I decided to copy him. Katya glanced over at me with a stern expression.

"What is he saying?" I asked.

"Goat fucker!" Katya replied.

The police quickly and non-violently restored order before things could get too out of hand. At one point during the second half, I noticed smoke rising from the stands across the field. The plume continued growing until it covered almost the entire stadium, obscuring the action down on the field.

"Oh my God, they've started a fire!" I said, panicked.

"No, it's not a fire," Katya assured me. "It's just a smoke bomb."

As the smoke began to clear, I could see a man being forcefully removed from the stadium by several police officers near from where the smoke had originated—never to be heard from again, no doubt. The rest of the game went by without incident and ended up scoreless—which is about what I had expected. Neither team had given the fans much to cheer, jeer, or riot over, and when the game ended, the crowd peacefully filed out of the stadium.

Katya described to me what the scenes were like in the stands when Dnipro would actually score a goal. Unfortunately, I did not get to experience that mayhem. But like everything else on this trip, my first professional soccer game had been a truly unforgettable experience.

15

DACHA

After we returned from the Dnipro game, we loaded up the car for our weekend trip to the dacha. Leaving the apartment for the weekend, however, was not as simple as walking out of the door, hopping into the car and driving away. Leaving meant unplugging every appliance, shutting off the water, double and triple checking every window, calling the security company, and then locking and double locking every door. All of this was excruciating enough. Even more excruciating was the realization that you had to go back inside because you forgot something, which meant unlocking each and every door and then calling the security company again to cancel the alarm, before going through the process all over again. And here's the kicker: once the alarm company has been notified, you only have *one minute* to clear out before the alarm sounds, notifying the police. This includes locking all the doors again. And the penalty should you not make it out on time? The cops show up at your door, guns pointing. It made going out almost seem futile. But like everything else in Ukrainian life, you grin and bear it, before moving on to the next obstacle.

With the fortress doors now securely bolted, we piled into the Zhiguli and were on our way. I was crammed into the back with Katya and Babushka. Nastya stayed behind, apparently to spend time with her boyfriend. Whenever we were going somewhere or had a family get together, Nastya was conspicuously absent. I started to develop a sneaking suspicion that her disappearing acts had more to do with me than with her boyfriend.

"I'm beginning to think it's me," I said.

"No, it's not you at all," Katya said … initially.

She later admitted that her sister thought of me as "physically weak," "sneaky," and "like a monkey in a bad suit." She had never even seen me in a suit! When I asked Katya why her sister felt that way, she simply said: "She dislikes most people. Just be glad you are not a Jew."

I tried not to take it personally. However, I had a much easier time accepting Babushka's disdain against me than Nastya's. Babushka was old and sick. Nastya was just ... plain nasty. *Nastya than the rest*, I guess.

As we made our way through the labyrinth of the city, our lives almost all came to a crashing halt as Sergei continually pulled out into the middle of busy intersections, without first looking to see if traffic was clear.

As we headed out of town, I was once again taken aback by how abruptly the city comes to an end. Unlike American cities, there is no gradual fade into suburban sprawl. The city morphs instantly into villages, farmland, and endless fields of sunflowers. No billboards littered the roadside. Instead, babushka vendors sold sunflower seeds and burly men sold watermelon from wooden carts.

We stopped at one of the vendors to buy some watermelon. Sergei began a prolonged negotiating process that included wild gesticulations, raised voices, the waving of arms, and pointing at various watermelons. This was serious business. And apparently it ended in clear victory for Sergei, as he strolled back to the car with an armful of watermelon and a broad smile on his face. The forlorn vendor sat down on his cart, bowing his head in defeat. Sergei loaded the watermelon into his trunk and we continued on our way.

For the first time, Ukraine actually looked beautiful to me. Even the dilapidated village shacks and shanties held a magical beauty, like a tranquil scene from a rural painting.

But just like anything else in Ukraine, it was only a matter of time before any semblance of peace and tranquility is interrupted by Ukrainian bullshit. This time, the bullshit arrived in the form of Ukrainian authorities.

Two policemen standing on the side of the road waved us over with black and white striped batons.

"What's happening?" I asked, as Sergei pulled over.

The officers slowly approached on opposite sides of the car.

"Shhh," Katya demanded. "Whatever you do, do not speak."

Sergei handed over his I.D. and several other documents to one of the officers. The other officer stuck his head through the passenger window, sneering at all of us, but mostly at the foreign darkie in the backseat.

Sergei was asked several questions, which he answered confidently without fear or hesitation. At one point, both officers looked at me with contempt and disdain.

After a lengthy discussion, Sergei handed the cop some cash and the cop handed Sergei back his documents, shook his hand, and returned to his post. And just like that, we were on our way.

"What just happened?" I asked.

"Nothing," Katya said, seemingly in denial. "Everything's fine."

"Was he speeding?"

"No. The police just pull people over from time to time."

"For no reason?"

"For money."

"Are you serious?!" I asked.

"Yes, of course. Why wouldn't I be?" Katya replied.

I was amazed yet again by how accepting Ukrainians were of this sort of thing. Nobody said a word. They just bent over and took it. Then again, they were smart enough to realize that any dissent would simply lead to retaliatory punishment ... or worse.

"And you won't believe what my dad told the cop," Katya added.

"What?"

"He said you were his son-in-law."

"Really? Why?"

"To keep you out of prison," Katya replied matter-of-factly. I couldn't tell whether or not she was serious.

For the remainder of our trip, Katya and I talked about our future. It felt strange to be talking so openly, despite her parents being within earshot of our conversation. However, they had no idea what we were saying. Despite this fact, there was a growing paranoia in me that maybe they *did* know English and just weren't letting on.

Sergei suddenly turned around and pointed: "Bobby! *Korova!*" he said in Russian as we passed by a field of cows.

"*Da!* Cows," I said, nodding in recognition.

Sergei turned off the main road, onto a very narrow, pothole-laden dirt road that seemed barely wide enough for a bike—let alone a car. Yet somehow Sergei managed to make the car fit, even if it meant scraping against a tree from time to time. The car rocked from side to side as we drove from one pothole to the next. I then noticed a car approaching from the opposite direction. *This is going to be interesting,* I thought to myself. Sergei continued to rumble down the bumpy road without slowing down. If anything, he seemed to pick up speed. As the two cars drew closer, neither driver seemed willing to pull off to the side let the other pass. *Something in this game of automobile-chicken eventually has to give, right?*

As the gap between both cars closed, I grabbed tightly onto Katya's hand and braced myself. Katya didn't seem fazed by our impending head-on collision in the least; and neither did Elena nor Babushka.

As the other car drew nearer, I realized that it was a mirror image of Sergei's, both in terms of make, age, and color. My heart began to race as it seemed less and likely that either driver was going to stop. I closed my eyes and hoped for the best. At the very last moment, both drivers slammed on their brakes. By some divine miracle, a head-on impact was avoided by mere inches as the game of chicken reached an impasse. Sergei uttered some kind of Russian expletive so loudly that it shook the car. He threw open the car door and stepped out. His "adversary" did the same. All that was missing now was the spaghetti western theme music.

The other driver was a shirtless, unshaven slob of a man in his mid-forties, wearing nothing but a pair of dirty, white boxers and holding a half-eaten chicken leg in his hand. Both men unleashed a flood of what were clearly obscenities, punctuated with matching hand gestures.

I could make out a couple of words that were being repeated and asked Katya what "Eblan" and "Dolboyob" meant.

"Bobby!" Katya replied, shocked, putting her finger to her mouth as if to say "quiet," as though I were the one out of order. Babushka simply shook her head and glared at me, muttering an obvious insult under her breath. Katya glanced over toward Babushka and narrowed her eyebrows—but refrained from saying anything. She knew better.

Meanwhile, the shirtless man wildly waved his chicken leg in the air for added emphasis. The tirade went on for close to five minutes, as both men stood their ground, refusing to budge. Finally, the shirtless man decided that enough was enough and threw the chicken leg at Sergei's head. Sergei ducked out of the way and the flying drumstick landed on our windshield, before sliding down slowly, leaving a greasy trail.

Seemingly happy with his parting gesture, and now out of options … and chicken … the man stumbled clumsily back into his car, backing away from us at speed, and pulling over as far off the road as possible.

Sergei got back into the car and, with a big smile on his face, proudly proclaimed: "Sila, Bobby! Sila!"

"Da! Sila!" I replied, as Sergei proceeded to drive forward.

There still wasn't quite enough space to pass, but that wasn't going to slow Sergei down. As we passed, Sergei's car scraped against the side of other driver's car. The driver shook his fist in anger. In his hand was another chicken leg, which he had already started to devour.

And just like that, we were back on our way—the forest-splintered sun glistening through the chicken grease on our windshield.

Ten minutes later, we arrived at the dacha—a small, plain cottage made of white brick, topped off with a tin roof. Entering the dacha involved walking up a very steep set of stairs consisting of ten or so uneven steps. Inside, a spiral, corrugated-steel staircase led upstairs to the master bathroom and a spare room snugly co-existing with flying buttresses.

"My father built this himself," Katya boasted. It was certainly nothing to write home about. Then again, I could barely construct a house out of Lincoln Logs.

On the main floor was the living room, consisting of a couch/fold-out bed, and a small, black and white television. A small dining room led to an even smaller kitchen, which then led to a closet of a bathroom, which was even smaller than the one at the apartment.

Since the dacha had no running water, the first order of business was for Katya and me to load a large, plastic barrel into an old, wooden wagon and head to the village pump.

While walking along the village road, we passed by a large, barren field. "This used to be my parents' plot," Katya began. "When I was little, we would work in this field from sunrise to sunset, picking tomatoes, potatoes, eggplant, peppers, beans and whatever else we had growing there."

"Sounds fun," I said.

"No, I hated it," Katya continued. "It was miserable! But that's what the government expected since they were giving us the dacha in exchange for a share of our crops."

"Sounds like slavery!" I said.

"Indentured servitude is how we preferred to call it," Katya said with a wink. "But it worked … at least for a while."

"So what happened to the plot?" I asked.

"After the Soviet Union fell," Katya replied, "it was easier just to go the market. I never thought I'd miss it …," she said, reminiscing. "I guess nothing stays the same."

"Life's one constant," I added.

Katya smiled.

We left the forgotten vegetable plot behind and made our way to the old, rusty pump. Katya placed the barrel under the pump and began filling it up, instructing me to hold the barrel steady. The pump creaked and groaned mournfully as we took turns pumping the water.

After about ten minutes, the barrel was full. I attempted to load it back into the wagon, but the weight of the barrel almost caused me to fall over backwards. When I finally regained my balance, Katya held the wagon steady so I could place the barrel into it.

Walking back to the dacha, I had to navigate the wagon over a wide array of bumps and ruts. At one point, I hit a bump, causing the wagon to topple over. The barrel began to roll down the road, forcing me to chase it until it landed in a ditch on the side of the road, much to the merriment of a couple of the villagers who were out tending to their gardens.

When we returned to the dacha, Elena greeted us, carrying two old-fashioned milk jugs. She asked us to accompany her into town.

"Are we going to milk a cow?" I asked.

"Not quite … but close," Katya said. And with that, we set off down the long village road, walking past several farms—and the occasional cow grazing on the side of the road. The orange-pink sunset covering the endless landscape of sunflowers provided a memorable backdrop, making it seem as though we were walking inside a Van Gogh painting.

At the end of the road was the village of Volosskoye, whose "downtown" consisted of a small market and a dark, decrepit apartment building. An old man sat on a rotted, wooden bench, drinking vodka and watching a chicken pecking in the dirt. A horse and buggy passed by.

"This reminds me of the Amish," I said.

"What's the Amish?" Katya asked.

I explained to them who the Amish were.

"Why would they choose to live that way?" Katya asked.

"It's their religion," I explained.

"Here, people don't *choose* to live that way," Elena explained. "It's the only option they have."

Before we went to get the milk, Katya and Elena decided that it was best for me to wait outside as they entered the small village grocery shop for some meat and cheese. While I waited, I noticed a goat chained to a fence. I decided that I had to take its picture. As I began snapping, an elderly man with a long, white beard came waddling up, angrily waving his finger at me, shouting something in Russian.

"Nyet, Russkiy," I said, pleading my case, but the man continued shouting at me. Moments later, Katya came running out of the shop, coming to my defense, while Elena finished up the grocery purchase.

"Is this your foreigner?" the man asked Katya in Russian.

"*Da*," Katya admitted nervously. "Did he do something wrong?"

"Get him the hell out of here! That cheap son of a bitch owes me!"

"What did you do?!" Katya asked me.

"No idea! All I did was take a picture of this goat," I explained, gesturing toward the bearded animal. The man continued to yell.

"What is he saying?" I asked.

"He said if you want to photograph his goat, then you have to pay the price."

"As in *literally* pay money … or is he threatening me?" I asked, equally amused and bemused by the whole situation.

"He wants you to pay him money."

"I'll butcher you like a cow if you take another picture of my goat, you hear me you son of a bitch?" the man shouted.

Katya apologized, took me by the hand, as though I were a small child in trouble, and escorted me back toward the shop, leaving the old man grumbling to himself.

"Never do that again!" Katya scolded.

"Do *what* again?" I asked, exasperated.

"You can't just take pictures of another man's goat."

"Why? What's the big deal?" I said in disbelief.

"Stop asking 'why' Bobby! That's just the way it is," Katya said, clearly annoyed.

"That doesn't really answer my question," I replied, standing my ground.

"You'll *scare* people, that's why!" Katya shouted, as everyone within earshot watched the drama unfold.

"*I'll* scare people?!" I said, losing my cool. "Look! This country scares me! Nothing works right. Nothing's logical. Nothing's rational!"

"If you're looking for rational," Katya snapped back "you're in the wrong country. It might not be perfect like America, but it's *my* country. *This is how it is.* If you can't handle it, no one's forcing you to stay."

"I'm sorry … but it's becoming more and more obvious that I don't belong here," I said, struggling to hold back my frustration.

"Bobby! Stop it! Stop talking like that!" Katya begged. "I'm supposed to come with you, remember?"

That helped settle me down.

We survived our first squabble, just in time for Elena to come out of the shop. We walked down the road in silence until we saw a middle-aged woman selling milk on the side of the road, her face worn and haggard.

"*Vechernee moloko?*" ("Evening milk"?) asked Elena.

"*Utrennee*" ("Morning"), the vendor replied sullenly.

Elena frowned, then carried on walking. Katya and I followed.

"What's wrong?" I asked.

"They don't have evening milk."

"What the hell's evening milk?" I asked.

"Milk that's milked in the evening," Katya succinctly explained as we headed towards the dark and dingy apartment building in search of the elusive "evening milk." From the outside, one could easily assume that the building was not only abandoned, but uninhabitable. Yet here we were, about to enter.

"So where are we going now? The black market?" I asked, as we crept around to the back of the building.

"Shh. Don't ask questions," Katya warned.

Of course not. Why would I question us entering what I was pretty sure was Ukraine's own Amityville?

As we entered, the stairwell was completely dark, making the dimly-lit stairwell of the family apartment in Dnipropetrovsk look like a sunroom.

We made our way up several flights, trusting that each step was evenly spaced since they were impossible to see in the darkness. When we finally reached our destination, Katya reminded me again: "No English." Clearly, we were on a top-secret reconnaissance mission.

Elena called out. Moments later, another haggard, middle-aged woman appeared through a bead curtain hanging from the doorframe.

"*Vechernee moloko?*" Elena asked the woman. The woman nodded and took the jugs from Elena before disappearing through the curtain, leaving us waiting in the dark hallway. Everything about this felt like a drug deal.

Moments later, the woman reappeared with the two jugs filled with warm, fresh milk. Elena handed over some money and we very carefully began our descent into darkness—a feat far more frightening than the way up. Each step felt as though we were about to stumble off a cliff into an abyss.

"Did she just milk a cow in there?" I asked, assuming it was now safe to speak.

"Don't speak!" Katya retorted. I guess we were still in danger after all.

It wasn't until we were back on the village road leading to the dacha that my speaking moratorium (*moo*-ratorium?) was lifted.

After we returned to the dacha, Elena took out some glasses and began pouring milk, as everyone eagerly awaited a straight-from-the-teat treat.

Elena handed me a glass.

"Oh, *nyet, spasibo*," I said.

"Why not? It's fresh," Katya said.

"It's maybe a little *too fresh* for my taste," I said. "I don't trust it," again making myself look like a spoiled, ungrateful misfit—and coward!

Once Katya finished drinking her milk, she took me by the hand and led me outside toward a sunflower field. When we reached a clearing, we lay down and stared up into the starry night. The bright moon was now half full.

"I've never seen so many stars in my life," I said. It was an incredible sight; I was inside yet another Van Gogh painting.

"You have no idea how many nights I wished you were here with me, Bobby" Katya said. "Sometimes, I would wake up in the middle of the night, see the moon and the stars through my window and wonder if you were looking at them too, at that exact moment. Somehow, it always made me feel closer to you."

"I know exactly what you mean," I said.

"But now, I can't stand the idea of living like that again when you leave next week," Katya continued.

"Don't think about that," I said, holding her closer to me.

"But I can't help it. And the fuller the moon gets, the closer it will be to when you leave."

"We still have another week," I said, trying to reassure her. "Think of it this way: when I leave, that means it will be even closer to the time when we will never have to be apart again."

This seemed to comfort her. We stared at the stars for several minutes, in deep contemplation.

I broke the silence, asking Katya, "Do you think everything we do is predestined?"

"Do you mean everything that *happens* to us?" asked Katya.

"Yeah, I guess so," I replied. "Is there a difference?"

"Of course," Katya began. "It all depends on how you look at it. We either *do* things, or things *happen* to us. Yes, I believe in fate. But I also believe we have something to do with our fate—so whether that's predestiny or not ... I don't know. I do believe that we were destined to meet and fall in love. But how we got there was up to us."

"Do you think we would have still found each other if we didn't meet that day?" I asked.

"Probably not," Katya replied. "Do you?"

"I think so, yes. I think fate gives us certain ingredients and it's up to us to mix them up and decide how to proceed. In other words, only the major events in our life are predestined. Take right now for instance. Lying here together under the stars. I don't believe this was written in the ..."

"Stars?" Katya said—helping me realize how cliché this conversation was becoming.

"Yeah," I said, smiling, embarrassed. "I don't believe this small moment in our lives was predestined. But us falling in love certainly was."

"If we went to high school together, would you have asked me out?" Katya asked.

"Probably not," I replied.

"Why not?" Katya asked, surprised.

"I would have been too afraid to back then."

"But wait a minute. Aren't you contradicting yourself?"

"How so?" I asked, confused.

"You said you wouldn't have asked me out in high school, right?"

"I said 'probably not.'"

"So doesn't that mean that it is possible to avoid your fate?"

"You're right. But I would have just asked you out after high school."

"What if you never came here?" Katya asked, testing my theory.

"There's no getting around it," I said, hoping to wrap up this conversation. "We are exactly where fate wants us."

But Katya wasn't about to give up her role as devil's advocate. "But what about people who miss out on an opportunity even when it comes knocking at their door and then spend the rest of their life regretting it?"

"Then *that's* their fate," I replied.

"So fate is cruel?"

"No. Fate isn't biased."

"I don't believe that," Katya said.

"I think in the end, everything eventually balances out," I said.

"Then does that mean someday, instead of being young and in love, we'll be old and hating one another?" Katya said.

"I can't see that happening," I replied.

"Isn't that what everyone thinks when they're madly in love?"

"That won't be us," I assured her, filled with overconfidence.

"But what if that's our fate?"

"Then we'll fight it," I said assuredly.

We held each other in moonlit silence until Katya spoke up: "Tell me something you've never told anyone else before."

"Hmm, let's see," I replied. After thinking for a moment, I said "Okay. I once had my face shoved in dog shit."

Katya burst out in a mixture of laughter and horror.

"What?! How did that happen?!"

"It was in fourth grade. We were out in the playground for recess and this bully named David Montroy—who was even smaller than me—saw a pile of dog shit and wrestled me to the ground. He then took me by the neck and shoved my face right into it. The rest of the class just stood and watched."

"How awful!"

"Well, fortunately, it was winter, and the shit was frozen, so smearing was avoided," I added.

"Did he get in trouble?"

"My teacher never saw it. And I knew things would only get worse if told on him. Plus, there were so many other incidents like that and so many other David Montroys, it would have been hard for them to keep track."

"If it makes you feel any better," Katya began, "I ate a thermometer when I was little."

"Ouch! Did it cut your mouth?" I asked.

"A little bit. My mom panicked because she was worried that I had swallowed mercury. She took me to the hospital. Fortunately, I had bitten off the end without the mercury."

"I don't know what's worse: poop or glass?"

"I think I'd rather eat glass than have a poop face," Katya replied. "But mercury on the other hand ..."

I smiled and said "Okay, you're turn. Tell *me* something you've never told anyone else before" I said.

"I just did!" Katya replied.

"That doesn't count."

"What do you mean? Why not?"

"Because. It just doesn't."

Katya thought long and hard, hesitated, then finally said: "Okay … the day we met … I not only thought you were cute, but I thought you looked like someone I would one day want to marry."

"Seriously?" I said, not believing her.

"Yes! 100% seriously," Katya replied, blushing.

I leaned in toward Katya and began kissing her passionately under the moonlit sunflowers. Just when it appeared that things might start to go even further, Katya broke free.

She whispered into my ear, "No, not here, Bobby … not now. Soon."

And before I had a chance to consider what "soon" might mean, Katya leaned back toward me and continued to kiss me with all her passion.

Following an unpleasant night of trying to sleep on what amounted to a prison cot in the dacha, a new day awaited. Sergei boastfully announced that he would be making his specialty—the one and only meal he cooks—shish kabob, or *shashlik*. Little did I know what a prolonged, precise science making this meal would turn out to be. It was no wonder that Sergei was rarely left in charge of cooking.

After spending half an hour or so preparing what was essentially a pyre on top of his handmade grill, Sergei handed me a box of long matches, giving me the honor of lighting his grill as though it were the Olympic torch. The only problem was, I have an irrational phobia of matches. Due to my fear and lack of experience, it took me several attempts to actually light one. Sensing that Sergei was growing impatient and that I was looking more and more like a wuss, I dug deep inside myself, stepped up to the plate, and lit the match. I quickly turned toward the grill to light it. With a *whoosh*, the resulting flame burst three feet into the air, singeing my arm hair and almost torching my face off. Ignoring my close call with death, Sergei proclaimed "Bobby! Hero! *Sila!*" and patted me hard on the back almost knocking me over onto the grill.

We were back in business.

Since it would be awhile before we could put the skewers on the grill, Katya decided to take me for a walk down the dirt road. The flame from the grill was still in view behind us, as a horse and buggy passed us by— the driver of which was swigging on an almost empty bottle of vodka.

At the end of road, we came upon a wooded area. As we headed into the woods, I heard what I assumed was a cuckoo clock.

"Do you hear that?" I asked.

"What?" asked Katya.

"A cuckoo clock," I replied.

"I don't hear a cuckoo *clock* … but I do hear a cuckoo *bird*," Katya clarified.

"Wow! A real cuckoo bird?" I exclaimed, surprised.

"Of course," Katya said in a manner deserving of the idiot that I am.

"I've never heard a *real* one," I said, with the sheer astonishment of a complete idiot. "I didn't realize just how much they sounded like the clock!"

We climbed to the top of a small cliff, overlooking the Sura River—a tributary of the Dnieper. Clearly, Katya had much more experience than me at climbing. I fell quickly behind. Once we had finally made it to the top, we sat on the edge of the cliff to admire the view and to catch our breath—or, rather, *my* breath.

We then headed down toward the river for a swim—Chernobyl-be-damned. The river was completely coated in a green, moss-like substance that I was certain would glow in the dark and give me a third testicle; or melt my existing ones. And suddenly, without warning, a bright green water snake popped its head above the surface, and turned toward us, slithering its pink tongue. I screamed like a schoolgirl and booked full steam ahead to the shore, slipping and sliding on the slimy, moss-covered rocks. Katya was right behind me, but not nearly as panicky. That's when I noticed the snake was swimming right toward us! Fortunately, we got out just in time. Disappointed, the snake disappeared beneath the surface, to await its next victim.

We headed back to the dacha. Sergei eagerly greeted us and took me by the arm, leading me to his homemade grill. He gently lifted up the grape leaves, and proudly showed off his skewers, carefully placed equally apart on the grill. Typically, once meat is on the grill, it is only a matter of minutes before it is ready to be consumed. However, in true Ukrainian fashion, it would be another two hours before our meal was ready.

"Bobby, *shashlik*," Segei said.

"Da! Shish kabob," I replied, as Sergei gently rotated the meat *just so*, before covering them back up with the grape leaves. I felt as though I had just been given a glimpse of the Holy Grail.

Sensing that I was expected to be impressed, I did my best to act in the manner of one who is indeed very impressed.

"What are the grape leaves for?" I asked.

"For flavor. And to keep the meat moist," Katya replied.

"Wait here," Katya said. She disappeared inside, leaving Sergei and I alone. Unsure of what to say, I smiled awkwardly and patted my stomach, uttering a rather lame "yum, yum." Sergei nodded and smiled back.

Sergei then pointed at me and exclaimed, "Bobby! *Schlong!*"

Schlong?? I was sure that I must have misunderstood.

"*Chto?*" ("What?") I asked.

"*Schlong!* Please Bobby!" Sergei repeated, again pointing toward me.

Here we go again, I thought to myself. First, *cock* ("kak") and now *schlong*. There was no mistaking him this time, however. He was clearly saying 'schlong.' But why?

Sergei continued to point. And I continued to be confused. Sergei started to make hand gestures, like somebody stretching out pizza dough. This did nothing to alleviate my confusion ... or anxiety.

"Katya!" Sergei and I both yelled toward the house. Moments later, Katya appeared in the door at the top of the steps.

"Everything okay?"

"Your dad keeps saying 'schlong.' I don't know what he wants!"

"*Schlang!*" Katya replied. "He wants you to get him the hose. For the meat."

I looked toward Sergei, who pointed toward a shed. Beside it was an old, kinked-up hose.

"*Da! Schlang!*" Sergei repeated, with a confident nod.

Now, it all made sense, and, suffice to say, I was quite relieved. Katya headed back inside as I retrieved Sergei's *schlang*, which he used to spray his meat for reasons I couldn't comprehend. I later asked Katya why he did this and all she could offer was: "Master chefs never reveal their secrets."

I then asked why we had to go through all the earlier trouble with the pump if they had a hose available with running water.

"Because that water is not safe for drinking," Katya explained.

"But it's safe for soaking our food with?"

"Yes, of course," Katya replied. "The heat kills all bacteria."

I was reminded that some questions are best left unasked.

Two hours later, it was finally time to eat. And what a feast it was! We gathered on the garden patio as Ukrainian folk music played from an old radio into the perfect late-summer night. Every square inch of the table was covered with food. Sergei and I washed our food down with shots of vodka.

Following dinner, Elena sliced up a watermelon. I had never eaten more watermelon than I did that night. Or rather, I have never been *forced* to eat as much watermelon. As Elena offered me yet another slice, I held onto my gut to indicate that I was full, but this didn't seem to matter.

"I'm going to burst," I pleaded.

But Elena insisted. I gave in once again, forcing myself to eat it. Sergei turned the volume on the radio up and began clapping along to the music—his personal favorite—a moving, operatic folk song called *Sharmanka* ("Organ Grinder") performed by Nickolai Baskov, "the people's artist of Ukraine."

Despite feeling as though I had a bowling ball sitting in my stomach, I joined in. Katya joined in, too, and Sergei coaxed a reluctant Elena to join us. I did a surprisingly solid imitation of a traditional Russian dance, drawing laughs from everyone—except for Babushka, of course, who just sat there and glared—not saying a word, but speaking volumes.

When we had finished dancing, Sergei poured me another shot, which I drank, despite Katya's flash of disapproval. Katya quickly poured me a cup of water in hopes of diluting the vodka already inside me.

And then, out of the blue, I suddenly decided that I was going to take a midnight stroll. I stood up and headed out through the gate and down the dirt road, carrying my cup of water with me for safekeeping.

Katya watched from the gate as I staggered around the corner at the end of the road. She called out my name, but I didn't respond. I was in my own little world, oblivious to my surroundings.

Katya ran after me and quickly caught up, taking me by the arm and turning me around, in the manner one would do to an escaped Alzheimer's patient.

"Where were you going?" Katya asked.

"That way," I pointed, zombie-like.

"Let's go back, Bobby. No more drinking,"

Katya led me back to the patio, helping me into my seat, where tea awaited.

That night, filled to the brim with food and vodka, I slept like a baby for the first time since my arrival in Ukraine.

16

THE FLOWERS OF DEATH

The next day, my watermelon and vodka-induced stomachache from the previous night had been reduced to a dull throbbing. Following breakfast, which consisted of open face cheese and "some-sort-of-salami" sandwiches, it was time to head back to the city. Sergei decided to let Katya get some driving practice. Even though she had her license, like most women in Ukraine, Katya rarely drove. Since owning a car was a luxury, the men that did own cars weren't too keen on sharing them with the women in their lives. As a result, mere inexperience was often interpreted as poor driving ability.

As Katya drove, Sergei barked instructions into her ear. Although she was clearly a beginner driver, Katya was actually a better driver than her father, despite her struggles with the manual transmission. Then again, I never used a manual transmission, so I had no room to talk.

"This is why women don't drive in our country," Sergei said, before demanding that Katya pull over, reminding her of her place.

Shortly after Sergei took back the controls and got back on the main road leading to Dnipropetrovsk, the car began to make a loud thumping noise. The noise grew louder as we continued. Moments later, the car began to repeatedly jerk back and forth. Black smoke emerged from under the hood until all visibility was lost. Finally, the car rolled to a stop in front of an enormous field of sunflowers.

"Kaput!" Sergei declared, calmly, in a manner that suggested that this was a regular occurrence.

"Not again," Katya said as Sergei got out of the car, confirming my theory.

"What are we going to do now?" I asked.

"First, we'll let the car cool down a bit and see if it starts up again," Katya explained.

Always the consummate hostess, Elena spread out a blanket on the side of the road. She then took a watermelon out of the trunk and proceeded to slice it up with a giant knife. We all sat down on the blanket, surrounded by various pieces of trash, and ate; it was the perfect *Nemiroff Rockwell* scene.

When we were finished, Sergei attempted to start the car again, but to no avail. He then opened the hood and began tinkering around with the engine.

"He'll fix it. He always does," Katya said with full confidence. I was skeptical.

Suddenly there was a loud *pop* and black smoke billowed in Sergei's face. After the smoke had cleared, Sergei got back into the car and attempted to start the engine. It actually started for a brief moment, before cutting out. Sergei got out again and tinkered with the engine. He got back into the car and tried again. By some divine miracle, the engine actually sputtered into life. Sergei cheered, and put the car into gear. He barely came to a complete stop, so we could all climb back in and then we were off again.

After one-hundred meters or so, the car sputtered to another stop. Sergei punched the steering wheel, before getting out again. After several moments, he emerged from behind the engine, wiping the sweat off his brow.

"Take a route van or trolley," he commanded.

"What about your dad?" I asked.

"He's going to stay and fix it," said Katya.

"I'll pay to have it taken to a shop," I offered.

"Nyet, nyet, nyet! I will fix," Sergei retorted.

"He'll fix it," Katya said with unwavering confidence.

Katya, Elena, Babushka, and myself headed down the road to a small bus stop. As the minutes passed, I began to feel as though we were players in a Ukrainian version of *Waiting for Godovich*. While the women sat on the bench, I walked over to some nearby wild flowers. I picked some and brought them back. In an attempt to get into her good graces, I handed the flowers to Babushka.

"How thoughtful!" Elena said, clearly impressed. Even Babushka seemed touched—that is until she counted them.

All of a sudden, her face was overcome with fear.

"Mama, what's wrong?" Elena asked, concerned.

Babushka counted out the flowers, one by one, for everyone to hear.

"One. Two. Three. Four."

Both Katya and Elena put their hand to their mouths in shared horror. I had no idea what to make of this, wondering if the flowers were perhaps poisonous.

"What is going on?" I asked.

"You never, *ever* give a Ukrainian an even number of flowers," Katya said.

"What difference does it make?" I asked with escalated confusion, as Babushka glared at me with even greater intensity than usual.

"It's the difference between *life* and *death*—that's what. Only dead people get an even number of flowers."

Babushka shook her fist, railing at me in Russian: "I'm not dead yet!"

"Please tell her I'm sorry. I didn't know!" I said, exasperated.

Katya translated, but Babushka simply waved it off. She wanted no part of my apology. I devised a plan to rectify this situation by obtaining one more flower to make it an odd number, adding it to Babushka's bunch.

"There. Problem solved," I said, fooling no one.

"Too late!" Babushka said. "Too late!"

I asked what the time frame was for the death I would now be blamed for. Or more specifically, to know if there was an expiration date as to when I would be off the hook.

There was none.

Fortunately, at that moment, a *marshrutka* (route van) arrived to distract from the tension. Nobody spoke during the ride.

The route van dropped us off at the edge of the city limits, where we proceeded to head toward a trolley stop. Suddenly I heard the honk of a car horn. It was Sergei in the car, good as new.

"Unbelievable!" I said.

"I told you he'd fix it," Katya said.

As we climbed into the car, Sergei immediately noticed Babushka's demeanor—even angrier than normal!

"What's wrong?" he asked.

"This boy!" Babushka barked in Russian, glaring and poking at me. As I slunk down into the car seat, I was quite sure that she had placed a curse on me.

17

PUBLIC SCHOOL #23

On two separate occasions, Sergei and Elena attempted to take me to the Yavornitskiy History Museum, which documents the history of Dnipropetrovsk—a reminder of how young the United States truly is in comparison with the rest of the world. Unfortunately, on both occasions, the museum was closed. On the third attempt, it was just Katya and me. And third time was a charm.

The museum is located on *Zhovtneva* (October) *Square* in downtown Dnipropetrovsk—alongside the oldest church in the city, the gloriously ornate Preobrazhensky Cathedral—a Russian Orthodox Church founded by Catherine the Great in 1787. Interestingly, from 1975–1988, the cathedral functioned as the museum of religion and atheism before returning to its primary function as a place of worship.

The museum's centerpiece was an enormous diorama depicting the bloody, brutal "Battle of the Dnieper" in 1944—one of the largest campaigns of World War II, involving close to 4,000,000 troops (with estimated casualties of up to 2,700,000). It was hard to imagine such a catastrophic toll and the effect that this must have had on the people of Ukraine.

Another important fact I learned at the museum was that prior to the Holocaust, Dnipropetrovsk was an important center of Jewish life, with 80,000 Jews living the city. However, after the Nazis captured the city in 1941, 11,000 Jews were executed. Persecution of Jews continues to this day throughout the former Soviet Union.

For me, the highlight of the museum was viewing the skeletal remains of a tribal family from around three thousand B.C., complete with broken skulls—no doubt indicating their brutal, grizzly end.

After we headed out of the museum, we walked past a display of ancient, gargoyle-esque Kipchak warrior statues. Kipchaks were a tribal federation who ruled much of eastern Europe in the 11th and 12th centuries. Based on their stone depiction, they also apparently had large, saggy breasts—males and females alike.

Katya led me past a row of WWII-era tanks and through a hole in the fence surrounding the museum, which led toward a gray, ominous-looking building.

"This was my high school," Katya said, pointing at the structure—which was exactly how I would have imagined a Soviet school to look like.

"Wow!" I exclaimed, trying to imagine life at the unimaginatively, but aptly named "Public School #23." Judging by Katya's description, the pedagogy there was also exactly what I would have expected from such a sinister, oppressive looking building. Straight rows of desks. Authoritarian teachers. Drills, drills, and more drills in lieu of freedom, creativity, and exploration, which probably translates into students better equipped with basic skills than the U.S., but less capable of independent thought.

"Looks pretty creepy," I said, staring at the drab building.

"Creepy? What's creepy?" Katya asked.

"Scary ... foreboding," I explained.

"It *was* scary," Katya replied.

We sat down on a nearby piece of rusted playground equipment.

"I hated every second of it here," Katya said.

"Why?" I asked.

"Mainly because there's nothing worse than having to pretend you're happy when you're not. And that's how it was here," Katya said sullenly.

"Why were you expected to be happy?" I asked.

"Because I could speak English. Because my parents made a little more money than everyone else. Because of my father's position and his connections," Katya replied.

"After I came back from Mississippi, my classmates made up a rumor that I said I hated Ukraine and wanted to live in America," Katya continued. "I would never say that about my country. To prove it, I even brought in an article from a newspaper in Mississippi, in which I was quoted about how proud I was of my heritage. But that didn't matter to them. Plus, there was the small fact that they couldn't read English," she said, smiling.

"Sounds like they were just jealous," I said.

"Yeah, you could say that," Katya replied, "Especially my English teachers."

"Why?"

"Well, it didn't help that I knew more English than they did, I think. But that was because my parents wanted to give me an opportunity to better my life—and learning English was the best way to ensure that. Unfortunately, my teachers—and my classmates—held that against me."

"Better to have people jealous of you, than to be jealous of them," I said.

"The grass is—what's the phrase—always greener on another side?"

"… on the other side," I replied, nodding in agreement.

We reflected on this before I added, "at least you never had your face shoved in dog shit!"

"True!" Katya replied. "I just don't understand why you were treated like that?"

"In America, if you're picked last in gym class, there's no hope," I explained.

"Why didn't you fight back?"

"I was always small for my age. A late bloomer."

"So?"

"I was scared."

"So you've never been in a fight before?" Katya asked.

"Nope."

"But you must have at least punched someone?"

"*I've been punched*. But I never punched back," I admitted. "Fortunately, I've always been fast, so I would just run. I'm also really good at curling up into a ball when necessary."

"Wow!" exclaimed Katya, laughing. "Now, that's a really great skill to have!"

"It really is," I reflected.

"You're such a nice guy, Bobby. It just seems so unfair."

"Well, you know the phrase …," I began.

"Good guys don't finish in first?" Katya suggested.

"Nice guys finish last," I replied.

We both laughed.

"So, how did you deal with all that stuff?" Katya asked.

"You really want to know?" I replied.

"Yes!" Katya said. "But only if you don't mind sharing."

I paused for a moment, taking a deep breath, before continuing. "By actually convincing myself that all my classmates were in on a big joke. That one day, I would come to school and they would all yell 'surprise!' and suddenly become my friends. So I kept waiting."

"And now look at you," Katya said, kissing me on the cheek.

"Surprise!" she added.

"In some ways, David Montroy and all the others like him were the best thing that ever happened to me. I learned not to give a shit about what others thought of me. And that's what led to me becoming a writer. It was either that, or sociopath. So 'thank you' David, wherever you are."

"I would have been your friend," Katya said.

"And I would have been yours," I replied, taking her hand.

After several moments of silence, Katya asked: "Do you want to try to go into the school?"

"Sure!" I replied. "Do you think it's open?"

"Let's check."

We walked up to the entrance. Katya tried the handle. It was unlocked. She slowly pulled open the large, heavy door and we entered. We were greeted by the strongest chemical fumes I have ever encountered. The smell immediately gripped my throat and seared my nostrils.

"What in the hell is that?" I gasped, choking.

"They must be painting," Katya explained.

"That's some pretty strong paint," I said. Between these fumes and swimming in two nuclear-waste-carrying rivers, I will know what to blame if I ever get cancer.

We began walking through the building, which was dark and surprisingly chilly, despite the sweltering heat outside. Windows were certainly in short supply. Being inside Katya's former high school was like being inside a chemical-soaked crypt. The further down the halls we walked, the stronger the fumes became. By this point, I could literally taste them. There were no workers or teachers in sight. Maybe they had all already been carted off to the nearest morgue?

Katya showed me her former classroom. The walls were painted gray. There was not a single poster or piece of artwork on the wall. This is where the future of Ukraine was educated.

After ten or so minutes of inhaling vapors—the source of which I never did figure out—I couldn't take it anymore. I could hardly breathe and was beginning to feel faint. Of course, it didn't faze Katya a single bit. She was probably used to it.

I begged that we leave before I passed out … or passed away.

We left, and headed out toward the river and a riverfront café, high on the fumes of Public School #23.

18

LOVE & CAVIAR

Life sometimes presents us with opportunities to try things we never thought we would try. Like, for instance, going to Ukraine. Or … trying caviar. Now, it's important to point out that I do not like fish. I will occasionally eat fish sticks, a *Filet o'Fish,* or shrimp. The "fishier" the fish, the less likely I am to eat it. So the idea of eating caviar was something I never deemed possible, but leave it to Ukraine to change all of that.

We found a café with an outdoor patio. Katya went inside to order while I sat at a table overlooking the Dnieper River. I tapped my feet along to the heavy beat of the blaring Russian techno-pop, still *tasting* the paint fumes from Katya's former high school. Katya appeared with a bottle of *Sovetskoye Shampanskoye* (champagne) and two glasses.

I poured out the champagne and raised my glass: "Here's to the past," I toasted. "And to getting rid of the taste of paint fumes!"

We clinked glasses, then downed their contents. It's amazing how quickly our bodies can adapt to a regular consumption of alcohol when given the chance.

A sullen-faced waitress brought us some bread and an orange, beady substance. *She forgot to ask how we were doing today!* I thought sarcastically to myself.

"Is that jelly?" I naively asked.

"No, it's caviar," Katya replied. "Fish eggs."

"Yeah, I know what caviar is," I replied, adding "and there's no way I'm eating that."

"You eat chicken eggs, don't you?" Katya asked.

"Yeah, but these don't come from chickens. I love chicken. Caviar comes from fish. I hate fish."

"How can you hate fish?" Katya asked.

"I just do," I said.

"Have you ever tried caviar?"

"Nope. And I plan on keeping it that way."

"Well … history's about to change," Katya replied with a sly smile.

"I've never been much of a revisionist," I said.

"You're not revising anything if you haven't done it yet," Katya insisted. "Just try it."

"No way," I replied, adamant in my conviction.

"Why?"

"'Because it's fish eggs!"

"Just try it!" Katya insisted.

"What do I have to gain?"

Katya flashed me a seductive glance.

"You already got me to eat cow tongue, Katya. I draw the line there."

"More for me then," Katya said, dipping a piece of bread into the caviar and removing a hearty portion.

"Mmmmm … you don't know what you're missing," Katya said with a mouth full of orange fish eggs.

Perhaps it was the combination of the champagne, the paint fumes, and Katya's "come on" glance, but I suddenly felt a desire to try it—*if only to prove my point.*

"Okay … alright … you win," I said, taking a piece of bread, dipping it into the caviar, and carefully removing two eggs.

I sniffed it, gagging slightly at the pungent fishy odor blending with the chemical fumes still inside my nostrils. That forced me to quickly change my mind.

"Way too fishy for me," I said. "No way. I'm not doing it!"

"Don't smell it, Bobby. Just eat it!" Katya said, laughing.

I realized I wasn't going to win this battle, so I poured myself another glass of champagne as a caviar chaser, then popped the bread into my mouth. It tasted as awful as I imagined it would. I quickly grabbed my champagne and downed it, much like a kindergartner insisting on taking a drink after a spoonful of medicine.

"Good, huh?" Katya said with a smirk.

I could still taste the fish. I grabbed a napkin and wiped my tongue vigorously. "I told you, I don't like fish and that tasted exactly the way fish smells."

"Well, at least you tried it. And for that, you deserve a hand," Katya said, giving me a slow, slightly sarcastic round of applause.

"Just for the record, Katya, you are the only person on this planet that could ever, *ever* get me to eat that," I said.

"I love you, too," Katya replied teasingly.

I looked across the café at a couple in their mid- to late-fifties gazing into each other's eyes.

"Look at that couple."

"What about them?" Katya asked.

"They've probably been married for twenty years, yet they look like they're on their first date."

"Maybe they are?" Katya said.

Katya glanced at another middle-aged couple sitting nearby. They stared blankly in opposite directions, clearly not interested in one another—or seemingly, in life in general.

"I think they are just comfortable with one another," Katya concluded.

"*Too* comfortable," I retorted.

"Is that really a bad thing?"

"Not necessarily bad or good. But just look at them."

As Katya looked, the woman said something to the man. He passed her the salt.

I continued with my observations: "They're so used to the repetition of their daily life that they just go through the motions, rather than truly living. No spontaneity. No unpredictability. It's like they have nothing left to say."

"I see your point," Katya said. "Promise that won't be us."

"I promise," I said.

And then suddenly, the couple got up and began to dance to a traditional Russian waltz. The music had snapped them out of their stupor and they danced together, looking as though they were having the time of their lives.

We both laughed at the realization that nobody ever really knows anything.

19

LOVE & CLUBBING

During dinner that evening, I committed the grave sin of spilling salt on the table. Everyone grew eerily quiet, as though I had just threatened to kill somebody, or remove my pants and dance on the table.

"No problem," I said, "I'll clean it up," sweeping the spilled salt into the palm of my hand.

"But ... you don't realize what this means, Bobby," Katya said, concerned.

"No, I guess I don't. Excuse me for being clumsy. Of course, if you had a regular salt shaker instead of a *bowl* of salt, this wouldn't have happened. What's the big deal anyway?"

"Spilled salt means that an argument is coming," Katya explained.

And judging by everybody's facial expressions, she was probably right.

Following dinner, while I was updating my journal in my bedroom, an argument did indeed ensue between Katya and her parents.

Moments later, Katya burst into my room.

"Is everything okay?" I asked

"Tonight, we're going to do something my parents never let me do," Katya declared.

"Stay out past nine?" I asked, half-serious.

"Yes!" Katya replied. "We're going out, to a dance club."

"Are you sure that's a good idea?" I asked.

"I'm so sick of them operating under the illusion that I'm sixteen," Katya exclaimed. "Well you know what? Tonight, there's nothing they can do to stop me."

"Aren't they likely to get upset at me?" I asked.

"No, they know it's not you ... it's me. They already know we're going, and that's that. I'm going to get ready. We're leaving in thirty minutes."

I fished around in my luggage for my "clubbing shirt"—a grey, short-sleeved shirt that I had bought in Germany.

Thirty minutes later, we headed out into the night.

Katya wore tight, leather pants along with hula-hoop-sized earrings, which I had earlier observed were in fashion in Ukraine. I never thought I would date a girl in leather pants; yet another expectation-defying moment in a trip chock-full with them.

We took a route van to a club—the succinctly named "King"—with an enormous, gaudy exterior that resembled a Czar's palace made out of Styrofoam.

We made our way over to the entrance. Two intimidating doormen—who looked like twin mixed martial arts specialists—stood in front of a thick, velvet rope, barring our entrance. As we approached, one of the doormen said something to Katya. As Katya replied, I watched as the second doorman slowly looked Katya up and down, nodding his head in appreciation. He then turned to me as if to say *I know you saw me doing that … so what are you going to do about it?* I smiled politely and nodded as if to say *it's all good.* The doorman acted as though I no longer existed as his twin unhooked the rope and motioned for us to enter.

Inside, the club's decor was minimalist and unassuming—especially compared to its garish, kitschy exterior. The perimeter of the dancefloor was lined with plush booths, framed with sheer curtains. The walls were mirrored, creating the illusion that the club was much larger than its actual size. A small bar was situated off to one side. As we entered, the bartender—who could easily have passed as the triplet brother of the doormen—looked up, but did not greet or even acknowledge us; he seemed to be more interested in cleaning dirt from his fingernails with a hunting knife and taking swigs of vodka from a huge bottle. Colored lights swirled and dashed across the empty dancefloor as Katya led me to a corner booth. As it turned out, we had the club all to ourselves.

"Where is everyone?!" I asked, confused.

"What do you mean?" Katya replied.

"It's so dead in here."

"It's Saturday!"

"Yeah, exactly!"

"It's not even ten o'clock yet. It will be packed later. After midnight. People are only just sitting down to dinner."

"When does the club close?" I asked.

"At the break of dawn," Katya replied.

"Like the Beastie Boys!" I said. The allusion was lost on her.

That's hardcore, I thought to myself. Only the most dedicated ravers do that back home.

"I'll be back in a minute Bobby. You stay here," Katya said.

Katya sauntered over to the bar and began chatting to the bartender. The bartender seemed to be congratulating Katya. I watched as he poured her a shot, which she downed in one go.

Moments later, Katya returned with a bottle of champagne, two glasses … and a lit cigarette in her mouth.

"You smoke?!" I asked, surprised.

"Yeah, on certain occasions," Katya replied. "It is my birthday after all!" she said smiling.

"It is??!" I asked.

"Well, that's what I told the bartender at least! It got me a free shot of vodka … and a cigarette!"

Although smoking had always been a turn off for me, I actually found myself intrigued by Katya's emerging wild side.

"You're nuts!" I said, adding "You're really mad at your parents, aren't you?"

"You can tell?" Katya replied, sarcastically.

"Just a bit," I said.

Katya placed the champagne and glasses onto the table and then, completely out of nowhere, threw herself on me. We kissed passionately for at least five minutes. By this point I was *extremely intrigued* and turned on by this "new" Katya. I reached over to the table and I poured out the champagne.

Katya held up her glass for a toast: "To freedom!"

We clinked glasses. I watched in astonishment as Katya downed the champagne in one go. I followed suit.

"More!" Katya commanded.

I poured us each another glass, which Katya again quickly downed. I decided to take it slower this time.

"Careful, Katya," I warned.

"Hey, I'm Ukrainian!" Katya replied. She was in no mood for compromise. She pulled me toward her again and began forcefully kissing me. I was *almost* intimidated.

"Well, I see you're in a better mood," I gasped, coming up for air.

At that moment, our song ("Not Going to Catch Us") came on.

Katya stubbed out her cigarette and grabbed me by the hand, practically dragging me out of the booth onto the dance floor. We danced in the swirl of lights and smoke on our own private dance floor, as Katya grinded herself against me seductively, kissing me until it hurt.

As we danced, I glanced over at the DJ. Dressed in black and wearing a plastic, jewel-encrusted, crown, he was the 'king' of "King"!

When the song was over, we headed back to the booth, where we polished off the rest of the champagne. Without saying a word, Katya grabbed the empty bottle, turned and stumbled off toward the bar, returning a few minutes later with yet another bottle of champagne … and another cigarette. She slammed the bottle down onto the table, and took a deep drag on the cigarette, blowing smoke over my head. She then poured the champagne out, filling both of our glasses to the very top, before grabbing her glass, and raising it to make another toast.

"To us! Forever! Bobby!!" Katya shouted exuberantly.

"To us!" I exclaimed. We clinked glasses and kissed again.

We headed back out onto the dancefloor where the DJ continued spinning a never-ending platter of cheesy, pulsating Euro-trance and techno. The music sounded so similar that he easily could have left the same song on a loop and it wouldn't have made any difference. I wasn't complaining however; the unique atmosphere, the amazing sound system, the buzz from the champagne, and Katya's crazy mood were making for a very memorable night.

As the evening wore on, the club continued to be all ours. We danced the night away, the VIPs of own private party. On a trip filled with endless movie-like moments, this was perhaps the most cinematic moment of all. It was a moment I never wanted to end, even though I knew it would have to, just like everything else.

During a rare break in the thump-thump beat of the music, we made our way back over to the booth and fell back into our seats. By now, I could tell that Katya was completely wasted. She sat there with her head tilted back and her eyes closed. After a few minutes, I leaned over to ask her if she was okay. Katya opened her eyes, and without a word, pulled me in toward her and began kissing me passionately. She then proceeded to grab my hand and force it onto her breast, knocking my champagne glass over in the process. Champagne flooded the table and began to drip onto the floor—and onto me. I stood up quickly to escape the river of champagne. Katya seemed oblivious and simply slumped back into the seat and tilted her head back again, closing her eyes, seemingly unaware of her surroundings.

At that point, I decided that enough was enough. I decided to make an executive decision.

"Katya, I'm taking you home" I said.

Katya did not seem to hear me; at least she did not respond.

"Katya!! I'm taking you home!" I repeated, louder.

This time, she did respond, slurring her words and waving her hands in my general direction, her eyes still closed. "No! Bobby! I'm staying out all night! I don't care what my parents think."

"No, Katya, we're leaving," I insisted. "Look, there's too much at stake here." It was not only past dark, but it was already well past midnight.

Katya resisted and I had to practically drag her out of the booth. She continued to protest as I helped her to her feet.

As we staggered toward the door—well, only one of us was staggering … I was simply struggling to remove the staggerer from the premises—I could hear Katya mumbling in Russian underneath her breath.

At the door, I was shocked to see a large number of clubbers waiting to go in. It was a sea of black clothes: halter tops and short leather skirts for the ladies; short-sleeved shirts, tank tops, and black pants for the guys. Practically everyone was decked out in gaudy, gold jewelry. And the smell of cheap, knock-off cologne was overpowering. It was the Ukrainian "Jersey Shore."

All eyes were suddenly focused on us, as snickers and, presumably, insults were tossed in our general direction. Of course, I had no idea what they were saying. And in Katya's drunken state, neither did she.

Once we made it outside, I noticed that the line snaked halfway around the Styrofoam palace—a human moat of douchebags and sluts. We continued to be mocked by "the pride of Dnipropetrovsk." I assumed that the mocking was aimed more toward Katya than me, although I'm sure that I wasn't helping matters. I heard maniacal laughter, and looked over to see the twin mixed martial arts King Asshole bouncers pointing and laughing at us. I carried/dragged Katya away from the club as quickly as I could. For once, I didn't need to be told—I knew it was best not to speak a lick of English.

Once we were a safe distance away from the idiot clubbers—and once my panic had subsided—it dawned on me that Katya was now rendered completely useless as a translator.

I was on my own.

My subsided panic retuned in an instant. I waved down a route van and helped Katya into it. I somehow even managed to provide the driver with directions that he understood. I held out a handful of coins—which the driver gleefully took one by one. I was quite certain that I was being ripped off, but was unconcerned. My only concern at that point was to make it safely back to the apartment.

After we took our seats in the back of the empty van, Katya seemed to come around. She continued to sloppily kiss and grope me all the way back. I could see the driver smiling and giving me knowing glances in his rearview mirror; once or twice he even gave me a thumbs-up. After we arrived back at the apartment, I opened the door of the route van and Katya almost fell out. Thankfully, I somehow managed to keep her on her feet.

I led Katya up the steps of the apartment building, pleading with her to punch in the key code. It took her several attempts, but she finally managed to punch in the correct code.

Once inside, I helped Katya into the elevator, deciding that the risk of one or both of us falling down the concrete steps far outweighed the risk of getting stuck in the elevator. Once inside the elevator, Katya pinned me against the wall. When we reached the second floor, she promptly sent the elevator all the way to the top of the building, before bringing it all the way back down to the ground floor.

"Katya, you're going to get us trapped in here," I exclaimed.

"You say that like it's a bad thing," Katya replied in a drunken slur.

"It would be!" I replied.

"We wouldn't even notice," she said, drunkenly. I was far from turned on at this point and started to become more and more irritated. The next time Katya reached for the buttons, I blocked her. The last thing I wanted to do was spend the night in a run-down, Soviet-era elevator.

I managed to get the elevator back to the second floor. The door opened and Katya fell to the ground. I struggled to help her up. She was giggling too hard to stand straight. Thankfully however, as we approached her apartment, Katya was able to find the ability to compose herself.

"I can't let them know I'm drunk," she said with sudden concern.

"I thought you didn't care what they thought anymore?" I replied.

"I don't … but you have no idea what my father would do to sober me up," Katya said, echoing her earlier warning to me.

She took several deep breaths—somehow quickly managing not to look like the intoxicated mess she really was—and rang the doorbell.

Thankfully, Elena answered the door. She looked exhausted. It was clear to me that she had been waiting up all night for us to return.

"*Privet, mama,*" Katya said, hugging her mother.

Elena expressed a few, calm words to Katya, before heading off to bed, outwardly happy that her daughter was home, but surely, inwardly hurt by her defiance. Elena was not one to make a scene.

We headed down the hall toward my bedroom.

"Are you going to be okay?" I asked.

Without responding, Katya pushed me into the room. She slowly closed the door behind her, and threw herself down on the couch, squirming seductively and unbuttoning her pants.

"I'm through waiting, Bobby. I want you. Now."

"Katya ..."

Katya ignored my plea, squeezing her legs around my neck and pulling me down on top of her.

"What about your parents?" I warned.

"Since when does that stop you?" Katya replied, without concern.

I tried my best to resist, but she was too strong for me. For some reason, I started thinking of the cult 90's alien flick *Species.*

"Bite me. On the neck," Katya commanded.

I nibbled on her neck.

"Harder. So it hurts."

I bit harder.

Katya hurriedly unbuttoned her blouse, exposing her snow white, ample breasts and pushed my face against them. She continued to squirm, fumbling for my pants, which she hastily unbuttoned.

By now, Katya was panting hard, I had to cover her mouth with my hand to muffle her moans. She wiggled her hips, pulling her pants down below her waist, and grabbed me by the wrist, forcing my hand onto her crotch.

"Take me. Now. *Trahni menya!*" she commanded.

As incredibly tempting as this moment was—it wasn't supposed to be this way. And if Katya were sober, I was pretty sure she would have agreed.

And so, despite myself, I resisted, forcing her off of me.

"Katya, no ... *please* ... not here ... not like this," I begged.

"What!? You don't want me anymore?" Katya replied, hurt.

"Yes! *I do!* Trust me. More than anything. Believe me, I've fantasized about this moment countless times. *But not like this.* You're totally wasted. We'd both regret this."

This seemed to have a sobering effect on her—or at least a calming effect. Rejected, she pulled up her pants, fastened up her blouse, and stumbled toward the door.

"Goodnight, Bobby," she whispered. She kissed her finger and placed it onto my lips.

"Goodnight, Katya. *I love you,*" I whispered back.

I lay on the bed for a few moments, my pants half down, trying to make sense of the last few minutes.

Seconds later, I heard vomiting.

I quickly pulled up my pants and crept out of my room and over to the bathroom.

"Katya. Are you okay?" I whispered as loud as I could outside the door. I knew that Elena had to be awake and wondered whether Sergei was, too. Neither Sergei nor Elena appeared. I prayed that they had not heard what was happening in the bedroom moments earlier. *But how could they not have heard?* If Sergei had burst in on us several minutes earlier, I'm quite sure that I would be off for a dip in the Dnieper in a nice pair of Ukrainian concrete boots.

The flow of vomit continued.

Moments later, the bathroom door opened. Katya stood there, zombified.

"I think ... I'm ... going ... to bed," she said slowly, before shuffling off to her room.

The next morning, I cautiously headed out into the hallway, not knowing what to expect. Katya was still asleep, but I was greeted by Elena. Fortunately, Sergei had gone to meet up with a colleague and had already left the house.

"*Dobroe utro*, Bobby!" Elena said cheerfully in Russian ("Good morning"). There was no indication whatsoever in her tone or demeanor that she was angry with me for bringing her daughter home in such a drunken state. I wondered whether she had somehow been able to piece together what had transpired in my room the night before and realized how much I truly respected her daughter. I hoped that was the case at least. *I couldn't very well ask.*

"*Dubro utra*," I replied back in butchered Russian.

"*Zaftrak*, Bobby?" ("Breakfast?") Elena asked, making the universal hand gestures for eating and drinking, and ushering me toward the kitchen.

"Breakfast?" I replied

"*Da!* Breakfast!" Elena said, smiling

"*Da! Spasibo*, Elena" I replied.

Elena led me into the kitchen, where she poured tea and offered me some *Risovaya Kasha* (rice porridge) and *blini* (crepes).

Elena sat down and said *something* to me in Russian.

"*Da!*" I said, smiling like a fool, having no idea what she just said.

Elena laughed.

She pointed to the various food items and taught me how to say each of them in Russian. She continued with body parts:

"*Golova!*" she said, patting the top of her head.

"*Golova!* Head!" I repeated.

"*Plechi!*" Elena continued, pointing to her shoulders.

"*Plechi!* Shoulders!" I repeated.

Together, we butchered one another's language beautifully.

Moments later, Katya entered, rubbing her head. We stared at one another in silence for a few moments until I finally asked.

"Are you okay?"

Katya moaned in pain. Elena proceeded to serve Katya her breakfast, despite flashing her daughter disapproving looks. Katya was too hungover to notice or worry. The three of us ate in awkward silence for a few moments until Katya finally said:

"About last night, Bobby … I owe you an apology."

"No apology," I interjected.

"Then I owe you a *thank you*."

"A thank you for what?" I asked.

"For passing my test," Katya replied.

"What test?"

"I wanted to see whether or not you would take advantage of me. And you didn't."

"Wait?! What?" I said, surprised and confused. "You're joking, right?"

"No … no, I'm not."

"That wasn't a *test*. You were completely wasted. And you were trying to get me to …" It suddenly occurred to me that Katya's mother was sitting not three feet away from me. I glanced over at Elena and smiled—thankful that she was unable to understand a single word that we were saying.

"Yes, I was drunk. And yes, I did want you to. But that doesn't mean I didn't know what I was doing."

I didn't know what to believe.

"You're … unbelievable!" I replied, incredulous. It was the only response I could come up with at that moment.

"I was *surprised* actually," Katya replied.

"You sound disappointed," I replied.

"No. Of course I'm not," Katya said. "Well … maybe a little," she added, smiling.

"I don't want you to think I didn't want to. Because I did."

"Look Bobby, just because I'm surprised doesn't mean I'm not *impressed*. I don't know how many guys would do what you did—*or didn't do.*"

"You wouldn't want to find out," I replied.

Katya nodded and sighed.

We continued to eat our breakfast in silence. Or rather, Elena and I ate. Katya struggled to eat about half a crepe.

After we had finished breakfast, I demonstrated the new vocabulary I learned from Elena: *golova* (head), *plechi* (shoulders), *koleni* (knees) and *paltzee* (toes). I felt like I should start singing the kindergarten nursery rhyme—"*Golova, Plechi, Koleni, Paltzee … Koleni, Paltzee!*"—but thought better of it.

"Very good!" Katya said, as though she were talking to a kindergartener. Elena then demonstrated what she had learned.

"Great job, mama!" Katya said in Russian, before explaining to me how testicles are affectionately referred to as 'eggs' in Russian and buttocks referred to as 'berries.'

After my vocabulary lesson, I began to clear the dishes.

"Not necessary. You're our guest," Elena insisted, waving her hands.

"No. I insist. Please. I want to," I replied, seeing yet another golden opportunity for approval.

I poured the remaining tea into Elena's cup and motioned for her to stay seated, relax, and enjoy her drink. I gathered up the dishes and took them into the kitchen.

"He's trained well," Elena said to Katya, smiling.

"In Ukraine, men aren't expected to do anything when it comes to help in the kitchen," Katya explained.

"Well, in America, things are different," I replied.

I washed and Katya dried.

I began to wonder whether my act of kindness would backfire, and that I would be seen as less of a man for offering to do—by Ukrainian standards—such a "womanly" task. However, when I turned around I saw Elena watching from the living room, with a broad smile on her face.

Meanwhile, the threat of Sergei's eventual return continued to hover over our heads, although neither of us spoke about it.

That afternoon, as Katya lay in bed nursing her hangover and Elena slaved in the kitchen, I sat in the living room, recording the events from the night before in my journal. Little did I know, a whole ream of new material was awaiting me.

One by one, I heard each lock and subsequent door open.

The Czar had returned ...

I heard keys slamming against the table by the door, followed by heavy footsteps. I glanced up to see Sergei standing in—or rather, *filling*—the doorway of the living room. Sergei glared at me. Without saying a word, he turned and proceeded down the hallway. I froze in terror, holding my breath.

"Sergei!?" Elena exclaimed, emerging from the kitchen hurriedly and running after her husband. I was no longer fearing for my own life. I was fearing for Katya's. I heard a door slam against a wall. This was followed by Katya's ear-piercing scream, as a rumble of Russian thunder emerged from Sergei's mouth. Of course, I had no clue as to what was being said, but I could certainly imagine. In fact, I was glad that I couldn't understand any of it. One thing I could understand loud and clear, however: *my name*, which was repeated over and over again.

I could hear Elena pleading with Sergei to calm down, but Sergei immediately cut her down to size, putting her "in her place" as she instantly became as quiet as a field mouse.

Sergei resumed his tirade against Katya ... and then Katya started to fight back! It was like an episode of *Okna!* I felt equally impressed and frightened.

Elena tried to intervene once again, but this time, it was Katya's turn to put her mother "in her place." Elena gave up at that point—shot by both sides.

The argument raged on. I could hear Sergei's and Katya's voices continually rising, along with the speed and intensity of delivery, as they attempted to overpower each other. In fact, their earth-shattering shouts made the screenless window frames rattle throughout the apartment. I wondered to myself whether any of the neighbors were attempting to take a nap. *Hopefully,* I thought to myself satisfying my thirst for nap-deprived revenge.

After a couple of minutes, I actually started to become numb to it, unable to understand a word, and resumed writing in my journal. After about five minutes of the non-stop onslaught, I began to feel more annoyed than anything. However, that's when I became aware that *the tables were now completely turned.* The only voice I could hear was Katya's. Sergei was completely silent, seemingly put "in his place," as Katya continued *her* tirade.

Not bad for someone with a hangover.

A few minutes later, presumably once he was no longer able to take any more, I heard Sergei retreat back down the hallway. Katya slammed her door shut. I held my breath, wondering if I was next on Sergei's hit list.

Sergei appeared in the doorway again and stood there motionless—staring, thinking—for what felt like an eternity. *Don't prolong the torture,* I thought to myself. *Please … just put me out of my misery now.*

Sergei approached and I braced myself for the inevitable strangling. To my surprise, however, he calmly sat down on the couch next to me, reached for my shoulder, and patted it several times. He then looked me square in the eyes, sighed, and said, in a low, quiet voice:

"Bobby … *Spasibo.*"

He then got up and walked out of the room. I could have been mistaken, but he appeared to be bowing his head in shame.

Later that afternoon, Katya, who still looked under the weather, finally emerged from her room. She walked past the living room and into the kitchen. I followed her. She was making a cup of tea.

"Are you okay?" I asked.

"I don't want to talk about it," Katya replied.

"What did your dad say?"

"He'll get over it."

"So, does this ..."

"Bobby! Did you not hear me? I said I don't want to talk about it!"

I decided that it was best not to press the issue.

I never did find out what exactly was said during the *Okna*-style blow out, but whatever it was, there remained no question that Katya was indeed in the clear victor.

Later that evening, the family gathered for dinner. Nobody said a word. For once, however, Babushka wasn't alone in her glare-fest. A Cold War had begun; a Cold War that would last two full days, much like Katya's hangover. As we ate in silence, I watched as Sergei reached for the salt. And then, suddenly, it all made sense. *Of course! The salt!* Maybe there really was some truth behind all of these Ukrainian superstitions? Maybe I was starting to see the light?

And just as Katya had predicted, Sergei did "get over it." In fact, once two days had elapsed, it was as though nothing had ever happened.

Despite not being aware of the intricacies of the argument, I couldn't help but feel that the whole "clubbing incident" and its aftermath had marked a turning point in my relationship with Sergei. I would think and wonder about that "Spasibo" many times.

20

BOBBY VS. THE CHAMPION

Each day of my trip promised new adventure. It's not too often that you have the opportunity to completely surrender to happenstance. Considering how routine the patterns of regular life can be, this was a refreshing change of pace. For instance: one moment, I was being mauled by a horny, out-of-control, vomiting Ukrainian woman, hell bent on getting back at her parents; the next moment, I was setting sail on a radioactive river, which was, of course, a safer alternative than swimming in it.

Two days after the infamous "clubbing incident," we were all invited on a boat trip by a former colleague of Sergei's from the university. While driving to the marina late that morning, Sergei threw me off guard when he asked out of the blue:

"Bobby, do you have a gift?"

"A gift?" I asked, confused.

"Da! For the Champion," Sergei replied.

"What champion?" I asked.

Katya explained that although Sergei's colleague's real name was Nicholai—he was affectionately known as "The Champion," a title he had earned as a world champion rower.

"Is it the Champion's birthday?" I naively asked.

"Nyet!" replied Sergei. "But in Ukraine it is customary to bring a gift when paying somebody a visit."

"I didn't know. I'm very sorry," I replied, flustered. "Can we stop at a store for some vodka or something?"

"I was hoping you had something from America to give to him," Sergei said, at which point Katya scolded her father for being so rude.

"Just ignore him," Katya said. "We're bringing candy and vodka. It'll be from all of us."

We arrived at a marina, which appeared to be pulling double duty as a junkyard. We were eagerly greeted by Nicholai, his wife, Svetlana, and their two über-athletic children, Kostya and Anastasia. I could tell immediately that if Kostya were American, he would undoubtedly be the star quarterback of his high school football team; and Anastasia would be the cheerleading captain.

It also didn't take me long to realize that Kostya had his sights set on Katya. I found myself desperately resisting the urge to grow jealous. After all, the quarterback always gets the girl—especially when the only competition is a scrawny little writer-*wannabe*.

Inside the marina, the Champion showed off his collection of rowing trophies.

"Were you in the Olympics?" I asked.

"No. However, I should have been," the Champion replied regretfully. Without further elaboration, and quickly changing the subject, the Champion turned toward his son.

"Kostya! Go and grab your weights. Show Bobby what you can do."

Kostya darted out of the room. Seconds later, he returned with two enormous, old-fashioned dumbbells.

"What's going on?" I asked Katya.

"Kostya will demonstrate his weight-lifting ability."

Of course, I thought to myself. *This was a perfectly normal thing to do to entertain your guests.*

Kostya began doing curls. Everyone counted along, clapping in rhythm to provide encouragement (as though he needed it). He grunted louder and louder with each curl. When he was done, he let out a wild, primal scream. For a brief moment, I was certain he was about turn into the Ukrainian Hulk.

"Well, then. Shall we set sail?" the Champion suggested.

As Sergei helped the Champion prepare the boat, Kostya approached, speaking in broken English peppered with a heavy Russian accent.

"Rice?"

"Excuse me?" I asked.

"You want rice?"

I turned to Katya. "Is he offering me some rice?"

"No!" Katya replied, laughing. "He wants to *race* you."

"Oh … a race?! You want to race *me*?"

Kostya nodded enthusiastically, pointing at me in a threatening manner. "Yes! *You!*" He then beat his chest, exclaiming loudly, "Kostya!"

What an asshole! I thought to myself.

"I don't know," I said, not liking where this was heading.

"What do you have to lose?" Katya said.

"How about my pride?" I replied.

"How do you know you won't win?" Katya asked.

"Well … first of all … look at me. And secondly … look at him!"

"You're smaller. So you might be faster," Katya replied.

"I doubt it," I said. "I've never won a race in my entire life."

Kostya began to run in place and stretch, preparing for "the rice."

"Is this what I get for not bringing a gift?" I whispered to Katya.

"No. He's just really competitive," Katya replied.

I realized then that I had no choice but to race him.

"We race from here to tree," Kostya said, "At count of three."

"I'll count," Katya said. For some reason, this prompted Kostya to wink at her as he hunched down into the 'ready' position.

"Get ready. On the count of three" Katya said. "One … two …" But before she could say "three," Kostya took off running, beating me by a landslide. Kostya celebrated his victory as though I was a worthy competitor that he had narrowly defeated after numerous attempts.

"Hey! He cheated!" I shouted.

"He still beat you by a lot," Katya replied.

"Yeah! Because he cheated!" I repeated.

Oblivious to my complaint, Kostya ran over to me with two rocks in his hand.

"Is this like a Ukrainian peace offer or something?" I asked as Kostya handed me one of the rocks.

"Let me see how far you throw," Kostya said.

Kostya prepared to throw his rock. The river itself was about twenty feet away from where we stood, with about fifteen feet of the space being riverbank. Of course, Kostya threw his stone halfway across the river. I should have just given up right then and there, but instead, I threw my rock. It didn't even reach the river. Kostya celebrated another landmark victory.

When he was finished with his over exuberant celebration, Kostya approached me, offering his hand. I shook it reluctantly, trying my best not to act like a sore loser. It wasn't so much that I had lost. It was more the fact that Kostya was such a sore *winner*.

"You are good sport," Kostya said.

"You are good sport!" I replied, good-sportsman-like.

"Good for ego," Kostya said, before playfully punching me in the arm, which, for the record, left a bruise.

The Champion called us over to the boat. As we followed Kostya, I whispered to Katya, "I'd like to see him write a poem."

"At least you tried," Katya said. I could sense pity in her voice.

"Story of my life," I said.

We boarded the medium-sized boat—which I referred to as the "champion-ship"—my pun flying completely over Katya's head and into the water.

We set sail. A few minutes later, we passed by Monastyrsky Island and the beach where I had proposed. I stared over at the golden dome of the church, which sparkled in the sun like a beacon of heavenly light.

"Out of curiosity," I said to Katya, "why didn't the Champion ever make it to the Olympics?"

Katya replied in a low voice. "I don't really know the whole story. Nobody talks about it."

Suddenly, the Champion handed the controls over to Kostya and headed over toward us.

Oh shit! He heard me! I thought to myself in a panic.

To my relief, the Champion passed by us and headed over to a table and picked up the bottle of vodka we had brought. *My gift to The Champion.* The Champion offered everyone a shot. I politely declined, considering my predisposition for seasickness and wandering aimlessly while under the influence.

About thirty minutes later, we anchored across from a small, seemingly desolate island and headed into the cabin for a meal, consisting of pickled herring, sausage, and a couple of salads that I deemed inedible due to their fish content. I nibbled on some stale bread and ate a couple of slices of sausage, which I washed down with sweet church wine as multiple toasts were shared.

As everyone became fully immersed in conversation, I was briefly left on the sidelines. I didn't mind at first, but eventually, I asked Katya to translate. Katya had either forgotten about me, or had figured that I wouldn't be interested in whatever they were talking about. I hoped it was the latter.

Katya explained to me that Kostya was telling everyone that he had pretty much bribed his way through college, without ever having to take a single test.

"Wow! And he's *proud* of that?" I said, forgetting that Kostya understood English.

"*Da!*" Kostya replied, turning around, staring at me menacingly. "Why wouldn't I be?"

"Well, shouldn't you have to *earn* a degree?" I replied, instantly regretting it.

With a sly grin, Kostya went on to explain, "In Ukraine, if you want to make money … you gotta *cheat*. It's simple. If you play by the rules, the rules play you."

I decided there was no point in arguing against Ukrainian ethics (or lack thereof), especially with Kostya. I let the grown-ups return to their conversation. For the first time on my trip, I felt truly alienated, disconnected, longing for home.

Moments later, the Champion appeared with a foul-smelling fish— eyes and all. There was clearly no escaping the odor, which quickly filled the entire cabin. And of course, *I* was the weirdo for turning down such a delicious treat. When offered a piece, I jokingly replied "Oh, no thanks … I'm trying to quit." No one laughed. This failed attempt at humor did not help my mood.

Within minutes, the fish was completely devoured and washed down with warm beer. The smell, however, continued to permeate the cabin. I considered excusing myself, but decided that it was in my best interest to tough it out. Besides, I didn't really want to leave Katya alone with Kostya.

Everyone grew quiet as the Champion began to tell a joke. Katya translated for me. It was about a group of men who took a winter boat trip on the Dnieper River. Of course, gallons of vodka were consumed, after which one of the men drunkenly fell overboard into the icy water. After much deliberation, one of his drunken comrades says, "Well, I suppose we have to do something!" So he dips his arm into the water, and fishes around. He finally grabs hold of his comrade's jacket and—with the aid of his friends—pulls the man out of the water and back onto the boat. The poor man wasn't breathing, and so they decide to perform CPR. It is no use. However, two conclusions are drawn: "Wow, I didn't realize how bad his breath was," said one of the men. "And I don't remember him wearing skates," added another.

Everyone erupted with hysterical laughter. Except for me, of course, who was left confused and empty inside as I struggled to make sense of it all. The punchline had to be there somewhere, but I was completely thrown for a loop. Perhaps I was thinking too deeply. Or, maybe I wasn't thinking deeply enough.

"I don't get it," I said to Katya.

"How can you not get it?" Katya replied.

"I am totally confused. Maybe you can explain it to me?"

"What is there not to get?"

"The joke itself!"

"But Bobby, it's so *simple!*"

"Is it?" I asked.

I was starting to feel simple myself once I became aware that everyone was watching our heated discussion, with a mixture of bewilderment and amusement. Kostya, of course, was more than willing to translate for everyone else's benefit ... at my expense.

"You see, Bobby," Kostya began, talking slowly on purpose, as if to an idiot. "The body... they pulled ... out of the river. It was not their friend. It was somebody else. And because of this, we laugh!"

"Oh! Yeah! Right!!" I said, feeling like a dumbass.

However, now that I "got it," it still didn't seem funny to me.

"You see now Bobby!?" Katya said, joining Kostya in laughing at my expense. "Simple!"

"Yeah. I get it," I said. "Sort of. But I just don't really get how's it a *joke*. It's more like a *story*."

"Da! A *funny* story. That makes a *joke*," Kostya interjected.

"A funny story isn't always necessarily a joke. And it's not exactly much of a joke. It's pretty morbid!"

"Whatever. It's Ukrainian humor," Katya replied.

"Yeah, that explains a lot."

"What is that supposed to mean?" Katya said, irritated.

"Nothing. Nevermind," I said, attempting to dismiss my sour mood.

Meanwhile, the Champion began telling another joke. But Katya didn't bother translating. And I was fine with that.

After everyone finished eating, the Champion threw a collapsible ladder bridge leading from the anchored boat to the island. The men headed off the boat, while the women stayed on board to clean up.

Sergei and I followed a dirt path into the woods to take a leak. We peed side-by-side; it felt like a true bonding moment.

"Sometimes!" Sergei blurted out, as he stood there peeing.

"*Da!*" I replied, somewhat confused and surprised by this random statement, hoping that my reply would suffice.

I decided to venture off on my own to explore the island and clear my head. I wandered into a nearby clearing and came across an abandoned playground, filled with rusty swings, slides, and ping-pong tables. Shattered concrete littered the ground. I walked over to the water's edge and discovered what appeared to be a relatively new pair of gym shoes by the shore. The whole setting reminded me of the post-nuclear holocaust playground scene in *Terminator 2*. No wonder Katya loved that movie so much! A bit spooked, I headed back toward the boat. Katya informed me that the island used to be used as a summer camp, but that it had closed down after the collapse of the Soviet Union.

The Champion and Champion, Jr. emerged from the woods. They both stripped down to matching, tight Speedos and dove into the water with perfect, synchronized form. It was a true sight to behold.

"Wanna swim?" Katya asked.

"I didn't bring my swimsuit," I replied.

"I told you to, Bobby," Katya said in a disappointed tone.

"I figured it was too cold."

"The Champion swims here in the middle of winter," Katya replied.

"Yeah, I'm sure he does," I said. "You can swim if you want to."

"No. I'm fine," Katya replied. "You're right. It does feel a little cold."

We watched the Champion and Kostya swim in spectacular, Olympic fashion for several minutes, before they climbed back aboard so that we could begin our voyage back to the junkyard marina. The Champion disappeared briefly to change into dry clothes. Kostya, however, remained in his Speedo, dripping wet, as he began chatting with Katya. Apparently, the cold was no match for Kostya.

After a few minutes of listening to untranslated conversation between Katya and Kostya, I headed to the front of the boat and sat down before the strong headwind blew me overboard. A few minutes later, Katya joined me, once again sensing that something was bothering me.

"Are you okay, Bobby?" she asked.

"I'm just not that good with boats," I replied.

"It's Kostya, isn't it?" Katya said, not buying my flimsy excuse—even though that truly was *part* of the problem.

"No. It's nothing to do with him," I said unconvincingly.

Katya began to laugh.

"Why are you laughing?" I asked.

"Bobby, I've known Kostya my whole life. He's like a cousin to me."

"Yeah. Mississippi cousins," I said.

"What does that mean?"

"Why wouldn't you have feelings for him?" I asked. "He's good looking, athletic, successful … and obviously madly in love with you."

"He's good looking, but arrogant. He's athletic, but dull. He's successful, but a cheat. And yes, he may be in love with me, but so are you. And I'd take brain over brawn any day. Beyond that, you're creative. You're interesting. You're funny. You're good looking. You're hard working. You're even *sort of semi-athletic*. And you love me more than I ever thought I could be loved. Would you like me to go on?"

"Sure!" I said with a smile, already feeling better about myself.

"You know what the meaning of true love is?" Katya asked.

"What?"

"When jealousy doesn't exist."

"I'm not jealous!" I exclaimed.

"Then how else do you explain your behavior?" Katya replied. "And how can I marry you, if I think that you don't trust me?"

"I *do* trust you, Katya" I replied.

"Then start acting like it," Katya replied, sternly.

Katya started to shiver. I put my arm around her.

Suddenly, the boat's horn blasted directly behind our heads. We turned around. It was Kostya, laughing at us and flexing his biceps, like a steroid-fueled maniac.

Like father, like son.

As I looked back at Katya, I realized who the real champion was.

21

DOWN ON THE FARM

After returning from our boating adventure, I asked Katya if perhaps the time had come to tell her parents about my proposal.

"After we get back from my Uncle Vladimir's farmhouse," Katya said, "... so you'd better be on your best behavior!"

I prepared myself for yet another frolic in the Ukrainian countryside. As it turned out, our trip to Uncle Vladimir's farm would become the single most humiliating experience of my life.

That evening, we set off on our journey to the village of Tomakovka, located south of Dnipropetrovsk, close to the industrial city of Zaporozh'e. Babushka stayed behind due to a mysterious ongoing feud with Sergei's family. It went without saying that Nastya also stayed behind.

As we drove through the Ukrainian countryside, Katya soon fell asleep, with her head on my shoulder. As we passed by farm after farm, village after village, I couldn't help but think of the suffering and misery that had been inflicted upon so many citizens of this very land by Stalin during his years of tyranny. It was hard to imagine that somewhere so scenic and idyllic had laid witness to so much suffering. And with those thoughts in mind, I drifted off to sleep too.

I awoke to find that night had fallen. The car was pulled over on the side of the road.

"What's going on? Did we break down again?" I asked, still in a daze.

Sergei offered no reply. He got out of the car, shining a Maglite—a gift given to him by Katya's host-father from Mississippi—in the direction of a barren field. He motioned for us to follow. And so we did, despite no sign of civilization, no lights, and no passing traffic. It was just us ... in the middle of a Ukrainian field ... in the middle of nowhere. *So this is how it ends,* I first thought to myself.

Sergei shut his flashlight off. In the pitch black I heard him say something in Russian. I reached for Katya's hand.

"Look up!" Katya translated.

A three-quarter moon shone brightly over our heads in a starry night sky. Never had I seen so many stars in my life. It looked more like a planetarium than reality. It was truly breathtaking.

Sergei turned his flashlight back on pointed it skywards, seemingly slicing the darkness in half. He traced a constellation.

"Orion," I said.

"Da! Orion!" Sergei repeated, seemingly impressed by my knowledge of astronomy.

"We all sleep under the same sky," I said under my breath, reiterating the words that Katya had said right before we said our goodbyes on the day we met. Katya smiled at me before we followed Sergei back to the car, leaving no trace that we were ever there.

Within ten minutes, we arrived in Tomakovka. The lack of street signs in Ukraine—especially in village areas—made finding any specific destination very difficult. As a result, Sergei was having trouble locating his brother's farm.

"You've been here before, right?" I asked.

"Yes! Of course!" Katya replied. "He's just not sure whether this is the right house. It's so *dark* out here." Sergei pulled into a driveway, got out of the car, and walked up to a house, before being chased away by the home's irate owner—who I had first assumed was Katya's uncle.

This search went on for a good ten minutes or so before we finally stumbled upon Uncle Vladimir's farmhouse. When we got out of the car, we were enthusiastically greeted with hugs and kisses from Uncle Vladimir, his wife Nina, and their six-year-old granddaughter, Karina. Karina was visiting for the summer so that, as Katya later told me, her whore-mother could strut her stuff in the city, in order to put borscht on the table.

Uncle Vladimir—an imposing character who resembled a redneck version of Sergei crossed with Frankenstein (minus a couple of bolts)— greeted me with a well-intentioned but ultimately confused, "Good morning!"

"Good morning!" I replied, laughing and going with the flow.

"Good evening Uncle," Katya corrected him.

"Da! Good evening!" Uncle Vladimir said. I found out later that this was about the extent of his knowledge of English.

"Bobby! Welcome to my farm," he said in Russian—something I never imagined I would ever hear spoken to me. "Have you been on a farm before?"

"Not a *real* one," I said.

Katya looked at me, confused, not sure how translate.

Even I wasn't exactly sure what my answer meant. *It was late!*

"Well, tomorrow, Bobby," Uncle Vladimir continued, "you must get up from your bed at three-thirty, to do *real* farm work."

"Okay?" I said, not really sure if he was being serious or not.

Vladimir stared at me, a stern look on his face, sizing me up.

And just as I began to feel uncomfortable, he laughed loudly and said "*Shutka!* (Joke!)." He then gave me a huge bear hug, kissed me on both cheeks, and said "Bobby! *Dobro pozhalovat!*" ("Welcome!").

In addition to being a farmer, Uncle Vladimir had once worked as an engineer at the top-secret Soviet missile plant, Yuzhmash. As far as the general population was led to believe, Yuzhmash "officially" only manufactured items such as kitchen appliances, screws, bolts, pipes, and vacuum cleaners. In reality, the plant played a tremendous role in the Cold War arms race. Uncle Vladimir's work was so top-secret at the height of the Cold War, not even *he* knew exactly what he was up to there—or so he claimed.

"Karina!" said Uncle Vladimir, followed by something in Russian. Karina approached.

"Hello, Bobby. It is nice … I meet you," she said hesitantly, in broken English.

"Nice to meet you Karina," I replied. "So you speak English?"

"Nyet," Karina replied, staring down on the ground, embarrassed. Katya explained that Karina had just started to take English lessons.

"Well, tell her that I am very impressed," I said. Katya translated. Karina smiled bashfully.

We headed inside, where warm borscht awaited. The borscht that Nina had prepared looked a lot paler than the borscht that Elena made for us. It also tasted quite different, although still delicious. Katya explained how borscht was like snowflakes—no two women's borscht was ever alike. And, "naturally," borscht was never prepared by men.

The farmhouse was a two-story, red-brick structure that Vladimir had designed and built virtually all by himself. It was plain, but cozy. Although it might sound like an insult, it was clear that the house was handmade—a true original, and an impressive feat. Despite the ragged edges and occasional misaligned seams, the house looked quite sturdy. The feeling of living in a house that you not only designed, but built, brick-by-brick, must be like no other. It is certainly a feeling I will never know. I struggle with basic Lego kits.

Following our late dinner, it was time for bed.

I was given Karina's bedroom, which was quite cozy ... and very pink. I resisted the kind offer, feeling bad that Karina was going to have to sleep on a couch in the living room, but Karina insisted.

"For Bobby," she said in English. "For Bobby."

How could I resist such innocent kindness?

Karina's room was filled with tons of stuffed animals, whose condition suggested that they had survived Chernobyl. Overall, I managed a decent night's sleep, despite sleeping on what felt like padded bricks. Some of Karina's stuffed toys—a lion, a giraffe, an(other) earless Mickey Mouse, and a fuzzy alien—proved to be accommodating hosts, helping to cushion my neck and back.

I was awoken at the crack of dawn to the sound of a rooster crowing. This was even more amazing to me than hearing the cuckoo bird. As the rooster continued to crow, I got up from my bed and trudged over to the window hoping to locate it, imagining it standing on the corner of a wooden fence. And sure enough, it was!

I crawled back to bed and fell back asleep, refusing to let a rooster dictate when I should begin my day. A couple of hours later, I awoke to what sounded like the Russian lovechild of Bob Dylan and Tom Waits blaring from the next room. I learned that this was actually a recording of Uncle Vladimir's favorite performer—Vladimir Vysotsky—a famous singer of Russian "prison" music: folk songs of protest, misery, and hardship, songs of dissidents, heroes, and political prisoners—all written, of course, from a strong anti-state perspective.

After breakfast, Karina led us outside to the backyard, which was bustling with chickens, turkeys, ducks, and geese, all wandering around like they owned the place. While the poultry roamed free, I noticed two puppies that were being kept inside a rotting, wooden barrel. The reason? So they wouldn't eat the livestock, apparently.

Two cats crossed each other's paths, hissing. Katya chased a chicken around the yard.

"Help me try to pick one up," she said.

"It's not going to attack me, is it?" I asked, nervously.

"It's a chicken!" Katya responded.

We chased several chickens around in circles with no success.

Finally, Katya managed to grab one. The poor fowl wiggled about in Katya's hand, kicking its feet in a desperate bid to escape. Katya plucked a feather from its butt and handed it to me.

"A present for you!" she announced, proudly.

"Gee, thanks! Just what I always wanted."

"Just think," Katya continued, "one of these will be our dinner tonight." And she wasn't joking. Then again, at least its meat wouldn't be sitting out in the summer heat like the meat I had seen in the open-air market in Dnipropetrovsk.

I looked across the yard and noticed a well.

"Is that real?" I asked, excitedly.

"What do you mean by 'real'?"

"I mean, is it decorative, or does it actually work?"

"Of course it works!" Katya replied. "Why would somebody have a well just for decoration?" she asked—clearly unfamiliar with American garden decor.

Katya cranked the spindle until a wooden bucket came up, full of algae and rusty, sulfur-scented water, before letting it fall back down.

"It's like a Disney movie!" I exclaimed, letting my true colors shine.

"Can I try it?" I asked.

"Of course, "Katya replied.

I cranked the spindle with the enthusiasm normally associated with small children.

"Make a wish!" Katya exclaimed.

I closed my eyes and made a wish, the sulfurous stench filling my nostrils.

"What did you wish for?" Katya asked.

"That would be telling," I replied. "But I think that's obvious," I added, with a wry smile.

After my "fun with the well," we headed back inside.

Sergei and Uncle Vladimir were embroiled in an intense game of chess—each with a half-empty bottle of vodka by their side.

"It's *war* when these two play chess," Katya explained. "See that vacuum cleaner over there behind my uncle?"

I nodded.

"It will be my dad's if he wins."

"And if your uncle wins?"

"Papa, what does Uncle win?" Katya asked her father in Russian.

"He won't win, so it doesn't matter!" Sergei boasted. "But if by some unfortunate twist of fate he does beat me, he wins my flashlight," Sergei said, pointing at the Maglite on the table behind him.

"That's one of my dad's favorite possessions," Katya said, highlighting the importance of this match.

"Wow, you aren't kidding. This is serious," I exclaimed.

"Yes! And one game can last the entire weekend."

"What if they don't finish it?"

"Whoever is winning by the end of the weekend is the winner. And if it's a tie, then nobody moves!"

Without taking his eye off the board, Sergei waved his arms furiously, demanding silence.

Karina motioned to us to follow her into her bedroom, and instructed us to sit down on her bed. She formally introduced me to her stuffed animal friends, telling me what each one was in Russian. I did the same in English.

"*Zaychik*" — "Bunny."

"*Koshka*" — "Cat."

"*Sobaka*" — "Dog."

"*Lev*" — "Lion."

"*Obezyana*" — "Monkey."

And last but not least, the very green and very fuzzy "*Inoplanetyanin*" ("Alien.").

After my zoology lesson was over, Karina led us on a walk through the village. She walked in between us, holding our hands as we ambled down a dirt road. Like the dacha, all the roads in the village were dirt.

A few hundred yards down the road we walked by a hospital— distinguished by a cow chained to its fence.

"Does this lone cow provide milk for all of the patients?" I asked in all seriousness.

"It was probably brought there by its owner to graze."

"Can't it graze on its own grass?"

"Not if it already ate it all."

Katya picked up some apples off the ground that had fallen from a nearby apple tree and approached the cow, which ate right from her hand.

"Its tongue is rough," she said.

"I remember," I said, alluding to the tongue I had earlier eaten.

"Here … you try," Katya said, handing me an apple. I held the apple up to the cow, who eagerly munched it off my hand, leaving a streak of warm cow drool across my hand and halfway up my arm.

As we continued our way along the road, we passed several vendors hawking sunflower seeds, goat milk, eggs, fruits, and vegetables. Goats were chained to stakes. Farmers walked cows down the road toward presumably unorthodox grazing spots. *And chickens crossed the road!*

Amused by this sight, I said to Katya, "Why did the chicken cross the road?" assuming that she would know where I was heading with this.

"Probably to find its family," Katya replied.

"No," I said laughing. "It's a joke. *Why did the chicken cross the road?*"

"I don't know. Why?" Katya replied, clearly unamused.

"To get to the other side!"

"I don't see the humor in this," Katya said, echoing my earlier sentiments regarding The Champion's Ukrainian "jokes."

"It's the most famous American joke!" I exclaimed.

"Yeah, but it's not funny," Katya replied.

I thought about this for a moment, and said "No … I guess it's not," but still reveling in how unique of an opportunity it was to tell this joke to virgin ears.

"And you thought Ukrainian humor wasn't funny?"

"Well, the thing is, this joke is so cliché, it isn't really a joke anymore."

"Yes … so then it's *not* a joke."

We both laughed at the full-circle nature of this conversation and decided to leave it at that, as we headed into the village shop, which — like so many other buildings in rural Ukraine—looked like collapse was imminent.

The store sold basic food items: bread, eggs, milk, deli meats. Liquor and chocolate were sold behind the counter. A selection of sun-faded stationary was on display, featuring Y2K American pop culture icons such as N'Sync and Britney Spears. We bought some chips and cola for ourselves and a candy bar and juice for Karina. The shopkeeper totaled our order up on an old, beat-up wooden abacus. There was no cash register. It reminded me of an abacus my grandmother bought me when I was five—a futile attempt at training me up to become an engineer, which was indeed the equivalent of fitting a square peg into a round hole.

We stepped out of the store and headed down a picturesque, tree-lined dirt road. Rays of golden sun shone through onto the brown, yellow, red, and golden leaves, which were already beginning to turn.

As we continued back toward the farmhouse, Karina asked Katya if we would swing her back and forth between us.

"Ready? *Adeen … dva … tree!*" Katya said, counting in Russian before we swung her. Just before we swung her again, Karina counted in English. "One … two… three!"

"Wow, very good, Karina!" I said.

"Thank you!" Karina replied, with a broad smile. She was starting to warm up to me, gaining in confidence.

Katya and I looked at one another and smiled.

Later that afternoon, Sergei and Uncle Vladimir took a much-needed break from their chess battle and headed over to a nearby basketball court, located on the grounds of a rather modern-looking school, which had been built by a Methodist missionary group (which, apparently, had realized that the trick to helping Ukrainians find Jesus was to build modern schools in impoverished Ukrainian villages).

Uncle Vladimir sat on a nearby swing, swigging vodka, while Karina swung on the swing next to him. Elena and Aunt Nina stayed behind to prepare dinner, presumably chopping the head off of the hapless chicken we had caught in the yard earlier.

Sergei and I prepared for some "one-on-one."

"Tell him I'll teach him how Americans play," I said, with empty bravado, considering my inferior basketball skills.

"And I'll show you how Ukrainians play!" Sergei retorted.

I imagined that the "Ukrainian way" might involve a fair amount of cheating.

With that in mind, I shook Sergei's hand in agreement. I, at least, had *age* on my side.

"Just to warn you," Katya said, "there's nothing my dad hates more than losing." I, on the other hand, was well used to it.

Sergei was surprisingly aggressive. But I held my own, using my speed to blaze past him for a few hard-earned buckets.

"If you know what's good for you, you'll let my father win," Katya warned.

"If he wants to win, he's gotta earn it," I replied.

Sergei proceeded to make a jump shot. I then made a jump shot from the same spot.

"One more point, the game's mine," I said.

"Two more points, the game is for Sergei," Sergei added, pointing to himself.

On the next play, Sergei drove hard into me, causing me to fall and scrape my leg on the concrete. Fortunately, he missed the shot.

"You're bleeding," Katya said with concern.

"I'm okay."

Uncle Vladimir came over, offering his vodka and a handkerchief.

"*Nyet, spasibo*," I said, assuming he was offering me a drink.

"Not to drink. For your wound," Uncle Vladimir said in Russian, soaking his handkerchief with vodka, before handing it over to Katya, who used it to clean my wound as I sat on a swing. I grimaced in pain, avoiding the temptation to shriek like a schoolgirl. When Katya was done, I headed back to the court.

"Okay, let's finish this," I said.

"Are you sure you can play, Bobby?" Katya asked, concerned.

"Of course! It's just a flesh wound," I said mock-cockily, even though it stung like hell.

Katya took my spot on the swing.

"OK, I'll stay here and watch," she said.

Despite the obvious foul that knocked me to the ground, I let Sergei keep his points. I missed my next shot and Sergei proceeded to miss a jumper which I rebounded.

As I prepared to finish him off, Katya called out: "Bobby, remember what I told you?!"

I disregarded her warning and drove to the basket. Sergei knocked me to the ground again—but not before I managed to throw the ball up into the air ... and into the basket. *Game over.*

Katya applauded, then helped me up. Sergei was not a happy camper. Once the heat of battle was over, I realized that maybe beating him wasn't such a good idea. But much to my surprise, Sergei approached me, offering a congratulatory handshake.

"You play well, Bobby," Sergei said. He didn't smile.

"You, too Sergei Andreovich," I replied.

Sergei then went over to Uncle Vladimir and took a big swig of vodka from his bottle, saying something in Russian, and gesturing toward the basket. Uncle Vladimir nodded in an attempt to look interested.

"My father has *never* shaken hands with anyone who defeated him," Katya said.

"This can only be a good thing then, right?" I said.

"*I think so*," Katya replied. There was very little confidence in her voice, however. And suddenly, I wasn't so sure, either.

Uncle Vladimir and Sergei headed back to the farmhouse. We remained at the school and pushed Karina on the swing. After about fifteen minutes, we also headed back to the farmhouse, where our chicken dinner awaited.

As we passed a goat chained to a stake, I decided to approach it.

"Bobby ... didn't you learn last time?" Katya exclaimed.

But before she was able to finish her sentence, the goat charged. If the chain had been an inch longer, I would have been sent flying. Karina giggled hysterically.

"What were you thinking?" Katya scolded.

"I only wanted to pet him."

"It's not a dog, Bobby! You scared him."

"I scared *him*?"

Karina continued to giggle.

"He's cute," she said to Katya in Russian.

"Tell Karina that I think she's cute, too," I said.

Katya translated.

Karina blushed, and said "Why did you tell him?"

"Because he *is* cute," Katya replied, winking at me.

22

THE SOBERING METHOD

Inside the house, Aunt Nina was checking on the chicken roasting in the oven. Sergei and Uncle Vladimir had resumed their epic chess match.

"Dinner will be ready in just a few minutes," Aunt Nina said.

I inquired about taking a shower, before realizing that the shower consisted of an outdoor, ramshackle wooden stall. I didn't even bother to ask about hot water, and opted instead to wait until we returned to the city. I proceeded to take a pee in a dilapidated outhouse located next to the shower stall. I tried my best to hurry as mice scuttled about at my feet and large, black flies buzzed around my face.

When I came back from the outhouse, the food was waiting on the table and we were all invited to take our seats. Everyone came to the table except for Sergei and Uncle Vladimir, who remained embroiled in their chess match.

Katya took a corner seat next to me, but Elena immediately grew concerned and asked her to switch with me.

"What's the problem?" I asked.

"My mom says that if a single woman sits at the corner of the table, she'll never get married," Katya explained.

We both chuckled at this. *Of course*, there would be a superstition for that.

"Are Ukrainians always this superstitious?" I asked.

"Well, you gotta believe in something," Katya replied.

As I learned throughout my trip, Ukrainians believe in *a lot*. For instance, I found out that you should never sit on concrete or you will catch a cold. This same logic applies to open windows and cold drinks (which explains why windows are rarely open and why most drinks are lukewarm, no matter how hot the temperature is outside); when moving into a new house, a cat should always enter first for good luck (even if you have to borrow one from a friend or grab one off the street). My personal favorite however, is the belief that witches appear on the Saturday before

Easter, begging for cheese. *Why not?* Even witches need cheese.

"Vladimir! Sergei! Kushat!" Aunt Nina shouted into the living room.

Sergei and Uncle Vladimir staggered in, their vodka bottles nearly empty, providing us with a stirring and extremely loud rendition of a Soviet military song. Sergei went to retrieve another bottle of vodka from what I was guessing was an endless supply.

"The difference between my father and my uncle is that my father only drinks for social occasions. My uncle drinks for all occasions," Katya said, as Sergei and Uncle Vladimir practically fell into their seats.

"But when my father and uncle get together," Katya added, "there's no difference."

Uncle Vladimir poured three shots—one for me, one for Sergei, and one for himself. He raised his glass for a toast: "Here's to food. May we eat to live, not live to eat."

After clinking our glasses, Sergei and Uncle Vladimir downed their shots, then immediately sniffed their sleeves.

"What's that all about?" I asked, confused.

"Just a tradition," Katya replied, "to help soften the harshness. Sometimes, people choose to eat a pickle instead." *Sure ... why not?!*

I took a baby sip from my shot glass. Uncle Vladimir noticed this and laughed, saying something in Russian to Sergei.

"What did he say?" I asked.

"Nothing," Katya replied. "Don't worry about it. He's an alcoholic."

"You not finish?" Uncle Vladimir asked, pointing to my glass.

"Da! Of course!" I replied, forcing myself to finish it off in two more sips, in a feeble attempt to impress. Involuntary gagging, however, ruined any chance for redemption. Uncle Vladimir immediately attempted to pour me another shot.

"Nyet! Spasibo!" I begged. But judging from the look on his face—not to mention Sergei's—something told me this was going to be a long night.

"A man who drinks *too much*, he has nothing to say," Uncle Vladimir proclaimed. "But a man who drinks *too little*, he also has nothing to say. So ... *I say chut-chut!*

I played along, flicking my neck.

"Bobby ... please don't," Katya warned as Uncle Vladimir eagerly filled up my glass. She tried to stop him at half, but it was no use.

Uncle Vladimir raised his glass for another toast.

"To Bobby! Control toast!"

We clinked glasses.

"What's a control toast?" I asked.

"It means to the bottom in one go," Katya replied.

"No … I can't," I said, nervously.

"Time to prove that you are a *man*, Bobby!" Sergei exclaimed.

With all eyes on me, I realized that it was now or never. It was time to take off the training wheels and knock back my first full shot of vodka. I looked over at Sergei, who saluted me in encouragement with his own glass, and slowly raised the glass to my lips.

"Don't say I didn't warn you," Katya said.

I took a deep breath, tilted my head back and let the vodka slide down my throat, before sniffing my sleeve. It went down surprisingly smooth. I was becoming accustomed to vodka consumption, which wasn't necessarily a good thing—but not necessarily a bad thing, either—especially if I were to marry into this family.

Everyone applauded. I pumped my fist in triumph. Sergei and Uncle Vladimir issued congratulatory handshakes. Even Katya applauded, despite her growing concern for my well-being.

I was surprised at how quickly I became buzzed. Uncle Vladimir poured another round of shots, finishing off the bottle.

Aunt Nina tried to stop him, but Uncle Vladimir barked at her in Russian. *How dare a woman interfere with this manly ritual!*

"I think I've had enough vodka for now," I said, holding my ground. But it was already too late. I stared down at the full shot glass in front of me on the table. "How about some wine instead?" I suggested, eyeing an unopened bottle of wine sitting on the table.

"Normally, wine is saved for women," Uncle Vladimir said, handing me the wine bottle and corkscrew. "But let's see how well you can handle a cork."

Never having used a traditional corkscrew before, I might as well have been handed the controls of a Soviet space shuttle.

I struggled mightily, causing several fragments of cork to fall into the bottle. When he could bare it no longer, Uncle Vladimir grabbed the bottle out of my hand and effortlessly removed the cork, before pouring a glass of wine for Elena, Katya, Aunt Nina … and lastly, me.

"Bobby, you should eat," Elena wisely suggested.

"Here. Have some chicken," Katya said, putting a roasted leg down on my plate. As I filled my plate with chicken and took a large helping of borscht, I could feel the effects of the vodka going to work on my system; my vision became a little blurry and my motor functions became slightly impaired. I started to feel detached.

I took a few bites of food, noticing how the rest of the family ravenously devoured their chicken legs until there was nothing left but bone, which they then gnawed on down to the nub. First lemons; now chicken bones.

Uncle Vladimir raised his glass for yet another toast.

"Here we go again," Katya said.

This time, both Uncle Vladimir and Sergei stood up.

"What's happening?" I asked.

"The third toast always goes to the women," Katya explained.

Sergei tipped his glass toward me.

"For women," Uncle Vladimir said in his thick Russian accent, tipping his glass toward me , winking, and chuckling. *Was he calling me a woman?* I quickly stood up with my glass of wine to join my fellow comrades.

"To women. And all their beauty. Like vodka, may it never run out," proclaimed Uncle Vladimir with great gusto.

Sergei and Uncle Vladimir downed their shots. Uncle Vladimir then reached over and took my shot glass, poured my vodka into his empty glass, and downed it in the blink of an eye.

"To women," I said, with not quite as much gusto as Uncle Vladimir, before taking a sip of wine.

After we had continued eating dinner for a while longer, Uncle Vladimir pulled a brand new bottle of vodka out from underneath the table, and passed it over for me to examine.

"*Ukrains'ka Horilka z pertsem,*" Vladimir said in Russian, referring to the popular Nemiroff honey and pepper-flavored vodka—which is made by steeping hot red peppers in vodka.

No way, I thought to myself. I smiled, and passed the bottle back to Uncle Vladimir, trying to look enthusiastic.

"Bobby ... I love honey!" Sergei added, as Uncle Vladimir quickly opened the bottle and began pouring a new round.

"No Bobby ... don't," Katya said with dread in her eyes.

Aunt Nina and Elena both shook their heads in disapproval, but said nothing. Uncle Vladimir and Sergei were firmly in control of the proceedings at this point.

"I'll just try a sip," I said, realizing that I had no choice if I wanted to prove myself to be a *real man*. "I ate a lot of chicken. It's fine."

Katya glanced down at the three discarded chicken bones on my plate.

"You only ate half the meat off of them," she observed. "And you didn't touch the bone."

I couldn't believe what I was hearing.

"Bobby! You are now ready to give a toast of your own, yes?" Sergei said, raising the stakes.

"Compared to your toasts, I'll only embarrass myself," I replied, echoing my response from my first evening in Ukraine.

"Not if you drink this," Uncle Vladimir said, raising his glass.

"To vodka!" I proclaimed. "Control toast."

I raised the glass to my lips, determined to down my shot in one gulp, thanks to the liquid courage I had already consumed.

"Always remember," Uncle Vladimir added. "A good, warmed vodka makes a carnation bloom inside your stomach."

Uncle Vladimir and Sergei downed their shots. I tried … but my body said *no*. And without warning, I immediately, involuntarily spat my pepper vodka out, all over the spread of food. *No carnation for me.*

"Ach! It tastes like varnish!" I exclaimed, quickly grabbing my wine and taking a big gulp in an effort to wash the burning sensation off my tongue.

Uncle Vladimir shook his head and once again poured the remainder of my shot into his glass.

"I'll be damned if I'm going to let good vodka go to waste," he said, slamming the empty glass back down in front of me.

Katya pushed it away. "No more, Uncle" she warned.

I grabbed it back. I hadn't quite given up on being a real man just yet.

I could sense Uncle Vladimir staring at me, but didn't look at him. And then, form out of nowhere, he asked me: "So, Bobby… how do you like Ukraine?"

"I've never been here before," I replied. I was kind of aware that my answer didn't make much sense. However, at this point, I was beginning to feel beyond buzzed … and beyond caring.

Everyone waited for Katya's translation. Katya simply shrugged.

Uncle Vladimir looked puzzled.

"And ... I am very happy that I don't live here," I continued, slurring my words.

I felt Katya kick my shin under the table.

All eyes were on Katya, awaiting her translation.

"Bobby said that he loves Ukraine and that he loves the food," Katya said in Russian. "Especially the chicken."

"Spasibo!" Aunt Nina said, smiling.

"Bobby ... let me tell you what I think of America," Uncle Vladimir began. "America's imperialist days are numbered. It's time for a new superpower to emerge in its place."

"Vladimir! Enough!" Aunt Nina demanded.

Uncle Vladimir actually seemed to take notice of Aunt Nina this time. We continued eating, in silence.

And that's when I noticed the plate of pickled herring, swimming in their own juice.

It is important at this juncture to point out that the course of events that transpired over the remainder of the evening are foggy and fragmented in my mind. I am simply piecing everything together based on descriptions given by eyewitness accounts and from my own brief flashbacks.

As I continued to stare transfixed at the herring, I began to grin from ear-to-ear like a fool, before mumbling to Katya:

"Look, the fish are swimming."

"No, Bobby. They're not."

"Yes! Look! They're swimming in their own fish juice," I insisted, poking at the fish.

Katya—realizing that she had no other choice, given that everyone wanted to know what I was saying—translated.

Sergei and Uncle Vladimir burst out in uncontrolled laughter.

"Are you trying to humiliate him?" Katya exclaimed, scolding her father and uncle. "This is your fault!"

"Don't worry," Uncle Vladimir replied, in between roars of laughter. "I've seen worse. And I've *been* worse."

At that point, as if on autopilot, I suddenly got up from my seat, shot glass firmly in hand, and turned to leave.

"Bobby, where are you going?" Katya exclaimed.

"*Piisss,*" I slurred.

"Are you okay?" she asked.

I either didn't hear Katya, or simply ignored her and kept on walking. I headed out of the backdoor and into the yard. This time, however, I mistook the puppy barrel for the outhouse and started to take a leak onto the unfortunate pups, before they began yapping. The yapping briefly shook me out of my stupor—enough to allow me to stagger around in a daze, unsuccessfully attempting to pick up a chicken to put into my shot glass. *Who needs a bucket?* At that moment in time, this made all the sense in the world to me, and was an extremely important task that took all of my concentration. Realizing, however, that this wasn't working, I did an about turn, left the yard and headed out onto the road. *Why did Bobby cross the road? Because he was drunk off his ass on vodka.*

It was at this point that Katya headed out to the yard to look for me. Once she realized that I had left the premises, she panicked and called the rest of the family. A search party was hastily formed.

Katya and Karina hurried off down the road in search of me.

Thankfully, I hadn't gone very far.

"There he is!" Karina said, pointing down the road, just as I turned a corner.

"Bobby!" Katya shouted down the road after me. But I kept on walking. Katya and Karina ran after me. When they turned the corner, they found me sitting at the side of the road, my head between my knees.

"What are you doing, Bobby? Where are you going?" Katya asked.

Without lifting up my head, I held up my glass and said "chut chut!"

"When are you going to learn?" Katya exclaimed.

"Learn what?" I mumbled, drunkenly.

"No more vodka!"

"But I have to. I'm trying to build up my resistance," I argued.

"Well … it's obviously not working." Katya said. "You don't always have to drink just because it's offered to you."

"I'm just trying to fit in," I replied. "I have to prove that I'm a *real man!*"

"By wandering off by yourself like a lost little boy?" Katya said. "C'mon, let's go."

Katya and Karina helped me up. As we walked back toward the house, I was now the one in the middle, asking to be swung back and forth.

Once we got back to the farmhouse, Uncle Vladimir, in his inimitable style, immediately offered me another shot. Aunt Nina scolded him. Katya and Elena helped sit me back down at the table.

I sat at the table and I stared blankly ahead at the kitchen wall, grinning like a village idiot.

Katya tried to get me to drink from a glass of water, to no avail.

"Bobby, drink this!" she commanded, putting the glass of mineral water up to my lips. I refused.

"Drink it!" she said, sternly.

"I have to go to sleep," I said.

"No sleep. Drink."

"I already drank too much."

"This is water!"

I finally gave in and took a sip, dribbling most of it onto my chin and down the front of my shirt.

"This is all your fault!" Katya said, angrily pointing to her uncle and father.

"It's not our fault that he can't drink," Uncle Vladimir retorted.

"We'd better get him to bed," Elena said, concerned.

Katya's worry deepened as I continued to stare at the wall, grinning.

"Maybe we should we take him to the hospital?" Katya suggested.

"No. I have a better idea," Sergei said. "Remove his shoes."

Katya knew immediately what Sergei was going to do next, and began removing my shoes.

"What are you doing?" I mumbled incoherently.

"We're helping you," Katya replied, as Sergei and Uncle Vladimir lifted me out of my seat.

"Where are we going?" I asked, as we headed for the door.

"For a walk."

"A walk?"

"Yes, a walk."

"Where?"

"Outside."

"Outside?"

"Yes, outside."

"For what?"

"For your own good."

As we headed down the porch steps, I lost my balance, almost taking

Uncle Vladimir and Sergei down with me.

"Yeah … I'm floating," I said, as Uncle Vladimir and Sergei struggled to help me regain my balance.

"That was fun," I said "But where are my shoes? I can't go for a walk without my shoes!"

"You'll get your shoes back later," Katya promised.

"Where are you taking me?" I asked, a small amount of concern and apprehension now starting to register in my vodka-addled brain.

"Siberia," Katya replied.

"I don't want to go to Siberia. What are you going to do to me?"

"Sober you up," Katya said.

"Am I drunk?"

Elena, Aunt Nina, and Karina followed us outside into the chilly night, as Uncle Vladimir and Sergei dragged me by the heels to the outdoor shower stall.

"Is that a gas chamber?" I asked in terror.

"Yes. Now take off your clothes," Katya commanded.

Sergei opened the door and turned the shower on.

"I don't want anyone to see me naked," I pleaded. "Too skinny," I added, echoing Babushka's earlier refrain.

"Then at least take off your shirt," Katya demanded.

"Nyet!" I said, like a petulant little schoolboy.

"Fine," Katya said, before helping Sergei shove me inside the stall, and slamming the door shut.

I screamed as the frigid water pierced through my clothing. So much for waiting until we returned to the apartment to shower.

I tried to escape, but Sergei and Uncle Vladimir held the door closed. This was waterboarding, Ukrainian-style. I pounded on the door, begging to be let out, but it was no use. I was completely at their mercy.

"Katya! Please! Let me out!" I pleaded, but to no avail.

After a few minutes, Sergei opened the door. I stumbled out, shivering like a wet dog, already starting to feel more sober. Aunt Nina handed me a towel.

And just when I assumed that the worst was over, little did I know that the worst was actually about to begin.

Still dripping wet from my arctic shower, Sergei and Katya proceeded to frogmarch me, barefoot, along the rocky, pothole-laden gravel driveway— beginning my own personal Bataan death march, Gulag-style, as the rest of the family watched along the sidelines.

Sergei counted in broken English: "One! Two! One! Two!" keeping me in step, as we marched back and forth along the broken path.

Hearing all of the commotion, a nosy neighbor approached, muttering: "Ah, to be young again."

"One! Two! One! Two!" commanded Sergei, trying to keep my drunken march in rhythm. "One! Two! One! Two!" he barked, leaving me yearning for an occasional "Three! Four!"

As I struggled to keep tempo, Katya joined in on the count. Before long, even I joined in, in a desperate attempt to distract myself from my sore, sure-to-be bleeding feet.

Fifteen minutes into this drunken parade, I demanded to know how much longer I would have to endure this torture.

"Until you're sober," Katya responded.

"I *am* sober. I'm fine," I said.

"You wouldn't be going through this if you were fine."

"I want my shoes back!"

"When we're done," Katya replied.

"Why?"

"Just trust us. We're professionals"

"I don't understand why I can't wear my shoes."

"Because a little pain will help sober you up."

"But I'm not drunk, any more" I pleaded.

Katya proceeded to kick off her own shoes in a show of solidarity.

"Look, now we're in this together."

"Put your shoes back on!"

"Don't worry about me."

"Just do as we say ... or else," Katya said, in a thick, exaggerated accent.

Minutes later, Sergei brought us to a halt. My feet were throbbing.

"Are we done?" I asked, hopeful that my ordeal was now at an end.

"Not quite," Katya replied.

And before Katya had finished answering, Sergei pushed down on my shoulders from behind.

"Up! Down! Up! Down!" Sergei commanded.

Previous to that night, I may have done squats once in my lifetime. And certainly not drunk.

"Up! Down! Up! Down!" Sergei continued.

Up and down I went. This went on for quite a while.

The worst was yet to come.

Sergei demonstrated the next step in his patented Ukrainian style sobering program, by pretending to stick his fingers down his throat.

I looked at Katya in desperation, who was now standing over by Elena.

"You gotta *vomit* now, Bobby," Katya stated, ever so matter-of-factly.

"What?! No way!" I exclaimed.

"*You have to!* If you don't, you're going to waste our last few days together with the worst hangover of your life."

Realizing that Katya was probably right, I attempted to stick a finger down my throat. All I produced was a dry heave. Sergei grabbed my hand and proceeded to "help" me stick *two* of my fingers further down my throat. Still nothing.

"This is inhumane," I pleaded, almost in tears. "Nobody should have to endure this."

"You'll thank us later," Katya said. "Trust me."

Sergei decided that he needed to lead me up and down the driveway of destruction one more time.

"One! Two! One! Two!"

"I gotta pee!" I said, grasping for any excuse to end this torture.

At Katya's request, Sergei led me behind a tree and held me up so I could pee. When I was done, Sergei forced me to do more squats. When my knees felt like they were about to burst open, Sergei held up *three* fingers and aimed them towards his mouth. I shook my head in protest. My refusal prompted him to grab me by the wrist, prying open three of my fingers from my fist. As he began to cram them down my throat, I shouted for Katya.

"I'm over here, Bobby" Katya yelled back. "You're doing great!"

"Your dad is trying to kill me!" I exclaimed.

"No, he's not trying to *kill* you. He's trying to *help* you."

I was no longer convinced. No longer able to resist, Sergei finally succeeded in shoving my fingers down my throat. You have not truly lived until you have had a grown man jam your own fingers down your throat in an attempt to sober you up.

I dry-heaved a couple more times before spitting up a tiny bit of vomit.

"There! I threw up!" I proudly proclaimed.

"That wasn't throw up!" Katya exclaimed.

"What do you mean it wasn't throw up? *Something was thrown up.* Didn't you see it?" I argued.

"Keep trying," Katya demanded.

"No! I refuse to be tortured any longer."

But my pleas went ignored, as Sergei once again began to march me back and forth.

"Be thankful you're drunk. And remember; you're in good hands," Katya continued.

I wasn't convinced.

"This is torture!" I exclaimed.

"It's not torture," Katya replied.

"Sometimes!" Sergei blurted out.

"I'm walking barefoot on this stone driveway and your dad is forcing my fingers down my throat. How is that not torture?"

"Okay, okay," Katya said, heading inside.

"Where are you going?" I asked.

"One! Two! One! Two!"

"Katya! … Katya!!!" I shouted.

Moments later, Katya returned—*with my shoes.*

"I'm here. And so are your shoes," she said, bringing them over.

"My shoes!"

I reached for them, but Katya pulled back.

"Not until you vomit," she insisted.

She had me!

"I told you, Katya. I already vomited. What else do you want from me?"

"That wasn't proper vomit."

"Please, tell your dad to stop. I'm fine. I'm completely sober."

"Just trust us, Bobby. We know what we're doing."

"Please. Katya. This is so embarrassing," I pleaded.

"You have nothing to be ashamed of. You're doing fine. And when you vomit, I promise to give you back your shoes."

Katya rejoined the rest of her family, reveling in the evening's entertainment. Aside from Katya, only Elena showed genuine concern.

"I'm sorry!" I blurted out, as Sergei continued marching me up and down the driveway.

"Why are you sorry?"

"I just am. I'm sorry, I'm really, really sorry!"

"Don't worry Bobby," Katya replied. "You don't have to be sorry."

"I love you, Katya!"

"I love you, too."

"No ... I mean, I *really* love you, *really, really* love you!"

"I love honey!" Sergei interjected.

"Marry me!"

"Bobby. Stop it."

"Marry me, Katya. Please, *marry* me!" I insisted.

"Bobby! No! Now's not the time."

"Marry me, marry me, please!"

"Ok! I'll marry you. But only if you vomit."

"And if I vomit, this will be all over?"

"Sometimes!" repeated Sergei, somewhat randomly.

"Yes, I promise."

"Okay. Okay. I'll vomit."

"He said he'll vomit!" Katya said to her father, in Russian.

And with that, Sergei brought me to halt. Knowing what I had to do, I shoved three fingers down my throat as everyone watched in eager anticipation. After several attempts, I finally managed to throw up. At first I panicked, thinking that I was throwing up blood—before realizing it was only borscht.

"Was that so bad?" Katya asked.

All I could do was stare down at my red vomit.

And with that, we headed inside, where Katya cleaned and bandaged my bloody feet.

Katya and Elena helped me into Karina's room and tucked me up in bed, surrounded by Karina's stuffed Chernobyl victims.

Within seconds, I drifted off into drunken darkness.

The next morning, I was awoken, once again, to the sound of the rooster. I sat up. Staring at me was a deranged stuffed elephant. I stared back at him for a few seconds before lying back down. As a lay there, random flashbacks from the previous evening began to seep into my still-fuzzy brain.

Did any of that really happen? Or was it all a bad dream?

I looked down at my bandaged feet. *It was no dream.* Despite feeling groggy, I managed to pull myself out of bed. I was in desperate need of water. I stumbled out of the bedroom and over toward the kitchen.

I quietly passed through the living room, where Sergei and Uncle Vladimir lay asleep on the floor, next to their unfinished chess match.

In the kitchen, I found an empty shot glass, which I filled several times over with mineral water, eagerly guzzling each glass. I then stumbled back to the bedroom, let out a loud belch, climbed back into bed, turned over and fell back into a deep sleep.

Next thing I knew, I woke up to a giggling Karina standing over me. Katya was standing next to her staring down at me and shaking her head.

"*Kuck-a-ree-kuu!*" Katya said (this was apparently what a Russian rooster says). Karina snapped a picture of me, and said something in Russian to Katya. Katya translated.

"Karina said you have needles."

"Needles?"

"Whiskers. How's your head?"

"Fine," I replied.

"I told you so."

"Why?"

"Remember last night?"

"Fragments," I replied, preferring to keep it that way. "I am so *embarrassed*. I don't know what happened. I don't even want to think about how this affects the chances of getting your parents' permission to marry you, or what this did to change your mind."

"Don't worry about it, Bobby. It's no big deal," Katya replied. "It happens to the best of us."

"It does?" I said in surprise.

"How do you think my dad learned about his sobering method? He learned from his father-in-law."

I laughed as I reflected on this.

"You do realize that you're *truly Ukrainian* now?" Katya pointed out.

"I thought I felt a little different," I said, thankful that Katya wasn't angry.

"We almost took you to the hospital," Katya said. "I was getting worried."

"I wasn't *that* drunk," I insisted.

Katya and Karina burst into laughter. I couldn't help but smile.

"So, what time is it?" I said, changing the subject.

"Almost noon," Katya replied.

"Wow. I'd better get up," I said.

Katya and Karina went off to the living room, leaving me to get dressed in private.

Once I was dressed, I headed out into the living room where Sergei and Uncle Vladimir were once again deeply embroiled in their chess war. Uncle Vladimir held out his bottle of vodka.

"Bobby! *Dobriy den'!* ("Good Afternoon!"). *Chut-chut?*" he said, laughing.

"Nyet, spasibio," I said, the mere sight of the bottle making me feel ill. "It's probably not a good idea."

"Vodka is *always* a good idea," Uncle Vladimir said, taking a massive swig. I shook my head in wonder.

The apparent lack of concern about—or, rather, complete indifference to—my drunken antics from the previous evening made me feel reassured that I hadn't irreparably damaged my reputation with Sergei. Sergei's, and everyone else's attitude was more a case of "been there, done that, no big deal." And, as Katya so aptly described it, I was now *truly Ukrainian* and less of an outsider in her family's eyes.

We headed outside to brush our teeth. As we walked along the driveway, more flashbacks from the previous evening raced through my mind. *And then I noticed the shower stall.*

"Look familiar?" Katya asked, with a wry smile.

Katya laughed as she observed the look of recognition on my face.

We passed a clothesline, where my underwear and pants were blowing in the wind.

"My underwear," I said, despondently.

Uncle Vladimir appeared, proclaiming: "For ever more, this driveway will be known as *Bobby's Path!*"

It would become my legacy.

Meanwhile, Elena was out in the garden picking tomatoes. Just beyond her were rows of cornstalks. As far back as I can remember, I always wanted to walk through cornstalks. And now I had my opportunity. I headed for the field.

"Where are you going?" Katya asked as I disappeared. Elena shouted something at me in Russian.

"That's not my Uncle's property!" Katya translated. "Come back!"

I quickly ran back, only to face a scolding from Katya. "You can't just run onto other people's property like that!"

Elena approached.

"How are you feeling, Bobby?" she asked, concerned.

"I'm fine today. Thank you, Elena," I replied.

Elena was holding several enormous tomatoes. She offered us each one. Katya took one and bit into it as though it were apple.

"Spasibo, mama."

I reluctantly took mine, asking "Don't they need to be washed?"

"That's what rain is for," Katya replied. "Just eat." So I did. And I don't even like tomatoes.

Suddenly, a loud, celebratory roar emerged from the house.

We rushed inside to find Sergei holding the vacuum cleaner over his head like a trophy.

"I take it your dad won?" I asked.

"Yes," Katya replied, "This also guarantees that we'll be leaving today. I was starting to worry that their match was going into overtime."

After lunch, we prepared to head back to Dnipropetrovsk. Sergei struggled to fit the vacuum into the trunk. Once it was in, Uncle Vladimir gently laid his hand upon it one last time before Sergei slammed the trunk shut.

Just before we got into the car, Uncle Vladimir handed Sergei a jar of honey, which quite honestly looked as though it were stolen from Winnie-the-Pooh. Sergei's eyes lit up with unadulterated joy as he proudly showed it off to me.

"Bobby, look! I love honey! *I love honey!*"

"*Da!* Honey!" I said.

This man sure loved honey.

Aunt Nina, who had otherwise shown little to no interest in my presence, hugged me tightly, much in the manner one would when saying goodbye to a dear loved one. It seemed like she would never let go. In fact, Uncle Vladimir had to gently nudge her away from me.

It was Karina's turn. She hugged me, as though holding on for dear life.

"I love Bobby," she said in broken English, muffled against my shirt. I was pretty sure I heard sniffling. "Bobby is kind. Bobby don't go," she pleaded. She simply refused to let go, holding on to me even more tightly. I continued to hug her back, looking around desperately for a cue. Finally, Katya responded and pulled her cousin away. My suspicious were accurate: Karina had tears in her eyes. In fact, my shirt was soaked with her tears. I couldn't help but tear up myself. She was such a cute little girl. Her mother had no idea what she was missing.

As I held out my hand to say goodbye, Uncle Vladimir took my hand into both of his, looked me squarely in the eyes and said: "Bobby, may God always light your path," at which point he embraced me as though I were a long-lost family member.

"Spasibo," I said in return, genuinely touched by the sincerity of his words.

As I crouched down to get into the car I turned and gave a final wave goodbye, at which point Uncle Vladimir—channeling Boris Karloff's Frankenstein—said "Bobby ... friennnd!"

As we drove away, we waved out of the back window until Uncle Vladimir, Aunt Nina, and Karina disappeared from view.

It was at that point that I realized that another, more painful goodbye was now less than a week away.

23

THE FELLOWSHIP
OF THE RING

On the way back home from Uncle Vladimir's farmhouse, we drove across the top of Zaporozh'e's infamous dam—a supposed symbol of Soviet efficiency and might—that had claimed the lives of countless workers during its construction at the height of the Soviet Union. Experts had predicted that the dam was now close to bursting—something you typically don't want to hear while you're driving over it. Another notable feature of this dam was the fact that sentries stood guard in towers, armed with AK-47's.

Within minutes, we were out of the city and back into the picturesque Ukrainian countryside.

"Let's talk to your parents this evening," I suggested to Katya, buoyed by my newly-earned status of *true Ukrainian*.

"No," Katya replied. "It'll be late by the time we get back; they'll be exhausted."

I was becoming increasingly paranoid that Katya was deliberately stalling, but she assured me that she wasn't.

"*Zavtra*" ("Tomorrow"), she said, echoing that old, familiar Soviet refrain. By my calculations, that left us with a total of three *zavtras* before my departure.

"We're running out of tomorrows," I reminded her. "What if something else comes up?"

"It won't. I promise."

"You can't promise something like that," I said. "Let's tell them now."

"What? In the car?"

"Why not? What do we have to lose?"

"No, Bobby. It's not a good time. You know that."

"Is there *ever* going to be a good time?"

"I told you. *Tomorrow.*"

"Do you want this to happen or not?" I asked. "Because I'm beginning to think that maybe you don't." I was starting to become agitated.

"Yes! Of course I do!" Katya exclaimed, her voice beginning to tremble. I could tell that Elena and Sergei could sense some kind of tension between us. However, they chose not to intervene.

"How can you say that?" Katya continued. "And besides … you can't just expect to march in here and steal me away from my family without letting them get to know you first."

Realizing that Katya was right, I put her hand in mine. Katya, however, was not nearly as eager to take my hand in return. She pulled her hand away and turned to look out of the window. *Conversation over.*

It was at that point that my left eye began to severely itch. This accounted for one of the reasons why I couldn't sleep that night. The other, of course, was due to anxiety about my proposal to Katya.

By morning, it was pretty clear that I had pink eye. This brought back some not-so-fond memories of my one previous experience with this condition, and an oozing eye—at Big Boy of all places—during a first, and last, date a couple of years prior.

Katya decided to take me over to the Soviet-era clinic where her sister, Nastya, worked, so that I could have my eye examined. This particular clinic looked like a place where you could quite easily *catch* pink eye— especially when taking into account the fact that the doctors dried their hands on a communal hand towel before examining their patients. Nastya prescribed some antibiotics for my eye, which ultimately worked.

We made our way back to the apartment, both nervous at the prospect of telling Sergei and Elena our Big News. *The time had finally arrived.* However, upon our return, we found out that Sergei had gone to meet up with some work colleagues. Our Big News was going to have to wait until dinnertime. *That's OK, more time to prepare,* I thought to myself. *Dinnertime isn't too long of a wait.*

With time to kill, Katya decided to call the airport to make sure that my flight was still set to depart from Dnipropetrovsk.

"Why wouldn't it be?" I asked, in the naïve manner of a non-Ukrainian.

"Flights are cancelled a lot here when airlines have disputes with the airports."

"Wait! What?!" I said, trying to make sense of the information I had just been given.

"Well …" Katya continued, "if there are disputes, the airports will try to assert their power by refusing to allow the airline's planes in."

"And what are these disputes about?" I asked.

"Money, of course," Katya replied.

"So what happens if my flight is cancelled?"

"Usually, the airline will arrange to have you driven to Kiev."

"How far is that?"

"About six hours."

Fortunately, as it turned out, my flight was still scheduled to depart from Dnipropetrovsk.

With a few hours left to spare before our big moment, we decided to take a walk along the riverfront. A crisp, autumn-like chill filled the air. Several wedding parties were posing for pictures as passing cars blared their horns in celebration.

Ukrainian wedding tradition usually includes a parade around the city to several scenic sites—the riverfront being the most popular, particularly the Monument of Glory. Of course, there's nothing quite like a white bridal gown contrasted against rusty, pipes and gray factories omitting green emissions over a river of contamination to create the perfect backdrop for that timeless wedding photo.

We headed over toward a market area so that I could purchase some vodka and chocolate for Sergei and Elena—a bribe in exchange for their daughter.

On the way back, while passing through a small park near Katya's apartment building, a single leaf fell between us. We exchanged glances, full of a bittersweet mix of optimism and the growing awareness that separation awaited us no matter what the outcome.

After we returned to the apartment, I headed straight to my room to get dressed up in my black pants, white dress shirt, tie, and jacket. We had decided to make our announcement in style. I paced from one side of the room to the other and back, looking over the speech I had prepared, nervously repeating the lines in my mind, over and over again. The door opened and there stood Katya, looking stunningly beautiful in a simple green sun dress.

"Ready?" she asked, nervously.

"Yep … let's do it" I said, taking a deep breath, reaching for the ring case and putting on my jacket. I took the ring out of the case and carefully placed it into my jacket pocket, before grabbing the chocolate and vodka.

Our big moment had finally arrived.

We made our way to the living room, where we found Elena, ironing, absorbed in the evening news program on TV.

"Mama," Katya said. Elena looked up.

"Hello!" Elena said.

She seemed surprised by the way we were dressed. "What's the occasion?" she asked.

"Oh, we just felt like dressing up," Katya replied. "Where's papa?"

"He's asleep in bed," Elena said. "He was out drinking with his colleagues and had one too many."

"We need to talk to the both of you," Katya said.

If Elena knew what we were up to, her expression certainly didn't let on. Then again, how could it not be obvious?

"Let me try to wake him," Elena said, leaving the room.

"Trust me," Katya said. "It will be like waking up a hibernating bear."

Moments later, Elena returned, shaking her head.

"Damn vodka," Katya said.

"He'll be up later, won't he?" I said, glancing at my watch. It was only seven.

"Well, if by later, you mean tomorrow morning …," Katya replied.

I tried to conceal my growing frustration.

"Tomorrow, Bobby, *I promise*," Katya said.

"But after tomorrow, we'll be out of tomorrows," I reminded her. Elena changed the channel.

We sat down on the couch hoping that the television would serve as a distraction. However, there's only so much pleasure one can gain from watching someone being hit over the head repeatedly with a frying pan on a Ukrainian reality show. *I was starting to lose faith.*

"Why didn't we do it earlier?" I asked.

"My dad was out," Katya replied.

"I don't mean earlier *today*. I mean *before today*. There were plenty of other opportunities."

"We didn't have much choice," Katya tried to reassure me. "We can't rush this, remember?"

"But time's running out! I just can't stand the thought of yet another day going by without seeing that ring on your finger."

"Believe me, Bobby," Katya said, "there's nothing *I* want more than to see that ring on my finger. And I promise you it will be, soon. This has nothing to do with *us* and everything to do with *them*. You know that, right?"

"Well, you sure seem to keep making it about them!" I snapped.

"They're my parents! And I'm their daughter. Nothing will change that."

"Well, you haven't exactly gone out of your way to make this happen," I replied, regretting it as soon as the words left my lips.

"Like I had anything to do with my dad getting drunk!" Katya snapped. She did have a point. We sat in frustrated silence, watching more Ukrainians getting hit over the head with more frying pans.

"*Bivaet huzhe,*" Katya finally said.

"What does that mean?" I asked.

"Things could be worse," Katya said.

"Sure," I replied back. "But then again, things could be better, too."

"True. But as my grandmother always told me, 'No matter how hard you try, the bull will never give you milk.'"

"What's that supposed to mean?" I asked, confused.

"Just that there are some things we can't control."

Katya took me by the hand and looked into my eyes reassuringly.

"We'll tell them tomorrow. After dinner. *I promise.*"

Every few seconds, I could hear what sounded like someone spitting.

I glanced over at Elena and discovered that yes, indeed, she was spitting onto one of my shirts as she ironed it.

"Why is your mom spitting on my clothes?" I asked, bemused.

"It helps with the ironing," Katya replied.

At the same time, from across the hall, I could hear Sergei's deep snore rumble through the apartment, shaking the walls.

So ... this is what I'm up against, I thought to myself.

24

A PROLONGED ENGAGEMENT

The next day, we prepared to give it another whirl, getting dressed up once again like actors in our own private stage show. This time, Elena had pleaded with Sergei not to go out and get drunk with his colleagues—explaining how we needed to talk with them together.

The time had finally arrived. No excuses. And no turning back. I stood in my room, staring at myself in the mirror, going over my speech in my mind, a mixture of nerves and excitement building up inside me. As I continued to stare at myself, I couldn't help but smile—at the simple thought: *how did I get here?*

I patted my jacket pocket for the umpteenth time, making sure that the ring case hadn't fallen out, and checked to make sure that my speech was safely tucked into my top pocket—even though I already knew it was. Now I had two things to OCD over! As I was putting on my tie, Katya entered, looking radiant in a silver dress with bright red lipstick and the large, hoop earrings I had bought for her. She held out two clenched fists.

"Pick one," she commanded. I chose her right hand, which she turned over and opened to reveal a silver chain.

"Now pick the other," she continued.

Inside was a silver crucifix. I gave her a big hug, before she helped me put it on.

"Close your eyes and make a wish," she said, holding on to the clasp. I did as instructed, at which point she pulled the necklace behind my neck and fastened it.

"Ready?" said Katya. I could tell she was nervous.

"No, not yet," I said. "Come here."

I gently reached up and held Katya's head, pressing her forehead against mine. We closed our eyes and remained silent for several seconds, breathing deeply and savoring the moment. I then kissed her softly on her forehead, and said "Okay … ready."

I picked up the chocolate and vodka and followed Katya toward the dining room, where Sergei and Elena were awaiting us like sitting judges.

I held my hand out to Sergei, who shook it. Sergei then stood up and gave me his patented bear hug greeting. Elena also stood up and I hugged her too. It all seemed so *formal*, so practiced. *How much did they know?* my paranoid self asked my rational self. I motioned for Sergei and Elena to sit back down, but I remained standing. I stood before them, and nervously began my prepared speech—expertly translated by Katya—speaking in a formal manner to which I was not typically accustomed.

"These past few weeks have been nothing short of memorable. I would first like to thank you for your generous hospitality during my stay here. You are the epitome of gracious hosts and I can only hope to be half the host you are if I am ever to return the favor. As a token of my gratitude, I would like to …"

My hands shook as I presented the chocolate and vodka to Sergei and Elena. Sergei's face lit up and he immediately proceeded to grab the shot glasses as I opened the bottle. I poured shots for all of us.

"I would like to give a toast," I said, taking a deep breath and removing the speech from my pocket.

Suddenly, I was overcome with nerves as I stood there for what felt like an eternity. I looked over at Katya for a confidence boost. Katya smiled and that was all the encouragement I needed. I took her by the hand and began the most important speech of my life.

"When I met your daughter just over two years ago, little did I know how much we had in common. It wasn't long before we became each other's biggest supporters. Katya changed my life in ways I never thought possible. She taught me what it means to not give up on something that you believe in. She also taught me that true love knows no boundaries and knows no distance. I believe everyone is a product of their upbringing, and judging by this beautiful girl that sits by my side, you couldn't have done a better job."

Sergei and Elena were touched—but I could tell that they were wondering what I might say next, and the nerves started to creep in once again. My throat felt dry and I started to wonder whether I would even be able to continue speaking.

I gulped and Katya gently squeezed my sweaty palm, adding a nod of encouragement. I put my prepared speech away and decided to do the rest off the cuff—*like a true Ukrainian.*

"Katya and I have discussed the possibility of a lifetime together. We understand all the obstacles that lie before us. Going back to school and finding a job will be my priority upon my return, as is ensuring that Katya completes her education. The one thing I can promise is your daughter's security and a lifetime filled with love. This woman ... this beautiful woman sitting next to me will be given more love anyone has ever received. So ... at this time ... I would like to ask for your daughter's hand in marriage and for your permission to let her live with me in Michigan."

I removed the ring case from my pocket. By this point, my hands were *really* starting to shake and I prayed that I wouldn't drop it. I opened the case up and placed it on the table in front of Sergei and Elena.

I stood there, frozen, for what seemed like an eternity.

Sergei stared at it blankly. Elena put her hand up to her cheek in shock.

Somebody ... say something ... please!

I wasn't sure if I should be the one to finally break the unbearable silence—or whether I should wait for Sergei or Elena. I squeezed Katya's hand harder, our mutual sweat joining forces and forming a pool.

"If you need some time alone ..." I offered, otherwise lost for words. Sergei shook this notion off and took the reins.

"Bobby ...," he said, taking a deep breath, "news such as this can only come as a shock. The last thing anyone should do in this situation is rush into an irrational decision."

Sergei looked toward Elena and put his arm around her.

"Together, Elena and I have raised two beautiful, intelligent daughters. We like to think we have raised them well. We sent them both to America to broaden their minds. We taught them how to make important decisions for themselves, preparing them to make their own lives. I just didn't expect something like this to happen so soon with Katya.

"But ... life rarely goes as planned. And, importantly, we must remember that life is also short. So one should never waste an opportunity. However, it is important that a decision like this is dictated by the heart, with no ulterior motives. To be married for any other reason would dishonor my family."

Sergei turned to his daughter: "So ... to be certain, Katya ... do you agree to Bobby's proposal for the reason of love?"

Katya nodded.

Sergei turned his attention back to me.

"Bobby ... I can see that you love my daughter. And that she loves you. Love can overcome any distance. Elena and I know this from our own experience, living two years apart after we got married. At the time, the government decided where we worked and it didn't matter to them that we were married. Elena worked as a doctor in a village 300 miles from here.

"Even after Nastya was born, it would take over another year before we could be in the same town again. I barely saw my wife and daughter during that time, and it was unclear how long this situation would last.

"Yet, despite all the uncertainty, nothing changed our devotion to one another. Our love got us through it all. And it continues to do so to this day. I hope your love for one another will do the same.

"You also promise our daughter a secure future. Your request is sound. Your intentions noble. Although we are losing a daughter, we are also gaining a son. You leave me no choice but to accept your offer. *But* ... under one condition: You must promise that we see Katya once a year. That's all we ask."

"I promise," I said, my brain still trying to process all that Sergei had said—marveling at his eloquence, and also in disbelief over the fact that this was actually happening *for real*.

"So ... Katya," Sergei continued, "I leave the final decision in your hands, knowing you have our complete love and support."

Everyone turned their attention to Katya. I took this as my cue to remove the ring from the case and turned to Katya, taking her left hand.

"Are you sure you want this?" I asked.

Katya nodded, her eyes filling with tears.

"Try it on!" Elena chimed up, with uncharacteristic excitement.

And with that, standing in front of Sergei and Elena, I slid the ring onto Katya's finger.

It fit perfectly.

We embraced.

And just like that, we were engaged.

Sergei raised a congratulatory glass. Katya rolled her eyes as if to say *here we go again*. However, Sergei had already said so much that what followed was quite likely the shortest—and, in my eyes at least, one of the best—toasts of his life: "To Bobby and Katya!"

We all downed our vodka.

Relieved, excited—and completely overwhelmed—we returned to the bedroom. Katya opened a drawer and removed a wooden, religious icon of the Virgin Mary holding the baby Jesus. She handed it to me.

"I was given this by my parents before I left for the U.S," she said. "Turn it over."

I flipped it over. Written in English, in Katya's handwriting was the following prayer: "Dear God, please help me reach my biggest dream." She had drawn an arrow which pointed to an American flag.

"As time passed," she continued, "I began to think that I had been so naïve. But then you came along. And now ..."

"Funny how things work out, isn't it?" I said, smiling.

"How do you manage to come here for less than three weeks and get away with what you did?" Katya asked, teasingly.

"I keep asking myself that same question," I replied. "And I have to keep pinching myself."

Still dressed up, we headed out into the Dnipropetrovsk evening to celebrate—after asking for permission from Sergei and Elena, of course.

25

BOAT TO NOWHERE

Katya and I strolled arm in arm along the riverfront, basking in the fact that—somehow, despite the odds—we were now an engaged couple, still finding it too good to be true. We had come so far since our first walk.

An autumn chill filled the air. Dark clouds hovered above us, leaving an opening just large enough to reveal a bright full moon. This dramatic backdrop seemed very fitting.

We approached a ferryboat café docked on the riverfront.

"Let's see if it's leaving soon," Katya suggested.

We headed down the entrance ramp. Not a soul was in sight.

"Hello?!" Katya called out. There was no reply. We walked further onto the boat, where we noticed a sullen, disinterested waitress, sitting at a table painting her nails, alternating puffs of her cigarette with sips of vodka.

"Excuse me. Will the boat be leaving soon?" Katya asked.

"Five minutes," the waitress replied, seemingly annoyed by our mere presence, and by the fact that she would now actually have to work.

We sat down at a table on the upper deck, overlooking the dark, foreboding water. A storm was on the horizon.

"The last time I was on this boat, I think I was about eight or nine," Katya said.

We ordered a bottle of champagne and some chocolate.

Katya grew quiet and melancholy.

"I can't believe you're leaving already. It feels like you only just got here. Although in some ways, I guess it feels like a lifetime ago."

"Or a different life altogether," I added.

I took Katya by the hand and stared intently at the ring, shaking my head, still in disbelief.

"You have no idea how many times I have tried to imagine this ring on your finger," I said.

"I can only imagine," Katya replied.

"But what if I had said *no*?" she continued, "… or my parents?"

"It was a risk I had to take," I replied.

"Not too many people would have the guts to do what you just did."

"Well … maybe not too many people are as nuts as me," I said.

"Probably not," Katya replied.

We stared across the river at the clouds that were growing more ominous. The wind was starting to pick up, blowing across the river. Katya shivered and I held her closer to me. I took my jacket off and placed it over her shoulders.

Moments later, the waitress appeared with our order and check— before informing us that due to the incoming storm, the boat would not be leaving. All rides were cancelled for the evening.

"Of course … she doesn't tell us this until *after* she brings our order," Katya said, clearly annoyed. "Do you still want to stay?"

"Yes, of course. Why not?" I replied.

"You know what, Bobby … you were right," Katya continued. "Nothing works right in this country. I am so sorry. I thought this would be romantic. We should just go."

"How is this not romantic?" I said.

And then—as if on cue—a band began to play. And being that we were the only customers on board, we realized—just like at "King"—that this moment was for us.

I poured the champagne and raised my glass for a toast.

"*To us.* May we never lose faith in fate—which made sitting here, this very evening, on this boat to nowhere possible."

We clinked our glasses and nibbled on the chocolate.

Katya grew quiet again. She was completely overwhelmed.

"What's wrong?" I asked.

"It's just … I get so down when I realize that a memorable experience is coming to an end," Katya said, tears in her eyes.

"You're not alone in that," I said.

"Here we are now together. Newly engaged. But tomorrow at this time, we'll be five thousand miles apart, I'll be heading back to school, and all of this will just feel like a dream."

"Katya, the world is only as big as we make it," I said, reassuringly. However, this did little to comfort her.

"Whatever happens, it can never be like this again," she said, "like these past few weeks have been."

"Sure it can," I said. "And it will be."

"Why does my life have to be filled with so many goodbyes?"

"This goodbye will be different," I replied.

"But there will *always* be goodbyes. When I leave my family. When I visit my family. When my family visits me."

"Isn't it better to be sad over good memories than not to have those memories at all?" I said.

"But there's just so much uncertainty," Katya replied.

"Over what?" I asked.

"Too many roadblocks. Too many things we have no control over. I have a year of school ahead of me. What if you get tired of waiting?" Katya said, staring down at the deck.

"Katya ... that ring is a *promise*," I said, tilting her chin upwards, looking directly into her tear-filled eyes.

She began to cry even harder.

"I'm going to miss you so much, Bobby."

As thunder began to rumble in the distance, and the wind began to whip around the boat, I held Katya closer to me, wiping away her tears.

I raised my glass for another toast.

"Here's to never being alone ever again," I said. We clinked glasses and downed our champagne. Katya even managed a half smile.

Above us, the moon was now fully obscured by clouds that had grown even darker and more ominous. The wind whipped around us violently. The waves morphed into a deeper shade of gray and intensified, rocking the boat back and forth as the world around us started to turn a surreal shade of green.

As we held each other tightly in the eye of the storm, we both cried, our tears melting into one another as rain began to fall.

"Well ... this isn't helping," I said, pointing skyward. "Let's get out of here."

We headed off the boat, champagne bottle in hand and strolled along the riverfront, arm in arm, in the pouring rain, passing the bottle back and forth. *And the band played on.*

"Hey ... now's our chance," I said, as the rain began to fall harder.

"Chance for what?" asked Katya.

"To dance in the rain," I said. "You told me once in an e-mail that you had always wanted to dance in the rain."

"I did?" Katya asked, before remembering. She smiled.

"May I have this dance, madame?" I asked, offering my hand. Katya took my hand and we slow-danced in the rain. When the song ended, I noticed that the clouds had cleared just enough to once again reveal the shimmering full moon.

Somewhere behind us, we heard a meow. We saw what could well have been the same kitten that we had encountered on the night of my arrival—further proof that the fates were aligned in our favor, bringing things full circle.

Katya stooped down to pet it.

As we continued on our way, we could hear the kitten continuing to meow.

"Ever get the feeling you're being followed?" I asked.

We turned around, and sure enough, the kitten was following us.

"Looks like we made a friend," Katya said. "I wish I could keep it, but my parents would never let me."

"And if you did keep it," I replied, "that would mean having to get a kitty visa, as well."

"Sorry, kitty," Katya said. "No green card for you."

We turned away from the river and the cat stopped following us.

That night, I never slept better.

26

THE LAST SUPPER

The last day of any trip always brings with it a mixture of sadness, acceptance that it is over, rejuvenation, and the realization that the time has come to return to the routine of everyday life. This trip was no different … although those emotions were intensified to the highest possible degree. Even though I felt an overwhelming sense of accomplishment and optimism for the future, it was almost impossible to accept the fact that the next time I would see Katya would be on a yet-to-be-determined date — and one over which we realistically had no control. Sure, I could come back to Ukraine anytime, but it wasn't really economically responsible, or entirely logistically feasible.

In the meantime, however, we still had one final night together, a night to be savored, to be remembered. The trip would end the same way it began — with a feast.

While she helped her mother prepare dinner, Katya asked me if I could run over to the store to buy some bread.

"By myself?!" I asked, as though I had just been handed the controls of a fighter jet.

"Yes! You can do it, Bobby" Katya said reassuringly. "Do you remember how to say bread?"

"*Hleb*," I said.

"Very good!" Katya replied.

Katya offered me some money, but I insisted on paying. And just like that, I ventured out into the Ukrainian world all by myself. Fortunately, I didn't have to venture far; the shop was only on the ground level of the apartment building.

As I headed through the courtyard, I heard Katya shouting from the apartment window: "Get some water, too, please. Ask for *voda*."

"Da! Voda! And hleb!" I said.

"*Molodetz!*" Katya said ("Well done!").

I headed into the shop, where I was met with cold stares that suggested "you're not from around here, are you boy?" I grabbed a bottle of "voda," before joining the long line. As I waited, beads of sweat formed on my forehead. I felt paranoid that I was only confirming everyone's suspicions that I was up to no good. Maybe it really was time for me to leave this country? Paranoia was really beginning to overtake me.

Finally, I was next in line. Just as I was about to approach the counter, an old babushka woman decided that my window of opportunity had passed, and cut in front of me.

When it was my turn again, the shopkeeper asked me what I assumed was something along the lines of: "What can I get you?"

"*Hleb, pozhaluista pazualzta,*" I said. The woman didn't understand me and seemed to be annoyed merely by my presence. Then again, I had already noticed that she was like this with every customer. I repeated my order, this time pointing to the bread. She handed me the smallest loaf in the pile. In fact, she went out of her way to do so. I didn't argue. I just wanted to get the hell out of this hostile environment and back into the familiar world that had been home for the past three weeks..

The shopkeeper rang up my purchase. Fortunately, the amount appeared on the register, which made figuring out how much I owed a cinch. I was certainly glad it was not an abacus. As I paid, I could see from the corner of my eye that the babushka woman behind me was inching closer, scrutinizing me with deep curiosity.

As the shopkeeper handed me my change, I exclaimed "Spasibo!" with a smile. The shopkeeper simply rolled her eyes, presumably for butchering her language. As I turned around, the babushka woman was right in my face.

"Americanetz?" she asked in a surprisingly cheerful tone and with keen interest.

"Da!" I said proudly. And with my head held high, I walked out of the store, realizing just how far I had come on this journey.

I returned to the apartment, bread and water in hand, and we all sat down for our final meal together, consisting of such staples as borscht and roasted chicken (*zharenyy tsyplenok*). To my surprise, Nastya graced us with her presence. Her boyfriend had gone out with his buddies, essentially leaving her without an excuse. She looked about as happy to dine with me as Babushka.

After we had dished up, Sergei began his goodbye speech.

It was at that moment that I realized just how similar Ukrainian toasts began to sound after a while. Despite their surface appearance of enormous depth, their recycled tendencies revealed an unexpected, prefabricated greeting-card quality. I was saddened by this realization, because their earlier appeal that so enamored me was fading—further proof that what was once so magical and new was morphing into mundane routine—just like anything else in life. Robert Frost nailed it when he said "Nothing gold can stay."

We ate mostly in silence, which allowed me the opportunity to reflect on my trip and everything that we had done (and achieved). Nastya didn't say a word, of course. Babushka used the silence to fall asleep, after her third—or was it fourth?—shot of vodka.

When dinner was over, Sergei and Elena lavished me with gifts to take back to my family in Michigan. Vodka, chocolate, and a few hand-made, wooden crafts, including some decorative eggs, a wooden bird-shaped whistle, and some *matrioshka* (nesting dolls). Despite the general poverty in Ukraine, I continued to be amazed by the hospitality and generosity of the Ukrainian people.

When the formalities were over and we had finished our dinner, Katya and I headed back to my room with a bottle of champagne and two glasses, as we desperately set out to make this final night together last forever.

We lay on the floor, looking up at the glow-in-the-dark stars, listening as a gentle rain fell against the window.

After filling our glasses with champagne, I raised my glass, proclaiming: "To the rest of our lives. And whatever comes next." We both smiled and clinked glasses. We drank until the bottle was empty and then made love for the first time, holding on to one another with no intention of ever letting go.

As the night wore on, we dozed in and out of sleep, wrapped around one another, listening as the gentle rain morphed into a downpour.

Soon, the stars lost their glow. Before long, the rain came to a stop and the dawn sun began to peep through the curtain, heralding its arrival as it does each and every day, without prejudice.

27

DO SVIDANIYA

The final morning had arrived. I took my final frigid shower, to which I had, strangely, grown accustomed—a feat I didn't think was humanly possible. I was once again reminded of how quickly we are able to adapt and begin to actually *miss* the things we didn't think we could ever miss. I now understand Stockholm Syndrome—as least from a bathroom perspective.

As I finished packing, Katya sat on the couch, her eyes welling with tears. I sat down next to her and wiped them away.

"No tears," I said.

Katya nodded, but didn't say a word.

"Just think of this time apart as a long journey back to each other," I said.

"Can't you just fit me into your suitcase?" Katya asked.

"Your dad could pay the customs inspectors a bribe, right?"

"Maybe in Ukraine ... but once we got to America?"

"Yeah, I guess we're just going to have to do things the legal way," I replied.

We ate breakfast in silence in the dark dining room—devoid of all the pomp and circumstance of which I had grown so accustomed to in that room. Breakfast consisted of open-faced salami sandwiches and juice.

Before we left for the airport, I hid a note under Katya's pillow that said "You're never alone," before spraying her teddy bear with my cologne. I then retrieved my suitcase and backpack. As I passed through the doorway, I turned around for a moment to take one last look, took a deep breath, and exited.

Upon stepping out into the hallway, I was taken aback at the sight of Katya, Sergei, and Elena in the living room, sitting in a semi-circle on stools. An empty stool awaited me.

"Is something wrong?" I asked.

"Have a seat," Katya said without further explanation.

I sat down, somewhat bewildered.

"It's customary in Ukraine for us all to sit down before a long journey," Katya explained.

We sat there in silent contemplation for several moments, before Sergei stood up, followed by the rest of us. Sergei stepped inside his office and returned with a bottle of cologne. And then, without warning, he proceeded to douse me with his cologne from head to toe. I jumped back, startled, but he continued spraying until he assumingly ran out.

"Is this part of the custom, too?" I asked. "I'm going to drown in this stuff ... or choke to death."

"No," Katya explained. "He just wants you to smell nice for your trip home."

I let out a huge sneeze—and would continue to sneeze for the remainder of my journey home. *Thank you, Sergei!*

Apparently, my sneeze awoke the elusive Nastya, who shuffled out of her room in a daze. She wore a 1980's-style nightgown and matching 80's-style coke-bottle glasses. I had previously only seen her in her contacts.

"Goodbye *Booby*," she said—apparently thinking that Booby was my name. She made a half-hearted attempt at a goodbye hug before shuffling off back to bed.

I heard the toilet flush and moments later Babushka appeared.

"Do svidaniya," she said, sleepily. I attempted to hug her, but she backed away. In fact, I was quite certain that she *pushed* me away from her.

"Mama!" Elena said, confirming my thought.

Babushka muttered something under her breath.

"Mama!" Elena repeated. Babushka waved her off and disappeared into the living room, presumably for her morning cup of vodka.

"I hope I'm not forgetting anything," I said as we headed toward the door.

"I hope you are," Katya said.

"Why?" I asked.

"Because if you leave something, that means you'll have to come back."

And with that, we headed down the dark, dank stairwell and out into the cool autumn morning. Once again, Sergei refused to let me carry any of my luggage. After he loaded everything into the trunk, we drove off toward the airport. Nobody said a word. Occasions like this demand silence. Taking Katya by the hand was all that needed to be said. This triggered a tear to fall down her cheek. She looked at me, then quickly looked away, staring out of the window.

"No tears," I reminded her.

"No tears," she said.

But we knew we weren't fooling anyone.

We passed by uniformed elementary school students parading through a park during a traditional first day of school ceremony, before heading out of town toward the airport.

The ending of any memorable trip is especially depressing when you pass the sights you recognize from your arrival, when you were filled with the sense of utter freedom and joy as your journey began. You wish you could close your eyes and transport yourself back to your first sight, with your whole trip lying in front of you. But then you realize that there is no going back. We are always pressing forward, no matter how hard we try to hang on to the past.

Twenty minutes later, we arrived at the airport.

At the check-in counter, I was instructed by the Dniproavia agent to put my suitcase up on the scale. I was certain I was about to be screwed with one final time. *Ukraine wasn't going to let me go without a fight.*

"Too heavy," the agent said in Russian. Katya translated.

"Twenty dollar," the agent said in broken in English.

"Are you serious?" I asked.

"Yes! Pay!" the agent demanded.

I removed a twenty-dollar bill from my wallet and handed it to her rather hastily. She examined the bill as though it was laced with anthrax, before asking her associate examine it – much in the manner of the custom agents who so thoroughly analyzed my passport upon my arrival. After several moments of intense investigation, she said:

"We cannot accept."

"Why not?" I asked.

The agent pointed to a tiny rip in the corner of the bill.

"Ripped," she replied.

"It's still good," I argued.

"No good. Ripped," the agent repeated.

"I don't have any other bills," I said. "Do you accept credit cards?"

"Not for this. But there is ATM machine around the corner with American currency."

"I don't believe this" was all I could muster in defense.

"Just imagine how much it would have cost if you had packed me in there?" Katya said. I couldn't help but crack a smile.

Katya led me to the ATM. I withdrew twenty dollars—and was charged a fifteen-dollar service fee for doing so—and headed back to the counter, only to be informed that I would have to get to the back of the line again.

Twenty minutes later, the agent grabbed the bill from my hand, examined it, and provided me with a curt, officious *thank you* in return, as she checked in my suitcase, tossing it onto the conveyor belt with a resounding thud.

"Yeah ... *you're not welcome*," I muttered under my breath.

We headed over to the security line—to the boundary that would soon separate us.

As my turn approached, we had no other choice but to say goodbye. I first hugged Elena.

"Goodbye, Bobby" Elena said in English. She hugged me tightly.

"Do svidaniya, Elena" I replied in Russian.

I then turned and offered Sergei my hand. Sergei dispensed with a handshake and instead gave me one of his giant bear hugs and kisses on both of my cheeks. And although I could not be certain, I'm pretty sure I saw tears in his eyes.

"I love Bobby!" he said in English.

"Ya lyublyu, Sergei," I said in reply.

And then, just like that, it was time for the hardest goodbye of all.

"No tears," I said as I approached Katya.

"No tears," she said, as we both succumbed to a cascade of tears.

Sergei and Elena stepped away to afford us some privacy.

During our tear-soaked embrace, I realized that we were now *that couple*—just like the couple I had observed saying their tearful goodbyes in Detroit. It felt like both yesterday *and* a lifetime ago.

"Goodbye, Katya" I said, "Ya lyublyu." I kissed Katya's warm, salty mouth. Both of our faces were streaked with tears.

"Goodbye, Bobby. I love you so much," Katya said, an unending stream of tears rolling down her red cheeks.

We both desperately wanted this moment to last—but an overly officious airport security guard waved us on.

I made my way toward passport control and security and was able to pass through without a hitch.

And just like that—within the blink of an eye—we were separated.

After attempting to regain some semblance of composure, I turned and waved to Katya. She smiled through tears and blew me a kiss. As I pushed my way forward, I stopped every couple of feet to get another glimpse of her, knowing full well that it could be my last. At one point, I lost her for a moment in the crowd, before finding her again, waving, just as she had on the day of my arrival.

I walked toward a flight of stairs that would take me to the second level. From that vantage point, I was able to see Katya, standing amidst the crowd. She pointed to the ring on her finger, as though to remind me of everything we had accomplished.

As soon as I made it to the top of the stairs, a barrier along the railing marked the point of no return. I paused to wave one last time, drawing the ire of another security guard who motioned for me to keep walking.

And then, with one more step forward, Katya was out of view.

In her place was the most intense feeling of loss and separation I had ever experienced. It emanated from the pit of my stomach, and spread throughout my whole body. It wasn't just a feeling. It was a throbbing, persistent pain—a pain that would take weeks to subside.

Before I reached the departure gate, I headed into a restroom, entered a stall and immediately and unexpectedly broke down into tears. I felt broken inside. I sat there for a few moments, breathing deeply in an effort to regain my composure, before heading out to find my gate.

As I sat at the gate, I struggled to hold back more tears. But no matter how hard I tried, I couldn't. It felt as though my mind was still in one place and my body in another. I could feel the same judgmental stares that I had experienced previously. This time, I couldn't blame them. Nor could I have cared less.

The time had finally come to board my flight. As soon as I sat down in my seat, I found myself suddenly battling a sneeze attack, courtesy of *eau de Sergei*. I felt sorry for my fellow passengers.

As my connecting flight to Frankfurt took off, I clutched the crucifix Katya had given me. Fortunately, this time there was no Christopher Llyod-esqe mechanic drilling while in mid-flight. Nor any vodka. Or smoked fish. Or dirty diapers. It was time to return home.

As the plane ascended I watched from the window as the neatly ordered patchwork of farms grew smaller and smaller until, suddenly, we were through the clouds, and Dnipropetrovsk instantly disappeared from sight.

As we reached altitude, I felt myself start to doze off. After what couldn't have been more than five, or ten minutes, I suddenly awoke with the certainty that Katya was standing before me. It was as close to an out-of-body experience as I had ever encountered. I was certain I was still in Ukraine. Of course, this sense of being elsewhere dissipated within a few tenths of a second—but the feeling lingered. This feeling was something I would experience several more times in the hours, days, weeks, and months that followed.

The rest of my journey passed without incident, unless you count my frequent, uncontrollable crying jags alternating with hallucinations of what I left behind.

At that point, I had no clue as to how drastically airline travel—and the world as we knew it—was about to change.

PART II

28

BEFORE : AFTER

As we pulled away from the arrivals terminal at Detroit Metro Airport, I nonchalantly mentioned to my parents: "I'm engaged." I figured that the more calm and collected I appeared, the less concerned they would be.

"What?! Are you fucking nuts?!" my dad exclaimed before falling completely mute on the subject. Every once in a while during our twenty-minute trip home, I would catch a roll of his eyes in the rearview mirror, as his head shook in disbelief.

My mom, on the other hand, was ecstatic.

"My son's getting married!" she exclaimed, prompting an even bigger eye roll from my dad.

She could now finally plan a wedding for her first born.

After her initial, instinctual reaction, she began to express concern.

"Are you sure about this?" she asked.

"Without a doubt," I responded with complete and, perhaps, over-confidence.

"You're not moving there, are you? Please don't tell me you're moving away."

"No, mom, I'm not. Don't worry."

We got into the car and headed home. Memories of the drive from Dnipropetrovsk airport to Katya's apartment flooded my mind. It seemed like yesterday, yet paradoxically, like forever ago. The whole trip had become one of those memories that seem to exist independent and free from the ordinary passage of time.

As we drove on, I couldn't believe how different everything in Michigan now seemed. Everything was familiar, but it all seemed so much bigger, cleaner, and somehow transformed, like a dream where a familiar place is not quite the way it is supposed to be, but you just sort of go with it because your mind is telling you to. I couldn't help but feel like an alien on my own planet.

"You okay?" my mom asked, breaking my train of thought.

"Just tired," I said, trying to mask my growing sadness.

"You miss her, don't you?"

I nodded, biting back tears.

I started thinking about how much I had to do before marriage could become a reality and suddenly, everything seemed less straightforward, less guaranteed than it had previous to my arrival.

Katya still had a full year of college ahead of her. And I was about to start my substitute teaching position at my former high school with the hope that it would lead to a full-time position when I finished my certification in the spring. On top of that, I was also taking a full load of college classes.

Upon my return to Michigan, I had less than half a week to prepare to teach for the first time. My days of vodka and wilted roses were over. During my trip, I gave little thought to teaching—and to just about everything else from the "real world" that I had left behind. Now, I was faced with reality. Jetlagged or not, I would soon be responsible for one-hundred and fifty teenagers on a daily basis. If that wasn't a sobering reminder of reality, then I don't know what is.

I should have started my lesson planning immediately. Instead, I focused my attention on the laborious visa process. In order for Katya to qualify for a fiancé visa, I had to gather every shred of evidence that proved that our engagement was legitimate: plane tickets, photos, e-mails, etc.—not to mention hundreds of dollars in application fees. And since I wasn't a full-time employee, my parents had to sign an affidavit of support, which essentially made them financially responsible for Katya in the event that I was unable to be—especially with student teaching looming the following semester and no guarantee of subsequent employment.

The visa process was going to be tricky enough to navigate.

And then came 9/11.

Suddenly, the distance separating us seemed to grow, as fear and uncertainty loomed over the entire country, not to mention the entire world.

The sky was a perfect, cloudless shade of blue that Tuesday morning, a slight hint of an autumn chill in the air. It was during my second hour, tenth grade English class that our world changed forever.

Shortly before 9:00 am, a student returning with a hallway pass matter-of-factly announced that "a plane crashed into the World Trade Center."

She had no other details. I assumed that a private, light aircraft had drifted off course, and struck one of the huge Twin Towers. The majority of students did not react in any way. She might as well have announced that the chess team won a match. In fact, many of my students were not even familiar with the World Trade Center. I described the Twin Towers, and how they represented an iconic part of the New York skyline and were the tallest buildings in the city.

It was during the next period that we first heard the crackle of the school's PA system. Time stood still as we listened to the principal announcing that another plane—a hijacked commercial passenger jet—had flown into the second of the Twin Towers. President Bush had already declared it an act of terrorism. Students reacted slightly more to this announcement than the previous one, but the majority still appeared to be casually indifferent.

The names Al-Qaeda and Osama bin Laden were quickly bandied about as "obvious suspects."

It is important to note that my hometown of Dearborn, Michigan has a substantial Muslim student body in a city with the largest Muslim population outside the Middle East. To ease the growing tension, I begged the class not to draw conclusions until more information could be ascertained. But it was already too late. Anti-Muslim sentiment was already mounting. Fortunately, most of the comments were kept in check. The majority of Arab American students in my classroom—including one unfortunately named Jihad—remained mute, perhaps out of fear of backlash and retaliation. However, one Muslim girl proclaimed: "It's happened to us for so long over there, I don't see how this is any different." At that point, I knew one thing was for certain: this was going to be a long fight.

After the initial announcement, the principal came back on the PA system and requested that nobody rush to judgment and that teachers take the time to discuss the matter with their students, despite having very little information to reasonably discuss. Fortunately, there was a planned half day that day for students. The professional development meeting following class was promptly canceled so teachers could head home to be with their families.

Suddenly, Katya seemed further away than ever. I wondered if she had heard the news. It was quite possible she had not—and might not for some time, since she had limited access both to television and to the Internet.

The remainder of the class was spent trying to explain to students the significance of what had happened, despite not fully understanding the significance myself. I was a bit shocked at how little the news seemed to be impacting students. For the most part, they were still acting as though it were any other ordinary day. As upsetting as their indifferent reaction was on one hand, it was a testament and reminder of their innocence on the other. Even though they had no idea, I knew they would never be the same after this day. None of us would be.

The bell rang along with an announcement that school was to be closed for the remainder of the day, in solidarity with numerous businesses and every airport in the nation. I joined some of my colleagues inside the teacher's lounge, silently huddled around a television as our national nightmare continued to unfold. Another plane had struck the Pentagon. There were reports of yet another plane heading toward the White House. The White House and Capitol were evacuated and closed. All U.S. airspace was shut down, with all incoming international flights being diverted to Canada.

And then—beyond all comprehension—one of the Twin Towers collapsed. I clearly remember one of my colleagues gasping in shock, then bursting into tears, her hand covering her mouth, simply saying "Oh my God … Oh my God!" over and over again. The rest of us simply stared in horror, struggling to process what we were seeing. *How many people were in there?* Within a few seconds, the huge tower was gone. One teacher told us that a triage area had just been set up just beneath the towers. Another teacher was desperately trying to reach her husband, who was flying that day to Minneapolis.

Stunned, I headed out of the building. I got into my car and immediately turned to the news station. It was then that I heard about another plane crashing into a field in Pennsylvania. I sat there for several minutes, unsure where to go or what to do.

I decided to drive to my grandmother's house in Dearborn Heights, about a fifteen-minute drive from the school. When I arrived, I found my grandmother glued to the television. We watched in disbelief and complete silence as the second Twin Tower collapsed. This was followed by looped replays of the second plane slamming into the tower. Numerous eyewitness observers described the horror they had witnessed. *The world was on fire.*

I headed home. My entire drive was a blur, as an endless stream of news reports filled my ears. Nothing was making any sense. Sadly, nothing ever truly would. After returning home, I spent the next several hours in front of the television, as Peter Jennings and Tom Brokaw worked overtime to deliver the latest news. I couldn't motivate myself to do anything else. Fortunately, my college class was canceled that night.

With the exception of a few clear memories, the rest of the day was a blur: my dad returning home from work early, parking his car in front of the house and walking up to the door, disbelief and anger on his face ... the collapse of World Trade Center Building #7 ... the plane crashing over and over again ... bodies falling ... the Twin Towers collapsing ... people desperately running from the plumes of dust and debris ... aerial views of the smoldering wreckage in Manhattan, in Washington, in Pennsylvania.

Later that afternoon, I checked my e-mail. Surely Katya would have heard about the attacks by now. What would she be thinking, thousands of miles away in Ukraine? What was the reaction over there? Although it was not foremost in my mind, I did wonder if the events of this most tragic day would affect Katya's visa, not to mention our entire future together. Katya had e-mailed me—but made no reference to the attacks. I attempted to call her, but as usual, all the lines were jammed. I e-mailed her, sharing my thoughts about what had transpired that day.

That evening, I lay in bed, the horrific images swirling through my head along with the words of President Bush: "Today, our way of life, our very freedom came under attack in a series of deliberate and deadly terrorist attacks."

Our whole way of life was going to change. I felt numb, confused, horrified. Since my return from Ukraine, I was already walking through life in a numb blurred state of reality as it was. Now, I was drifting in it. Where was the vodka when one truly needed it?

The next morning, following a sleepless night, I immediately checked my e-mail. A message from Katya awaited me.

Katya hadn't heard until she got to school the following morning. She expressed her shock and disbelief and had written that the tragedy served to make her miss me even more. I reassured her that nothing would get in the way of us being together. In fact, I indicated that this tragedy only made me want to be with her even more, making me even more determined to do whatever I could to help her obtain her visa as soon as humanly possible. Of course, I knew deep down that there was virtually nothing I could do to affect the outcome. I also realized that the odds were now even more stacked against us, but we took comfort in knowing that we still had one another and that, eventually, we would be together. Yet,

I couldn't help but feel an extreme sense of guilt and sadness. I knew that I would see Katya again, even though I didn't know when. For thousands of others, there was no "when."

I now look back at September 2001 as dividing point, separating both my life and the life of my country into two halves.

And as our nation prepared for war, I began my own personal battle to bring my future wife to the U.S.

29

THE WAIT

Two weeks later—and after much soul-searching—I decided to leave my substitute teaching position in order to focus on my full load of college courses. I just didn't feel like I could do my students justice—or myself for that matter. I was giving up a golden opportunity, but I knew in my heart that this was the right decision. Even though it had lasted less than one month, I will never forget my first teaching experience. Not only was it my first experience of full-time teaching, but the coinciding timing of both my return from Ukraine and 9/11 left an even deeper, lasting imprint.

It was also time to become adjusted to the "new normal"—a post 9/11 world and a post-Ukraine/pre-life-with-Katya one.

To help ease the passage of time, I set my sights on various calendar landmarks leading up to our reunion. Life became an endless game of ... *if I can just get to Halloween ... to Thanksgiving ... to Christmas ... New Year's Eve ... Valentine's Day ... Easter.*

With the aid of my local congressman's office, we were told that, short of any unforeseen problems, Katya would most likely receive her visa in April.

In the meantime, all we could do was *wait* ... and plan. We set a tentative July date for our wedding in the U.S., preceded by an engagement party in Dnipropetrovsk in May.

Katya and I continued to e-mail each other as much as possible, despite her limited Internet access. We also utilized instant messenger and talked on the phone at least once a week after finding a relatively inexpensive calling card plan. This came on the heels of my finding out the hard way that a fifteen-minute phone conversation without a calling card cost over $100.

Autumn morphed into the start of another never-ending Michigan winter, and before I knew it, the holidays were upon us. I sent Katya a box filled with presents: some blouses, a University of Michigan sweatshirt, a pair of earrings, and an "Our First Christmas" ornament. As it turned out, it was a Christmas miracle that she actually received them at all, since mail sent from the U.S. has a frequent habit of "disappearing" once it arrives in Ukraine. I felt fortunate not to be sharing "our first Christmas" ornament with a crooked Ukrainian postal worker named Boris.

New Year's Eve arrived. This is Ukraine's biggest holiday of the year, when their version of Santa Claus—*Ded Moroz* or "Grandfather Frost"— comes to town, accompanied by his granddaughter, *Snegurochka*, the Snow Maiden. During the seventy years of religious persecution during the Soviet Union, Christmas—like all religious traditions—was essentially illegal. To get around this, the majority of citizens who "believed" simply transferred their Christmas traditions over to New Year's Eve. This, of course, allowed them to combine their love for gift-giving and vodka into one glorious day!

I attempted to call Katya at the stroke of *her* midnight—six hours ahead of Michigan—but apparently every other person with loved ones in Ukraine had the same idea. The phone lines were jammed and I grew worried that I wouldn't be able to reach her until *my* midnight. I continued calling and was finally able to get through about thirty minutes later. Katya was celebrating with her family, drunk on champagne. It was crazy to think that she was not only a vast ocean and continent away from me—she was now already in a different year.

The ringing in of the New Year heralded the arrival of two additional chapters in my life: student teaching—again at Edsel Ford High—which upon completion would mean being awarded my teaching certificate. And the fulfillment of my New Year's resolution: beefing up through weightlifting to transform my—as Babushka was apt to describe—"too skinny" body into that of a *real man*. From January until I left for Ukraine in May, I went to the gym every day, supplementing my health regime with gas-inducing protein shakes. By the time May rolled around, my body had completely transformed.

I like to think that Babushka would have been impressed by the "new me" and would have given me half a chance upon my return. But unfortunately she passed away before I would get an opportunity to redeem myself. She died in late February, finally losing her battle with cancer (and an even number of roses). I still couldn't help but feel partially responsible for her death, dating back to the flower fiasco. Fortunately, Katya never mentioned it again. I certainly wasn't going to.

No matter what, I felt awful that I couldn't be there for the funeral. I have a hunch, however, that Babushka would have preferred it that way.

Fortunately, both Katya and Elena handled it as well as could be expected, seeking comfort in the realization that Babushka no longer had to suffer.

Spring finally arrived. On April 12, Katya officially received her visa at the American Embassy in Warsaw, Poland. She took an overnight train—the highlight of which included having to stop at the Ukraine-Poland border so that the wheels of the train could be removed and swapped with different ones that would fit on Polish rails. There was also a scary moment in the middle of the night when Katya was almost kicked off the train for not having her signature on her ticket. She pleaded in tears for the agent to have mercy on her, begging not to be left stranded in the middle of an open field in the middle of nowhere at three in the morning. She was given the option of paying a modest bribe and was allowed to sign her ticket. Fortunately, the rest of her trip passed without incident.

Even though getting the visa had been a fairly safe bet, until it became a reality, there was always that underlying feeling of anxiety and "what if" scenarios playing through our heads.

On the day of Katya's interview, I came home from work during my lunch period to check my parents' answering machine, just to make sure that everything had gone as planned. Sure enough, it did. *Nothing could catch us now.*

I returned to work, so full of excitement, I could barely contain myself. One of the hardest challenges a teacher faces is knowing how to maintain a poker face at all times—whether it be absolute joy, anger, or the urge to laugh at a student's inappropriate joke. Incidentally, it was at this time—just as my student teaching position at my alma mater was ending—that a rumor was started that I was bringing home a mail-order bride. And not by a student, but by a colleague. It's unfortunate that my combined experience as a former student, substitute teacher, and student teacher at Edsel Ford High had to end on such a sour note.

But that was behind me now. I was a certified teacher. And Katya was officially certified to come to live with me in the U.S.

Our future was here.

30

RETURN TO "THE" UKRAINE

After nine months, our time apart had finally come to an end. I was heading back to Ukraine. To Katya. I was going to spend three weeks in Dnipropetrovsk before returning to Michigan with Katya. And unlike my first trip, this time I knew exactly what to expect: *the unexpected.*

At the airport in Detroit, the shadow of 9/11 loomed heavily, filling my heart both with grief and anxiety. Unlike my previous trip—when my parents literally saw me off at the departure gate—security was exceptionally tight. We now had to say our goodbyes before the security checkpoint.

"Here we are again," I said.

"Well, unlike the last trip, we're hoping you don't return by yourself this time," my mom joked.

"I don't see that happening," I said with *almost* complete confidence.

"I still think you're nuts," my dad added with a wink.

"Yeah ... probably," I said, laughing.

"Just make sure to let us know once you arrive ... and don't forget to keep in touch," my mom said.

"I'll try, mom," I said. "But I'm at the mercy of Ukrainian Internet service."

"Just be careful, okay?" my mom said—echoing *exactly* what she had said at the airport gate eight months earlier.

"And remember ... it's not too late for second thoughts," my dad added, with a sly grin.

"Bob!" my mom scolded.

"We love you, son," my mom said. "We just want you to be happy."

"I am, mom. Katya makes me happy."

We hugged goodbye, knowing that things were truly never going to be the same from this point forward. Another chapter was coming to an end; a happy ending, but an end all the same.

I got in line, turning around to wave to my parents one last time. My mom was wiping away tears. Next thing I knew, I was, too. Then, it was time to look only forward.

The line now moved much slower due to more thorough inspections and random searches of old ladies and small children for bomb-making materials. Shoes also had to be removed. Forty-five minutes later, I finally made it to the front of the security checkpoint line.

"Please step aside, sir," the security official sternly instructed. I had been selected for a random check. Suddenly, I felt like I was already back in Ukraine. After a thorough check of my carry-on bag, I was allowed to continue toward my departure gate. I wondered whether my olive-skin tone had something to do with my "random" selection. If I was dark enough for Ukraine, then apparently, I was dark enough for a post-9/11 United States of America. Then again, it could well have just been paranoia. I settled on the "better safe than sorry" mindset and tried to not let it get me down.

Of course, once I got to the gate, I couldn't help but scan my fellow-passengers for potential "threats." *Everyone looks "ordinary,"* I thought to myself, with a sense of relief. My paranoia would return upon take-off.

As I continued to wait for my flight to Amsterdam, my thoughts turned to a Muslim man who I remembered seeing at the departure gate in Frankfurt on my return trip eight months prior. He had been dressed from head-to-toe in traditional Muslim garb. I remember having the same fears then—two weeks *before* 9/11 and realized at that point that I could no longer simply use 9/11 as an excuse for my airport prejudice.

Eventually, the time had come to board. I continued to evaluate every passenger as they came on board. During take-off, I held on tightly to the crucifix that Katya had given me with one hand and clenched the armrest with the other. Despite a smooth flight, my mind kept returning to 9/11 imagery.

Once we landed in Amsterdam, my anxiety quickly morphed into excitement for my reunion with Katya. However, a five-hour layover is enough to dampen any amount of excitement. The mall-esque nature of the airport kept me entertained for a while, but one can only get so much enjoyment out of duty-free shops. Layovers are about as close to purgatory on earth as one can get.

I finally settled into a lounge, where a player piano kept me entertained me with old jazz chestnuts and ballad classics. Things turned serendipitous when it started playing *As Time Goes By*.

After a seemingly endless wait, the time had finally come to head to the departure gate for my flight to Kiev. While waiting, I encountered a group of college-age missionaries from Iowa, who were headed to Ukraine for the first time. I wondered if they had any idea what they were getting themselves into. I thought about warning them. Then again, they had God on their side. They would be fine.

I boarded the flight for the final leg of my nine-month pilgrimage back to Katya. It seemed almost surreal to think that I was just a few hours away from the girl who consumed my every thought day after day, week after week, month after month. In the back of my mind, I couldn't help but think that *something* would block my path at some point on my journey. But by some divine miracle, the plane landed on time. I even passed through Ukrainian customs without incident. Even my suitcase was still zipped up! *Was I in the Ukrainian Twilight Zone?*

Next thing I knew, all that stood between us was a sliding door. Barring any malfunction on the door's part, the moment we had we been longing for had finally arrived. I passed through the sliding door and spotted Katya almost immediately. She looked like a vision of Christmas in a red shirt and green pants. Sergei stood by her side. Everything was beginning to feel so déjà vu, especially as we finally melted into one another's arms. Separation was no longer our reality. We were finally together.

"I missed you so much," I whispered into Katya's ear.

"I missed you, too, Bobby," she replied softly.

Sergei greeted me with a bear hug and kisses on both cheeks—not to mention the all too recognizable stench of his cologne. It felt as though I had never left.

Waiting for us outside the terminal in Kiev was a driver by the name of Maxim—as in *Maxim*um overdrive. Dressed in black from head to toe—including his shades—Maxim was one of Sergei's former students who owed him some kind of favor. In this instance, he had been roped into making the twelve-hour roundtrip drive from Dnipropetrovsk to Kiev and back.

After I thanked Maxim for loading my luggage into his trunk, he replied "special service, for special people." This, apparently, was the limit of his English-speaking ability.

Sergei sat in the front passenger seat while Katya and I sat in the back, where we held onto each other for the entirety of our six-hour trip, as though failing to do so would lead to another prolonged separation. We also held on to one another for dear life, as Maxim treated the narrow, one-lane road that made up the majority of our trip as his own personal racetrack. Only unlike a real race, the other drivers were not willful participants.

Shortly after leaving the airport, I began to feel car sick. I tried in vain to wish the nausea away, but finally got to the point where I had no other choice but to beg for Maxim to pull over. I stumbled through a thicket of weeds and proceeded to vomit—the first time I had vomited since the night of "Bobby's path." I stumbled back to the car and clambered back in. I felt a little better, but the lingering car sickness, combined with my jet-lag was not helping matters. At least there was no need for Sergei to ram his fingers down my throat this time. I marked that down as progress.

At around eleven that evening—almost 24 hours after I had left Michigan—we arrived in the familiar surroundings of Dnipropetrovsk and then, finally, the family's apartment. Unlike the previous time, Sergei did not carry my luggage. He now had Maxim to shoulder the burden.

"Special service, for special people!" Maxim cheerfully reminded me. We headed indoors, where everything smelled the same and *felt* the same. It's amazing how little time it takes for something to become nostalgic. Over the past nine months, I had tried desperately to recreate these comforting smells in my mind. And every now and then—usually triggered by either a song or a photograph—it came to me. But it was always all too fleeting.

"Dobro pozhalovat obratno!" ("Welcome back!") Elena said, greeting me with an enormous hug. In an attempt to kiss her cheek, I accidentally landed a kiss on her ear. Fortunately, she didn't seem to let it bother her and nobody else seemed to notice.

There were a couple of notable absences since my first visit. Nastya was now all-but-living with her now fiancé, despite her parents' disapproval and spent as little time at home as possible—my first night there being no exception. And of course, also missing was Babushka. Despite all logic, I still felt somewhat responsible for her passing.

There were also a few new additions. First off, Sergei had obtained a "new" (as in five-years-old) computer from one of his connections. And with a faster modem ... and seemingly less viruses. I was now able to send a single e-mail to my parents in a record time.

An enormous Ukrainian feast awaited us all—all except for poor Maxim. He had not been invited to join us. *Special service for special people* indeed, I thought to myself.

The second—very welcome—addition was even more of a shocker. Before we ate, I took a shower and—lo and behold—there was *hot water,* thanks to a newly-installed water heater. Progress in Ukraine does happen, however slowly. In place of piercing cold, however, was scalding hot— proving that there is never really a happy medium in Ukraine. I ended up burning my hand on the blistering hot faucet and suddenly found myself yearning for the icy cold days of yore.

As we ate a feast that was almost an exact carbon-copy of my first meal in Ukraine eight months prior, I couldn't help but feel an undertone of melancholy permeating through all of us, especially when compared to the more carefree nature of the first trip. The reasons were clear: I was there to steal Katya away from her parents. And no matter how joyous of an occasion this was on one hand, it was anything but on the other.

Furthermore, an empty chair was kept at the table in Babushka's memory, along with a place setting and shot glass. Her absence was certainly felt. Even though the woman despised me, I couldn't help but miss her frosty glares.

After pouring everyone a shot—including Babushka—Sergei stood up before us and delivered another of his vintage toasts:

"Bobby ... like a ship returning to harbor following a long journey across a vast ocean, we welcome you back with open arms. We understand the excitement you and Katya feel to be reunited, especially with the prospect of your entire future together ahead of you. This is certainly a reason to celebrate."

Sergei's eyes began to well up. Meanwhile, Elena looked at the spot where her mother once sat, with a forlorn, but steadfast expression.

"You have made my daughter so happy," Sergei continued, "And that is the most important thing on earth. We wish you both all the very best for the future."

We clinked glasses. Sergei wiped the tears away from his eyes. I could sense his sadness, but there was nothing I could say. Soon enough, there would be another empty chair at the table.

After we had finished eating, Sergei and Elena headed off to bed. Katya and I sat on the sofa and embraced for the longest time without saying a word, letting the months of separation melt away, bridging the gap between our last embrace and the present.

Katya suddenly lay back and closed her eyes.

"Pretend I'm sleeping," Katya said. "How would you wake me up?"

With her eyes still shut, I leaned and kissed her softly on the forehead, then gently on the lips, before we quietly consummated our reunion, before heading off to bed.

Despite our engagement, Katya and I were still expected by Sergei and Elena to sleep in separate beds. As a result, the sleeping arrangements remained the same as they were on my first trip.

And just like my first trip, I lay awake for most of the night—but this time for a different reason: *guilt*.

31

SHIST FEET UNDER

The following afternoon, Katya, Elena and I hopped on a route van and headed just outside the city limits to the cemetery where Babushka was laid to rest. Elena carried an old-fashioned picnic basket filled with wine and food. This was Elena's weekly ritual. She usually preferred to go alone, but had decided this day to take Katya and me along. Apparently, she *wanted* her mother to roll in her grave.

"Are we going to have a picnic there?" I asked half-jokingly, still jet-lagged and sleep deprived.

"Sort of," Katya said. "It's customary to leave food for loved ones at their grave."

"Do we get to eat it, too?" I asked.

"Of course!" Katya explained. "But just not Babushka's." I wasn't sure how to respond to this.

The route van dropped us off a half-mile or so from the cemetery. Just ahead of us were a dozen or so mourners—each carrying a rose—following behind a wooden, seemingly handmade casket that looked barely fit for a pauper. And I don't mean mourners in a generic sense. I never saw mourning this intense and this *real*. Veiled women dressed all in black wailed heavily. Men, of course, remained men in the Ukrainian sense: half way between stoic and stern. What really topped the whole deal off was the actual repeated playing of Chopin's somber funeral march. I used to think that this song was only used in cartoon funerals. Catholic funerals by comparison were like going to the circus.

Holding hands with Katya, the three of us followed the procession into the cemetery—one which would have made Edgar Allen Poe blush. It was completely overgrown with weeds. And then there were the crows. Big, black crows sitting on old, crumbling tombstones. It was though I had stumbled upon the set of a Victorian-era Hammer House of Horror movie. It was almost too cliché to be true.

When the mourners reached the already prepared grave with the casket, the priest opened it up, revealing the decaying body of an old man who—judging from the intensity of the wails—was clearly beloved (although Katya explained that it is customary to hire professional "mourners" to enhance the mood). A religious icon was placed over the deceased's forehead, which everyone kissed upon approaching the casket for the final time, as the priest stood over it, swinging a thurible of incense back and forth, creating a smoky haze that fit in perfectly with the ghostly surroundings. This ritual caused the mourners to mourn even deeper, all but flooding the casket with tears.

Once everyone was done saying their final goodbyes, the casket was closed and nailed shut by two grubby, shirtless men in overalls, before being crudely and clumsily lowered into the grave.

As the men began shoveling dirt over the casket, mourners threw their roses on top of it, then aided the gravediggers by throwing in clumps of dirt, while rivulets of tears flowed into their loved one's final resting place.

After watching this macabre spectacle unfold, we headed over to Babushka's grave. The tombstone featured an embossed photograph of Babushka from middle age. She looked so vibrant and alive—completely unlike the sunken husk I remembered so well from my previous visit. Her rough edges were gone and in their place, stoic beauty.

We stared at the grave in silence for a couple of minutes before Elena removed a blanket out of the picnic basket, which she laid down on the ground in front of the tombstone. She removed a loaf of bread, a container filled with borscht, and four bowls, before handing me a bottle of wine and a corkscrew. As Elena began distributing the bowls and slicing the bread, I tried my best to open the bottle. I struggled, but was finally able to figure it out; my prior experience at Uncle Vladimir's was finally beginning to pay dividends.

I watched as Elena placed a full bowl of soup in front against Babushka's tombstone, along with a slice of bread and an empty wine glass. I poured full glasses of wine for everyone, including Babushka. Initially, I poured less for Babushka—but was immediately urged by Elena to fill it up.

"Does she not deserve equal treatment?" Elena asked. I not only gave Babushka an equal amount, but I actually filled it a smidgeon more than the rest of the glasses.

Elena and Katya silently raised their glasses toward the tombstone. I followed suit. Not a word was said. After a moment of silence, they raised the glasses to their mouths. I awkwardly anticipated that we would clink glasses, but I learned that this wasn't done when the toast was directed toward the deceased.

In fact, our entire meal continued in silence. When we were done, we packed up our items, before standing—heads bowed—before the grave for one final moment of silence. Elena then propped the half-empty bottle of wine against the tombstone, next to the uneaten bread and borscht before we headed out of the cemetery in silence. I walked hand-in-hand with Katya, who in turn, linked arms with her mother.

32

A DAY AT THE CIRCUS

Refreshed from a decent night's sleep, Katya and I headed downtown. It didn't take me long to become reacquainted with the city, which now felt like a second home, as opposed to my first trip when it felt like another planet. For the most part, everything was pretty much how I remembered it, however I did notice a couple of new residential skyscrapers taking shape not far from Katya's apartment building. Unlike the drab, cinderblock style of Soviet-era apartments, these new buildings were both modern and very western-world glass and metal structures.

One of my regrets from my first trip was not visiting the Dnipropetrovsk State Circus. This time, I was determined to rectify the situation. I was especially intrigued by promotional posters and billboards throughout the city, advertising "The Flying Dogs of Dnipropetrovsk." I had to see this for myself. As if on cue, a stray mutt passed by.

"I guess there's no shortage of performers," I remarked, half-serious.

"You're probably right," Katya said, fully-serious.

I had been to a few circuses in my lifetime, but nothing could prepare me for the experience of a Ukrainian one. Unlike circuses back in the U.S., which roll into town for a day or two, the circus in Dnipropetrovsk runs from early spring through early fall. As is turns out, Ukraine is a hotbed of circus talent. In fact, many circus performers in the U.S. hail from the various parts of the former Soviet Union.

After purchasing tickets for a matinee performance, we headed to a nearby market to purchase warm beer and peanuts. We then entered the circus building, which had been built in 1980. For some odd reason, the lobby included a pet store. Various souvenirs were offered for sale around the perimeter of the lobby concourse by vendors dressed as clowns. As somebody who has a complete and utter fear towards these sinister spawns of Satan, it's a wonder I didn't head for the closest exit. The fact that they spoke Russian somehow made them even more horrifying.

We headed to our seats in the back row of the 300–400 seat arena, which was probably about three-quarters full. This was quite impressive considering that the circus is pretty much *always* in town in Dnipropetrovsk.

As we waited for the show to begin, Katya used an armrest to pop the caps of our beer off just before the chimes of what sounded like a very depressed clock rang—a cue for the audience to be aware that the show would begin in ten minutes. We used that time to make out in our seats, because nothing says romance like a Ukrainian circus. Five minutes later, the clock chimed again. A buzz filled the air. Katya explained that the chimes were ringing out the melody of the Moscow Circus. It sounded more like a funeral dirge to me. Finally, the lights dimmed and a spotlight shined upon the house band, perched in a balcony overlooking the crowd, which was now going bananas in anticipation. The band provided accompaniment for the performers throughout the entire show, which included everything one would expect to see at a circus: tightrope walkers, gymnasts, lion tamers, monkeys, clowns and performers inside giant, glow-in-the-dark worm-like creatures that resembled Slinkys on acid.

Prior to the intermission, a woman was brought into the ring from the crowd. She looked understandably shocked and confused. Moments later, a man was *rolled* out by a gang of clowns. He was positioned inside a giant ring—his arms and legs spread out like da Vinci's "Vitruvian Man" drawing. After the clowns released him from the wheel, he got down on one knee in front of the woman and proposed. She accepted. How could she not? The crowd went crazy. All I could think was, *why didn't I think of that?*

During the intermission, children lined up for elephant rides. More impressive was an enormous swing that was lowered from the rafters. And when I say enormous swing, I mean a swing that almost spanned the entire circus ring. I watched in utter fascination as approximately twenty children were strapped in at a time before being swung back and forth by some sort of contraption made up of levers, whirligigs, and gizmos.

The second half of the show began innocently enough with a half-naked gymnast twirling up and down a rope like a stripper on a pole. The next act became the realization of my worst nightmare as a posse of clowns ran into the ring, then up and down the aisles, searching for some poor soul to include in their act. I made it a point not to make any eye contact with any of them whatsoever. In retrospect, I think this may have been the wrong tactic, because as it turned out, that poor, unsuspecting soul happened to be *me*. Next thing I knew, I was being pulled from my seat and dragged down the aisle and into the ring below. Katya, meanwhile, couldn't stop laughing as I looked back at her in a desperate plea for help.

The procurer clowns brought me down into the dirt-floored ring, where I was instantly surrounded by at least a dozen more clowns. One clown in particular kept running around me in circles, making funny faces three inches from mine. This had to be—indubitably—what Dante's Seventh Circle of Hell is like.

The leader of the clowns commanded me to do something—in Russian.

"Nyet, Russiky," I pleaded in desperation.

Apparently, he either couldn't understand me, or chose not to. He continued barking at me in Russian, repeating the same command over and over—until it finally occurred to him that I couldn't understand Russian. Once this understanding was finally established, he instead gestured for me to sit upon the raised feet of a clown who was laying on his back. A third clown was positioned in the same manner five feet away. I did as instructed—or at least I thought I did—but I was apparently not positioned the way they wanted me to be. Another clown helped adjust me into the proper position, at which point the clown that was holding me up began bouncing me up and down on his feet, as though they were spring-loaded. However, my position was still apparently not to his liking. The more they tried, the more it was becoming evident that it was no use. The poor clown holding me up was struggling to withstand my weight. Finally, his legs buckled and I fell right on top of his face. He rolled over, holding his nose in pain, as blood gushed out, soaking the front of his costume.

As the crowd booed, I was scolded by the clown leader, who pointed toward my seat. I trudged back toward Katya, head bowed, equally ashamed and traumatized. Just what it was that the clowns wanted me to do, I'll never know. But I imagine it had something to do with being catapulted from one clown to the other. I couldn't really imagine any good coming from that, so I am quite sure that it was for the best that it didn't work out.

When I got back to my seat, Katya was laughing even harder.

"It's not funny," I said.

"It is *hilarious*," Katya replied, cracking up.

Meanwhile, the clown whose face I fell on was being helped out of the ring, holding a bloody rag up to his possibly broken nose. One might assume that considering the way I felt about clowns, I would have claimed this moment as a victory. But instead, I felt sorry for the poor clown. I never thought it possible that a clown could elicit my sympathy. Then again, the more time I spent in Ukraine, the more I learned that anything was possible.

When the clowns finished up their act — which I had clearly curtailed — it was time for the grand finale: the Flying Dogs of Dnipropetrovsk! I was dying to know how they would manage to make dogs fly. Would they be shot out of a cannon? Surely, they wouldn't be that cruel.

Initially, this trick was accomplished by having dogs wearing little backpacks walk up a ladder practically to the roof — a height of at least one-hundred feet. When the dogs reached the top, they would walk across a diving-board-like platform and then jump. Half way down, a little parachute would open, allowing them to land safely in the arms of their trainers.

And then, they brought out the cannon, which was pointed straight up into the air. And — just as I imagined — dogs were shot out of it.

33

THE JIM BELUSHI FILM FESTIVAL

Following the surreal experience of the circus, combined with a hearty meal, Sergei drove us to the Dnipropetrovsk bus terminal—the largest in Eastern Europe—located near the Central Railway Station. Katya and I were taking an overnight bus to Yalta in Crimea (or, as some still call it, *the* Crimea) to visit Katya's cousin, Andrei, and his family as part of the Katya goodbye tour. I was looking forward to leaving the dirty, claustrophobic confines of Dnipropetrovsk. Little did I know that I was simply trading that in for the dirty, claustrophobic confines of Yalta.

The Dnipropetrovsk bus terminal was a depressingly dingy building with a pervasive Soviet feel to it. After waiting far too long in a line not nearly long enough to warrant the wait, we were finally able to purchase our bus tickets from a less than enthusiastic and clearly bitter ticket agent, before setting off on our journey to what many considered to be the crown jewel of Ukraine.

A peninsula notable for its picturesque and mountainous terrain along an otherwise flat northern Black Sea coastline, Crimea is a popular tourist destination, brimming with resorts and a wide array of attractions, vineyards, and orchards. The peninsula was transferred to the Ukrainian Soviet Socialist Republic within the Soviet Union in 1954. In 1991 it became part of independent Ukraine, known as the Autonomous Republic of Crimea. Russia has since regretted this decision and the general sense was that it would only be a matter of time before Russia would try to take Crimea back.

We climbed into the hot, stuffy bus to begin our own personal Crimean adventure. I was hoping that the air conditioning would be turned on after we left. As we departed, Sergei stood outside our window, waving goodbye enthusiastically, like a mad man, even running alongside the bus until he could no longer keep up. He then continued waving until we were out of sight.

Our twelve-hour journey into southern Ukraine had begun. Despite the oppressive heat, the air conditioning was never turned on (assuming there was any to begin with).

"Do you know if these busses have A.C.," I whispered to Katya.

"What's A.C.?" Katya asked in response.

"Air conditioning," I replied.

"Oh, no ... I doubt it." Katya said "And if there was, it's probably broken or won't be turned on."

What was turned on instead was the cinematic masterpiece *Taking Care of Business*, starring the legendary Jim Belushi. In fact, the entire trip became a full-blown Jim Belushi film festival! As if one Jim Belushi film wasn't enough, *Taking Care of Business* was followed up with *Red Heat* and *K-9*. These three films were looped over and over again throughout the entirety of the trip. As Katya later explained, Ukrainians love Jim Belushi, who is apparently to Ukraine what Jerry Lewis is to France, and David Hasselhof to Germany.

As we drove through downtown Dnipropetrovsk, I began to notice something rather unusual. Every couple of minutes or so, the bus driver would pull over and another passenger would climb on board, paying the driver cash before finding a spot to stand in the aisle. After observing this several times, I asked Katya what was going on. She explained that these were people who had made arrangements with the driver to pick them up at a pre-arranged location. It was cheaper than paying for a route van and the driver was able to make some extra money on the side. It was a perfect arrangement, because for once, nobody was screwed over (well, except for the system itself, which made its living continually screwing the entire nation). Some of these rogue passengers were dropped off along our route before we left town. Others were dropped off along the main highway outside of town. These people were villagers who worked in the city and were looking for a cheap way to travel.

Soon, night fell. I attempted to doze off, but felt nowhere close to sleep. I would have read or written in my journal, but there were no reading lights. Nor were there any streetlights. Talking to Katya wasn't really an option, either, since she had advised me not to speak English, out of fear that I would be robbed, beaten (or both) if the driver – or *passengers* – knew that an American was on board. That left me no choice but to watch Jim Belushi's antics and lame attempts at humor, dubbed in Russian, as my fellow passengers rolled in the aisles with laughter. I never saw Ukrainians look happier.

About three or four hours into the trip, a rancid odor filled my nostrils. *Wow … that's different*, I thought to myself. The stench was a little on the sweet side—a cross between bacon, burning trash, and body odor—with a slight hint of nut. And it was drifting in from somewhere outside. It lingered for miles.

"What the hell is that smell?" I finally whispered to Katya.

"No idea," Katya replied.

As curious as I was to find out what it was, I was also relieved not to know. For all I knew, it was an unregulated chemical plant leaking toxins into the environment. Eventually—and thankfully—the mystery stench dissipated.

Katya fell asleep against my shoulder. I was left with two choices: stare at the pitch-black darkness outside; or watch Jim Belushi bicker with Charles Grodin, a German Shepherd, or the Soviets. I decided to go with the pitch-black darkness.

At some point, I finally began to drift off to sleep. Just as I reached that half-asleep, half-awake state, I was jolted awake by the loud hiss of the bus's air brakes and bright lights that the driver turned on without warning. We had pulled into a market area literally in the middle of nowhere. The sole purpose of this area was for the use of travelers en route to Crimea. It was the Ukrainian equivalent of a rest stop.

I stepped off the bus, slightly dazed and trying to adjust my eyes to the light. I couldn't help but dread the thought of being stranded out here. We purchased some snacks and I asked if there was a restroom nearby. Katya pointed in the direction of a small, brick building that looked like a nineteenth-century jailhouse.

"*That's* a bathroom?" I asked.

"Yep," she said, handing me some change.

"What's this for?" I asked.

"To pay, of course," Katya replied.

"You're kidding, right?!" I exclaimed.

"Why would I be kidding?" replied Katya.

"I have to pay? To piss? In *that*?" I said, incredulous.

"Hey … people have to make money somehow," Katya said, matter-of-factly.

I reluctantly took the money. The stench was noticeable from the first second we had exited the bus, which was parked a good fifty yards away. And now I was heading closer to the source. As I drew closer, the stench became unbearable. I held my breath and entered. But that was still no defense against the putrid odor. I gagged. A babushka bathroom attendant glared at me from behind her desk. Yes, there was a desk *inside* the outhouse. And upon the desk sat a rusty moneybox.

I decided that I had seen—and smelled—enough. You couldn't pay me to piss in that stink-hole, let alone make me pay! I turned around and headed out, deciding that my best course of action would be to head toward some nearby bushes. But before I got there, I realized that I was being followed by the babushka bathroom attendant. She was wearing a dirty apron, suggesting that she was also responsible for cleaning the outhouse, on top of collecting money for it—therefore making it highly advisable to carry exact change.

Realizing that I put myself into a potentially tricky situation, Katya quickly rushed to my aid as the attendant yelled at me in Russian:

"Hey, boy. Where are you going? I'm sick and tired of you rich assholes always pissing in the bushes instead of my toilet!"

"You can keep talking all you want," Katya told her in Russian. "He doesn't speak Russian."

"Is this your foreigner?" the woman demanded to know.

"Yes," Katya replied.

"Then you tell your foreigner if he dares piss or shit in the bushes, I'll throw chlorine on him. You hear me?"

Clearly, the chlorine wasn't being used to clean the outhouse.

"Bobby, I strongly recommend that you pay this woman and use her toilet," Katya said.

Realizing that I had no other choice, I reluctantly paid the babushka and headed back toward the foul-smelling outhouse—refusing to take my change from her shit-stained hand.

I struggled to hold my breath for as long as possible as I pissed into a seemingly bottomless pit. An empty toilet paper roll hung on a roller, which was loosely anchored to the vomit and shit-smeared wall.

And before I was finished, the babushka entered the bathroom and— standing no more than five feet behind me—continued to berate me in Russian, which, of course, made it almost impossible for me to continue to pee, despite that my bladder was still half full. Meanwhile, Katya stood outside, listening to all of this take place.

"You rich assholes think you can piss and shit wherever you want and go to Yalta, while I spend my life slaving away in this restroom."

I tried my best to ignore her and to continue peeing, knowing that it would be my last chance for a while. After I shook off the last drops of urine, I walked past the attendant and over to the sink, where I washed my hands with water more yellow than my pee. I decided to pass on using the filthy remnants of what used to be a bar of soap.

"You're lucky I don't lock you in here!" the attendant shouted, shaking her ring of keys, reminiscent of a prison warden, before returning to her desk.

As I walked out, I nervously smiled and muttered a meek "Spasibo," but was quickly reminded again that Ukraine is not for the meek and mild. The attendant gave me the Ukrainian equivalent of a middle finger— putting her thumb between her fore and middle fingers. I had learned this earlier when playing a seemingly innocent game of "got your nose" with Katya, standing there in confusion as she slapped my hand away, deeply offended.

Katya was waiting for me outside, shaking her head, and laughing at the absurdity of the situation. She took my arm, and as we headed back toward the bus, filled me in on what the babushka attendant had been shouting at me.

34

GASPRA

We arrived at our destination, the resort town of Gaspra, just after the break of dawn. Located on the Black Sea, this was the place Leo Tolstoy called home in the early twentieth century. But despite its impressive landscape, Gaspra was essentially Dnipropetrovsk on a mountain, in terms of architecture and everyday hassles.

My first clue that our stay there was going to be anything but relaxing was right after the bus dropped us off at the base of the mountain. Cousin Andrei's apartment building was quite a ways up. So with luggage in tow, we climbed upward ... and upward. Already feeling out of sorts from the bus ride, this sweaty uphill walk was not helping in any way. Just like anywhere else in Ukraine—no matter how seemingly beautiful on the surface—it isn't long before you just want to say "fuck this" and leave. This was most definitely a "fuck this" moment.

We passed by the shell of an unfinished apartment building, which Katya explained had been abandoned since the collapse of the Soviet Union, much like the Hotel Parus on the riverfront in Dnipropetrovsk. A hundred feet or so away was Andrei's apartment building. Looming over it was Ai-Petri Mountain, rising high above the Black Sea.

Once inside, we headed up a dark stairwell until we reached Andrei's apartment. Andrei—who spoke very limited English—greeted us enthusiastically, introducing us to his wife, Tanya and their two cute little girls—Masha and Dasha (who, to me, sounded like two of Santa's reindeer). Both Andrei and Tanya kissed us eagerly on both cheeks. The whole greeting process took over five minutes. Dasha was instantly afraid of me and would *dash* out of a room whenever I entered. Andrei was a doctor in his late thirties with a mischievous, boyish face, a "know-it-all" attitude, and a tendency to answer questions with a long, drawn-out "Daaaa." He was the son of Sergei's older brother—Anatoliy—who had passed away from cancer when Katya was seven.

Tanya showed us to our room, which featured a majestic view of the Black Sea (which was not black, but rather more of a bright, vivid blue) hundreds of feet below. Of course, the screenless windows were closed tight and shrouded in curtains. God forbid that such a beautiful view be on display and accompanied by a relaxing sea breeze. Once Tanya had left us to our own devices, I decided to take matters into my own hands and open curtains and windows. The breeze was absolutely splendid.

Before our brunch, I took a much-needed shower. I already knew that taking a shower in Ukraine is easier said than done. This time, I was treated to the unique concept of a shower that shared the same faucet as the sink. And there was also no shower curtain. So essentially, you had to stand in the tub, turn the sink faucet towards the tub and splash yourself with water, while simultaneously trying not to get any water on the floor.

Following my shower, I headed into my room, only to discover that the windows had been closed again and the curtains drawn. I was determined not to lose this battle, so I opened them again and went to meet up with everyone for our meal. This window war would be on-going for the duration of our stay.

Tanya had prepared a delicious meal of borscht and roast chicken. The borscht was much different than the kind I was accustomed to from Elena. It had the same basic flavor, but it was a lighter color than Elena's and did not have meat.

As we ate, the discussion—masterfully translated by Katya—centered on politics and history, most of which made little sense to me. Asking questions seemed to only confuse me more. At some point, we got onto the topic of World War II. This is where I "learned" from Andrei that the U.S. had nothing to do with winning the war—at least against the Nazis. I tried to remain diplomatic, suggesting that both the U.S. *and* Soviet forces had a hand in this, but it did little to convince Andrei otherwise. Considering what the Nazis had put Ukrainians through, I decided to leave well enough alone. I also learned from Andrei that the U.S. Olympic hockey team had, in fact, not beaten the Soviet Union in the 1984 Olympics—a "miracle on ice" indeed! And furthermore, U.S. astronauts had never actually set foot on the moon. Turns out, I had a lot to learn about the U.S. and its complete lack of achievements.

Following our meal, Andrei brought out a bottle of Madeira wine. Since both Katya and I were not familiar with this particular wine, Andrei told us the story of how it came to be. Apparently, the Madeira Islands were a port of call for most ships heading to both the New World and the East Indies. Legend has it, over the course of long sea voyages, wines from Madeira were exposed to extreme heat under the harsh sun, which transformed their flavor ... and potency. This was first discovered when an unsold shipment of wine returned to the islands following a round trip. The locals took to the taste and before long, Madeira was putting out a label called *vinho da roda* ("wines that have made a round trip"), which became popular in Great Britain, Russia, North Africa, and the American colonies. I later found out that Madeira wine had been used to toast the U.S. Declaration of Independence—although I'm quite sure that Andrei would refute that fact. Madeira wine is now made by heating the wine up to high temperatures for an extended period of time. As a result, the wine is extremely robust and can live quite a while after being opened.

I have a feeling the particular bottle we had was both left out in the sun and opened longer than recommended. Perhaps it was from the original shipment? The effect it had on me was hallucinogenic to say the least, much in the manner I would have expected from absinthe. According to Katya, after drinking a couple of glasses, I got up from the table and wandered off to my room. When she looked in on me, I was staring at the billowing curtains, proclaiming that I was seeing a ghost. Katya tried her best to convince me that there was no ghost, but it was to no avail. Tanya used this as an opportunity to shut the windows yet again.

None of this mattered to me, as I was now completely on my own planet, laughing much in the manner I did when under the influence of vodka. But the overall effect was quite different than vodka. For starters, it made me more giddy and less zombie-like. Furthermore, I seemed to have more control of my body. In fact, at one point during the evening, I vaguely remember attempting to do the splits in the hallway. My sore groin attested to that very fact the next morning. Katya forced me to eat some more food, which helped bring me back down to earth.

Later that night, while Katya was helping me turn my couch into a bed, Tanya came in, noticing the once-again opened windows and announced:

"You might want to shut your window. They're burning trash."

Burning trash? I stared blankly, struggling to fully process her warning. I had so many questions. Questions such as: *what exactly did this trash entail?* Not wanting to find out exactly what this would smell like, I heeded her warning and shut the windows.

Only in Ukraine could a calm, relaxing sea breeze be ruined by the stench of burning trash.

35

FAT MAN AND THE SEA

The following afternoon, Katya and I set out for a beach—or *Plyazh* in Russian—which I had initially misheard as "splash," thinking that Katya was asking me if I wanted to "go for a splash." I was initially excited, but my enthusiasm quickly waned from the moment we walked out of the door of the apartment building. To get to the beach, we had to walk all the way down the mountain. Perhaps, if it were a direct path, it wouldn't have been so bad. But the road zigzagged, taking its good old time. By the time we reached the beach, I was ready for a nap.

The first thing I noticed was a hand-painted sign showing a happy couple holding drinks in their hand, while their helpless child was drowning in the water behind them. The message? "Please don't leave your children unattended by the water while you get wasted."

Being that we were at a beach, I mistakenly assumed that several hours of relaxation lay ahead. But when the beach consists of large pebbles and stones about three inches in diameter, rather than warm, soft sand, relaxation is difficult. Walking on it hurt like hell. And lying on it was no picnic, either. How Katya could so gracefully walk upon the rocks showing zero discomfort whatsoever was beyond me. Apparently, I was just an all-American wimp. Then again, the rocks were further evidence of the constant state of discomfort known as Ukraine. The only thing more uncomfortable to deal with than the rocks was the abundance of men in Speedos.

I persuaded Katya to head toward a cement patio area overlooking the beach. Surely some temporary comfort could be found on the deckchairs there. And by temporary, I mean until the arrival of a swarm of angry Ukrainian bees that forced us back down onto the rocks. As it turned out, there was a trick to achieving some level of "beach" comfort. This consisted of essentially wiggling yourself into the rocks, until they formed a sort of a rocky mold that conformed to your body position. The trick was to make sure the position you settled into was a comfortable one, otherwise, you would be forced to re-shape the rocks to fit your new position.

Shortly after we had settled into our rocky molds, something caught my eye: a rather large gentleman in a tight Speedo. Any man in a Speedo is a disturbing sight. But this particular man weighed at least 300 pounds. He was standing on the edge of a pier, surrounded by friends who were urging him to jump. However, perhaps out of fear of displacing every drop of water out of the Black Sea, he was having major doubts. I watched, transfixed, as he struggled with his existentialist crisis, staring into the water for at least two full minutes. His friends continued to goad him into jumping.

"Bobby … stop staring!" Katya exclaimed.

"I can't stop now. I have way too much time invested into this," I said, as Mr. Speedo stepped closer to the edge. I could sense that he was finally reaching the level of courage needed to take the plunge. But then, he took a step back. For a split second, I feared that he was going to simply walk away. But no, he was taking a step back so he could gain enough momentum to clear the pier. I was fully expecting that he would simply plop himself down into the water. But not Mr. Speedo. He was going in with grace. And by grace, I mean an elegant, perfectly formed dive that was Olympian in every sense of the word. In fact, his form was so amazingly aerodynamic, he hardly registered a splash.

Several seconds went by and Mr. Speedo still had not surfaced. I began to worry that something had gone horribly awry. But I just wasn't looking in the right place. He was already about two hundred feet away from the pier. Not only was he a skilled diver, but he also had the speed and agility of Michael Phelps. This was further confirmed by the speed with which he swam back to the pier. From that moment forward, I vowed never to make assumptions about girth and athletic prowess ever again.

Inspired by the display we had just witnessed, Katya and I headed into the warm water of the Black Sea.

Several hours later, we headed back to the apartment. And by the time we had finished our arduous climb back up the mountain, we were drenched in sweat and utterly exhausted. At that point, there was nothing I wanted more than a refreshing swim.

Later that night, we returned to the beach with Andrei, who drove us down, along with some of his friends. At night, the Black Sea truly did earn its name. It was like staring out into a black abyss and an incredible sight to behold.

That evening marked my first night swim in the ocean—a truly unforgettable experience. After swimming out about one hundred feet or so, I decided it was too dark and too deep to go any further and found a large rock to stand on, which allowed me to keep my head above water with my feet firmly planted. Katya, on the other hand, insisted on swimming out another hundred feet. I knew that the gentlemanly thing to do would have been to accompany her. However, I was hoping my gentle plea not to swim any further would have done the trick. It did not. Within seconds, it was too dark to see her. Fortunately, I could still hear the splashing of her feet, so I knew she was okay. But suddenly, the splashing stopped.

"Katya?" I said, fearfully.

No response.

"Katya?!" I said louder.

Suddenly, the splashing was heard again.

"Are you okay?" I asked.

"Yeah. Just went under. Thought I saw something."

"What do you mean by *something?*" I asked.

These are words you normally don't like hearing when you are standing out in the middle of a vast sea. Despite my fear, it was an incredibly beautiful sight to behold. Everything was so calm and peaceful. Above was a clear, starry sky punctuated with a full moon.

But like everything else in Ukraine, it was only a matter of time before something ruins the moment. Suddenly, two lights appeared below me, slowly drawing nearer. *What in the hell was that? A Russian submarine? Aliens?* The lights began to circle the rock upon which I was standing.

From nowhere, Katya emerged onto the rock, scaring the hell out of me.

"Relax! It's me," Katya said, calming my nerves.

"What the hell is that?" I whispered, pointing toward the lights.

"Scuba divers."

They continued encircling the rock. Upon closer inspection, I not only saw the scuba divers, but I saw the flashlights they carried in one hand … and the pointed spear guns they held in the other. Fearful that climbing off the rock would inspire them to shoot, we waited several minutes for them to leave. Once they had left, we decided that it was probably in our best interest to head back to shore and call it a night.

36

YALTA EXCURSIO

The next morning, Katya and I headed into Yalta, which was about a fifteen-minute route van drive away. Yalta—much like Kiev—had a more modern, "westernized" feel to it. What Yalta also had in its favor was that it was located on the Black Sea—which is perhaps the only thing Ukraine can't find a way to totally uglify. But they certainly tried. If Yalta was in the United States, it probably would have looked something like Miami Beach, lined with luxury resorts and condos that took full advantage of its seaside setting. Instead, there were rows of Soviet-style apartment buildings nowhere close to the water. At least the city square was on the water. A large stage stood in the center of it, where an amateur Russian hip-hop group attempted to rap. The rest of the square was filled with numerous attractions and kiosks, including rides, bungee jumping and exotic animals, including monkeys, muzzled bear cubs, and parrots forced to pose with tourists for a photograph if one was so inclined to shell out fifty grivnas.

Across the square, opposite the stage, I noticed a small set featuring a jungle backdrop. I assumed that some entrepreneurial Ukrainian with an exotic pet had decided to go all out. But what I saw just about made my jaw drop. As we got closer, I saw two African men in full tribal garb— including grass skirts and spears, dancing to the beat of their own bongos. I had to take a picture of this obscenely racially stereotypical display, so I pulled out my camera. But just as I was about to snap a photo, both men waved their fingers at me—in rhythm—as if to say "Don't you dare … unless you are willing to pay" as they continued to dance. So we walked away. And when I was at a safe enough distance, I pretended to take a picture of the entire landscape, aiming the camera in their general direction and then zooming in. Moments later, a group of girls paid to pose with the tribesman. Apparently, a black man in Ukraine is truly an exotic novelty, on the same scale as bear cubs and parrots wearing skull-and-crossbones eye patches.

We headed toward a booth that was advertising excursions to various historical sites around Crimea. As we perused the various options, a shady-looking man wearing tight leather pants, an untucked white dress shirt, and sandals with black socks approached us.

"You want best tour?" he said, "... well follow me." And so we did, toward a row of route vans. Of course, I had no idea what was going on because I was once again under a strict "no English" ordinance.

"Wait here," the man instructed as he approached one of the vans and started speaking with the driver. After a few moments of intense negotiation, he walked back over to us and presented us with two tickets. Katya paid him and next thing I knew, we were climbing into the back of a hot, stuffy van that would take us on our grand tour of Crimea. The tour was officially sold out, but "sold out" in Ukraine simply means "let's negotiate." And that's exactly what Katya had done.

In an attempt to breathe in the oppressive heat, I tried to open a window, but it only went down two inches, doing next to nothing to improve airflow. I knew better than to expect air conditioning this time around. And this was even worse than the bus.

"Bobby ... can you wait here?" Katya asked. Then, out of the blue, she stood up and made toward the door.

"Where are you going?" I asked in a panic.

"Since we have a few minutes to spare, I'm going to see an old aunt who lives nearby. She's been sick, so I think I'd better stop in to say hello while I have the chance. It could well be the last time I'll get to see her."

"You're going to leave me here by myself?" I asked, confused by this sudden turn of events.

"You need to hold our spot," Katya replied, adding "don't worry ... we have plenty of time. I'll be back before we have to leave."

As apprehensive as I was to be left alone, Katya convinced me that I would be fine. But it turned out, my concerns were completely justified. After about fifteen minutes, the driver started up the engine. *Should I be worried? What if they leave without Katya?* I looked at my watch and realized that we still had fifteen minutes before our scheduled departure. But judging by the driver's body language, it was time to go. After about a minute or so, the driver shut off the engine, got up, walked to the back of the van, and stood before me. He said something in Russian that I couldn't understand.

"*Nyet*, English," I said in desperation, drawing stares from all of the other passengers.

But apparently, that meant nothing to him, so he repeated what he had told me, only louder.

"*Nyet*, English!" I repeated, louder.

An attractive, young woman seated a row in front of me turned and said in broken English: "He wants to know where your friend went."

"She went to visit a relative. She'll be back any minute."

The woman translated for me.

"When will she be back?" the man demanded. The woman translated for me again. However, her English was so choppy, I had to ask her to repeat it several times.

"Any minute," I said.

The driver muttered something else in Russian, kicked my backpack, and returned to his seat.

The woman did not translate this final comment, but instead simply offered me a look of pity. It was all she could do. In the meantime, there was nothing I wanted to do more than to disappear off the face of the earth, as all of the other passengers continued staring at me.

Several minutes later, Katya returned. The driver greeted her by pointing at me, shouting: "Is this your foreigner?"

"*Da*," Katya said, heading to the back of the van to join me in embarrassment—not to mention the increasingly oppressive heat.

Several minutes into our trip, when I couldn't take it any longer, I once again risked the ire of our driver by begging Katya to ask if he could put on the air conditioning. And lo and behold, he did! But less than two minutes later, he turned it off, never to be turned on again. I should have known better.

Meanwhile, Katya quietly translated all of the historical information that the tour guide was passing along—clearly to the annoyance of the other passengers. I found a great deal of it interesting, but for the most part, it was irrelevant without further context. And considering the heat, it was really hard to focus. The large amount of body odor swirling around the packed route van certainly didn't help matters.

Our first stop was the Livadia Palace, the site of the Yalta Conference, where Stalin, Churchill, and Roosevelt had convened in 1945 to discuss Europe's post-war reorganization. The Livadia Palace itself was the former summer retreat of Nicholas II, the last Tsar of Russia. It now functioned as a museum. But of course, as Ukrainian luck would have it, we happened to arrive on the only day of the week that the museum was closed—on a Wednesday of all days. But even though we couldn't go inside, I was able to stand on the exact spot where the triumvirate of world leaders had posed for their famous photo.

Our second stop was the popular resort town of Sevastopol, the second largest port in Ukraine (after Odessa). The city was formerly home of the Soviet Navy's Black Sea Fleet and still retains a significant Russian naval presence. The city also has one of the warmest climates in Ukraine, attracting many tourists. Our driver informed us that the Soviet Navy used to carry out top secret training missions for dolphins that were used in special undersea missions.

We approached a small foot bridge that is affectionately known as the "Bridge of Loving Couples." On this particular afternoon, however, it appeared to be anything but, as evidenced by a young couple having an all-out screaming match. In fact, they were the only couple on the bridge, as everyone else stayed well clear. A dozen or so people, including those on our tour, stopped to watch the spectacle unfold.

To be more specific, the shouting was very one-sided — as in the woman shouting unmercifully at her hapless lover. Translation proved difficult, as even Katya couldn't make out the gist of the argument. The woman began repeatedly striking her man over the head with her enormous purse, never minding the fact that its contents were pouring out all over the bridge. The poor man threw his arms over his head in self-protection, but the beating was so severe, he was on the ground within seconds. The woman continued to beat him with her purse, while simultaneously shouting an endless barrage of insults at him. He half-crawled, half-slithered off the bridge, before finally managing to pull himself to safety. By this point, it appeared that the woman had decided that her man had either been punished enough, or was simply out of energy. She helped him up, and crudely dusted him off before retrieving the scattered contents of her purse. The couple then walked away, hand-in-hand, as though nothing had happened.

With the coast clear, the pedestrians who had been watching the real-life soap opera traversed the bridge for the obligatory "Bridge of Loving Couples" hugs, kisses, and photos. Katya and I followed suit.

Our next stop was the Inkerman Cave Monastery of St. Clement, a medieval Byzantine monastery near Sevastopol, an incredible structure that was literally built into the side of a mountain. Contemplative Ukrainian Orthodox Christian priests with long beards and traditional cloth *klobuks* on their heads roamed the premises. I imagined that sustained contemplation must have been difficult, considering the constant rumble of passing trains directly across the road.

By now, I should have known that Ukraine was a place where *nothing* should come as a surprise. Being forced to wear a skirt before I could enter a monastery took surprise to a whole new level. And yet, there I was, putting on a skirt before entering a monastery. There was a reasonable explanation, however. Since I was committing the grievous sin of wearing shorts, it was imperative that I covered my bare legs upon entry. We were directed over to a chest filled with various articles of clothing, where I found a random cloth with a floral pattern that I wrapped around my waist. Katya located a scarf to wear on her head before we headed inside.

Once inside, I stood there in my skirt, awe-inspired, contemplating the centuries of devotion and spirituality that the stone monastery walls must have absorbed. But then, of course, a passing train rumbled the walls, breaking my concentration.

Our final stop was the ruins of an ancient Greek settlement. I had no idea that the Greeks had anything to do with Ukraine. Yet sure enough, here were the ruins to prove it, sitting on the shore of the vivid blue Black Sea, which glistened and sparkled in the sun. I learned that Greek settlers had actually inhabited a number of colonies along the peninsula, including this particular one—the city of *Chersonesos Taurica* (Tauris Peninsula) near modern-day Sevastopol.

Before we could enter the site of the ruins, I had to first endure yet another babushka battle. And once again it was on account of my camera. As the babushka gatekeeper took my ticket, Katya went on ahead, unaware that I was being denied entry because of the camera case attached to my hip. At least that's what I interpreted the woman pointing at my camera case to mean. I naturally assumed no cameras allowed. But I was apparently being asked a question … a question I could not understand. I desperately peered through the gate in hopes of spotting Katya, but I couldn't locate her. In the meantime, the attendant was growing impatient, as was the line of people behind me. As the woman continued jabbering away at me in Russian, clearly refusing to accept the fact that we did not share a common language, Katya thankfully and finally appeared back at the gate and to clarify the situation.

I was essentially being told that if I wanted to take my camera inside, I would have to pay extra. On principle, I refused to have to pay to use my own camera, so we took the camera back to the route van. I would later regret this decision, considering how absolutely breathtaking the site was. It now only exists in my memory.

As we headed back to Yalta, Katya realized that we were going to be passing right through Gaspra. So rather than driving all the way back to Yalta, Katya asked the driver if he could drop us off on the side of the road. To my surprise, he obliged and dropped us off … free of charge! We headed toward what we assumed was Andrei's apartment. After a few minutes, however, Katya began to realize that things just didn't seem right (all of the buildings looked the same to me, so I was no help). This became especially obvious when we arrived at a spot that *should* have been Andrei's apartment building. We assumed that we had walked down the wrong street, since street signs are a foreign concept in much of Ukraine. After more futile searching, Katya stopped a couple walking toward us:

"Excuse me? Is this Gaspra?" she asked the couple.

"Gaspra?" the man said with a chuckle.

"What's going on?" I asked.

"This isn't Gaspra," the man explained. "Gaspra is the next village over."

Katya thanked them and we started making our way down to the main road in search of a route van stop. As much as we wanted to give him the benefit of the doubt, we were pretty sure that the driver purposely did this to get back at us for daring to ask him to drop us off without any form of payment—or perhaps, to get back at Katya for making us all wait to depart for our journey to begin with. In any event, we finally found a route van stop on the main road and headed back to the real Gaspra, a ten-minute drive down the road.

Katya later told me how this incident reminded her of a famous Russian TV movie—*Irony of Fate*—which is shown every New Year's Eve in Ukraine and Russia—a sort of Russian equivalent to *It's a Wonderful Life*. The plot revolves around the fact that all of the Soviet-era apartment blocks look completely identical, and even have identical door keys—as alluded to in the introductory narration, "building standard apartments with standard locks."

In the movie, a group of friends meet up in Moscow to celebrate New Year's Eve. They all get drunk toasting the upcoming marriage of the central male character, Zhenya. One of the friends, Pavlik, has to catch a plane to Leningrad. Both Zhenya and Pavlik pass out. The others cannot remember which of their unconscious friends is supposed to be catching the plane, and they mistakenly decide that it is Zhenya and put him on a plane. He wakes up in Leningrad, believing he is still in Moscow, stumbles to a taxi and, gives the driver his address. It turns out that in Leningrad there is a street with the same name, with a building at his address which looks exactly like Zhenya's. The key fits in the door of the apartment with the same number. Inside, even the furniture is nearly identical to that of Zhenya's apartment. Zhenya is too drunk to notice any difference, climbs into bed, and falls asleep.

Later, the real tenant, Nadya, arrives home to find a strange man sleeping in her bed. To make matters worse, her fiancé arrives before she can convince Zhenya to get up and leave. Her fiancé becomes furious and storms out. Zhenya leaves to get back to Moscow but there are no flights until the next morning. Thus the two are compelled to spend New Year's Eve together. At first they continue to treat each other with animosity, but gradually their behavior softens and they fall in love. In the morning, and with a heavy heart, Zhenya returns to Moscow. Meanwhile Nadya reconsiders everything and, deciding that she might have let her chance at happiness slip away, takes a plane to Moscow following Zhenya, easily finding him in Moscow, since their addresses are the same. Life certainly imitates art. More often than we usually care to admit.

37

ON TOP OF AI-PETRI

It should be abundantly clear by now that I'm not exactly the most physically gifted person on the planet. I am certainly not out of shape, but when it comes to sports and coordination, I pretty much suck. I might surprise myself every now and then, but am usually brought back down to earth fairly quickly.

After embarrassing myself against Kostya, the Champion's son, on my previous visit, I was about to get a second chance.

"Bobby ... get dressed," Katya said, waking me from a deep sleep. "We're going mountain climbing."

I must have misheard. Or was I dreaming?

"What?" I asked.

"Get dressed. We're going mountain climbing today," Katya repeated.

"Seriously?" I asked.

"Yes, seriously. Why not?"

Mountain climbing—for many reasons—had never been high on my list of ambitions. Yet, here I was in Ukraine, about to be dragged against my will to the top of the looming monstrosity behind Andrei's apartment building, aka *Ai-Petri*.

It certainly didn't help that my shoes weren't equipped to handle the rigors of mountain climbing. They were both new and white. By the end of the day, they would be neither. And they had zero traction.

While I was putting on my shoes, Andrei appeared with an enormous hiking bag on his back.

"Are we camping?" I asked, half-joking and half thinking it wouldn't surprise me if we were.

"Nyet," Andrei replied, not offering any indication as to what would possibly necessitate the need for a bag of that magnitude. He carried a hiking stick and his shirt was also unbuttoned, shamelessly revealing his pudgy mid-section. The Ukrainian dough boy.

After a quick breakfast, we headed out the door and toward the base of the mountain. I snapped a photo as we stood at the base. Andrei told us that as far as mountain standards go, Ai-Petri was considered small. It was a mere 4,000 feet tall. *Small my ass!* And with that, we began our grueling climb. Of course, Katya and Andrei had no trouble whatsoever. So naturally, I kept falling behind. Katya and Andrei demanded that I pick up my pace. I insisted that I was pacing myself so I could actually make it to the top alive.

"You're too slow," Katya said.

"Well go on without me then," I retorted, struggling to catch my breath. "I'll be fine on my own."

There were a few times when I completely lost sight of my climbing companions, but then I would finally spot Katya, waiting for me five hundred feet or so away. For Andrei, this was a *daily* form of relaxation. I had never felt *less* relaxed.

"How can you do this every day?" I asked, panting, as I tried to catch up for the umpteenth time.

"It is easy," Andrei said with a sly grin. "My only regret is that this mountain is not bigger."

Another thing I didn't understand was the complete and utter lack of wildlife. I didn't see a single woodland critter, or hear the chirping of any birds. I did see a small lizard of some sort, sitting on a sun-drenched rock. It may have been dead.

Hindering my ability to keep up had less to do with motivation and more with the lack of traction on my shoes. Anytime we came across a steep grade, for every ten feet forward, I would slide five or six feet backwards. Although this might be a suitable metaphor for life, it is certainly not the most efficient way to climb a mountain. This especially became disconcerting during moments when we had to walk on the edge of a very steep—not to mention high—ledge. At one point, I wedged a rock out of place, causing it to fall far, far below. My first concern was falling to my death. My second concern was that the fallen rock could have resulted in somebody else's death, hundreds of feet below.

After watching me struggle for far too long, Andrei finally pulled out two collapsible walking sticks from his pack, which were essentially ski poles. Unfortunately, rather than aiding me on my journey, all these sticks managed to do was give me two additional, uncoordinated limbs to wrestle into a twisted mess. I never fully mastered proper usage of these poles, using them instead as spears or stakes that I drove into the ground, creating a sort of leverage that would help pull me up, until the next time I fell, moments later.

The fact that the poles were velcroed to my wrists turned this experiment into an unmitigated disaster that resulted in me helplessly falling flat on my back like an overturned turtle. Meanwhile, Katya and Andrei watched from a ledge up above as I struggled to get up. But could anyone really blame me? It didn't dawn on me that once I was down for the count, the rational thing to do would have been to remove the straps from my wrists, rather than rolling haplessly with all my limbs and poles in the air like an overturned roly-poly.

"Take the poles off!" Katya shouted down at me.

And so I did. Permanently. I was better off without them (but not by much). And so, our climb dragged on. And on. At one point, I thought we had reached the top, only to find out we had reached the half-way point. Two hours later, we were finally close to the summit. Andrei, clearly not impressed with my hiking abilities, pointed out that it normally took him a half hour to accomplish what had taken us four hours.

As we approached the summit, I noticed a dozen or so tourists milling around. I found this surprising because we had not encountered any other people during our entire hike. Once we reached the summit, an entire Tatar village came into view. It turned out that there was actually a road to the summit. We had just happened to take "the path less traveled."

Tatars (or Tartars)—a name most likely known to the outside world from the white, creamy sauce that compliments fish dishes—are a tribal group indigenous to Crimea. In 1944, they were forcibly expelled to Central Asia by Stalin's government, as a form of collective punishment on the grounds that they had "collaborated" with the Nazi occupation forces. After the collapse of the Soviet Union, the Tatars, although not exactly welcomed with open arms, began to return to Crimea. And apparently, one of the places they returned to was the top of ol' Ai-Petri.

The last thing I expected to find atop this mountain was human life. It felt as though we had stumbled upon an undiscovered planet—or at least continent. The camels and Tatars walking around in traditional garb certainly added to this sense that we discovered a hidden world. Like the land of Oz. Or Lawrence of Ukrainia.

We followed Andrei through the village center, which consisted of several ramshackle shops and cafes, reminiscent of a Western frontier town. Along the way was another batch of exotic animals muzzled and ready for their photo opportunities with tourists. The smell of shish-kabob wafted from enormous grills. After all, it is the Tatars whom Sergei can thank for his wonderful shish-kabob (*shashlik*). It was as though we had found an oasis in the desert. But as it turned out, it was all a mirage—a proverbial pulling out the tablecloth from beneath us: Andrei had no intention of letting us stop for a bite. After all, why should we have rewarded ourselves with food and drink after our arduous climb? Instead, we headed out of the village center and toward another summit way out in the distance.

"Wait! Can we stop to eat?" I asked.

Katya translated for Andrei, who replied:

"No. We must keep climbing. We eat later."

"But we still have to climb back down," I said, barely able to stomach the thought.

"The food ... it's no good," Andrei said. "It smells great. But it will make you sick." And he was probably right. After all, if a Ukrainian was telling me this, then it was most likely a good idea to listen. But that didn't negate the fact that I was starving. In fact, I even surprised myself in that I was considering eating food prepared in an ancient mountain village. But that was how hungry I felt. I may well have eaten out of a dumpster had the opportunity presented itself.

As we headed out of the market area, we walked along a road that was essentially a minefield of horseshit. Passing us by on horseback were Tatars, some of whom were galloping at full speed, bareback and bare-chested, toward an unknown destination.

"Where are we going?" I asked, praying that it wasn't to the aforementioned second peak.

"There!" Andrei said, pointing directly toward the aforementioned second peak.

"Seriously?!" I exclaimed.

At this point, I was having difficulty hiding my displeasure. Not that it was going to make any difference.

After heading through a patch of woods, we entered a clearing at the base of the next mountain. Out of nowhere, the sound of stampeding horses suddenly became audible. Seconds later, two horses burst out of the woods, riderless and galloping towards us at full speed. The horses raced past us. Moments later, two Tatars ran out of the woods, screaming for their runaway horses to return. They, too, also charged toward us, passing us by without even a glance. We never saw them—or their horses—again.

The meadow ended at a sloped edge overlooking Gaspra way down below. It was a breathtaking view—and for a brief moment, it made the long journey almost worth it. But as I stared at the town below, I was reminded of how far of a climb *down* we had, realizing just how truly breathtaking (as in literally taking my breath away) the descent was going to be.

I decided there and then that enough was enough. I was not going to climb the second peak.

Andrei suggested that we rest awhile before making a final decision. He produced some blankets from his giant backpack and what looked like food, wrapped in a newspaper. *So, there is food*, I thought to myself, relieved. Andrei proceeded to unwrap two smoked fish. Hungry I would remain. I may have been willing to eat out of a dumpster—but not smoked fish. Andrei handed one of the fish to Katya and we spread a blanket down under a nearby tree. Andrei found a tree of his own; he took a pee on one side before laying down on the other. Exhausted, Katya and I both quickly drifted off to sleep. We awoke to the sight of Andrei standing directly over us, gnawing on the remnants of his fish.

"So, Bobby! Ready to climb?" he asked.

I stood my ground and told him that I was going to stay behind. Katya decided to stay with me.

"Fine. I can do it faster alone," Andrei said. As he turned around to begin his ascent, his unbuttoned shirt flapped in the wind, as though he were the hero of a cheesy romance novel.

It turned out that he was right. Andrei made it up and back down the second peak in what seemed like a world record time. In fact, he was so fast that he caught me with my pants down—*literally!* Since there was seemingly nobody around for miles, Katya and I had decided to have a little "outdoor fun." Just as I had pulled my shorts all the way down to my ankles, I heard the rustling of footsteps through fallen foliage. And before I could pull them back up again, there was Andrei, standing before us, his unbuttoned shirt still fluttering in the breeze—an image branded into my memory for all eternity (just as I'm sure that the image of me with my shorts down was branded into his memory!). In one hand, he held his hiking stick, planted firmly into the ground. His other hand was hoisted above his waist, beneath the flap of his shirt.

We momentarily froze. Andrei simply uttered in a dispassionate, deadpan tone: "We should go."

Andrei gave no indication that he saw a single thing. Or maybe it was no big deal to him? He simply turned around and headed back into the clearing, leaving me to scramble to pull up my shorts.

Taking a deep breath and puffing out his chest, Andrei proclaimed: "There's nothing like mountain air," before we began our long, awkward journey back down the mountain. I guess five months of daily visits to the gym couldn't compare to a lifetime of "being Andrei."

As we passed through the Tatar market again, something caught my eye. It was a funicular tram, whose sole purpose was to take tourists all the way down the mountain, eliminating the painfully unnecessary need to descend by foot.

"Hey, let's take this!" I suggested excitedly, as though I was the only one who was aware of its existence and wanted to share my great discovery with Katya and Andrei.

"Nyet. We walk," Andrei said sternly.

I pleaded my case a little harder.

"Okay. Fine," Andrei said, clearly annoyed. "You take the funicular. I go by foot."

"Sounds good to me," I said. Andrei seemed surprised that I was actually taking him up on his offer. We headed toward the funicular's entrance, only to discover that there was a two-and-a-half hour wait.

"You've got to be kidding me!" I said in what was becoming my familiar Ukrainian refrain.

"Let's take a cab," Katya suggested.

"Even better," I said. Across the road were dozens of cabs, desperate for desperate tourists like us. Katya negotiated a fair price, before parting ways with Andrei, who told us that he would still beat us back to the apartment.

Katya and I got into the cab, which like most cabs in Ukraine was a beat-up clunker with all of the requisite religious icons on display. Considering the ride we had to endure, we needed every possible bit of religious guidance. If there was a patron saint of taxi passengers, he certainly saved us that day.

The ride began casually enough, mostly due to the swarms of people, camels, and muzzled bears blocking the flow of traffic. But once we had made our way out of the market area and onto the long, winding road down the mountain, our nightmare journey began. Let me put it this way: the driver — who couldn't have been more than twenty — made Maxim look like a novice. At least Maxim had mostly straight roads on which to drive like a maniac. This guy did not, but he drove as though he did, oncoming traffic be damned. In fact, there were moments where I wondered if maybe his brake lines were cut, especially as we were whipped and jerked back and forth in the seatbelt-less backseat. This didn't seem to faze Katya, but at times, it literally felt as though we were spinning around and around in circles. As we approached yet another sharp turn, rather than slowing down to make sure there was no oncoming traffic, our driver simply honked his horn. There were definitely a few close calls, which resulted in oncoming traffic having to quickly swerve to the side of the road, narrowly avoiding hitting a tree head-on, or worse, swerving off the mountain entirely. Pedestrians simply had to dive or dart into the woods.

Forty-five minutes later (still more time than it typically takes Andrei to climb *up* the mountain), we made it to the base of the mountain ... somehow, miraculously, alive.

Sure enough, waiting for us at the apartment was Andrei. In fact, he had already taken a shower and was preparing shashlik for our final meal before we took the overnight bus back to Dnipropetrovsk. Andrei assured us that his meal would be far better than anything served up on that mountain.

We headed over to the nearby daycare facility where Tanya worked to make use of their grill and outdoor seating. Tanya showed around inside the facility, while Masha and Dasha played outside on the rusted playground equipment. A tabby cat roamed the grounds, following us wherever we went.

After the tour, we headed outside and squatted at a table designed for children under the age of five. The meal was excellent, but it was slightly marred by the constant reminder that another twelve hours on a stuffy Ukrainian bus was a mere couple of hours away.

Andrei had brought more Madeira wine. Like his uncles, Sergei and Vladimir, he had a propensity to fill my glass at every chance—sometimes when I wasn't looking. I somehow managed to convince myself that I was drinking very little since my glass was always full. I was just fortunate it wasn't vodka. But much like vodka, the wine created the desire for me to wander off like a toddler. Only this time, it was down a mountain.

I told Katya that I was going to use the restroom, which I did. And I vaguely remember spending a long time unsuccessfully trying to figure out how to flush the toilet, after which I wandered out through a different door. By the time Katya realized I had wandered off, I was nowhere in sight.

Katya, now used to this, teamed up with Masha to find me. They located me quite a ways down the road, sitting in a bus shelter.

"Where do you think you're going?" Katya asked, sitting down next to me on the bench.

"Waiting … for the bus," I mumbled.

"A bus to where?" she replied.

"Dnipropetrovsk," I slurred.

"That's not our bus stop. And, it's not time to leave yet," Katya explained.

By now, my alcohol-fueled escapes were becoming old hat.

And with that, Katya dragged me back to the daycare facility, where Andrei attempted to pour me more wine. Katya cut him off, reminding him of the long bus ride that awaited us that night.

"It is fine," Andrei rationalized. "It will help him to sleep on bus."

Still buzzing from the wine, the time had finally come to say our goodbyes. I looked up at Ai-Petri one last time in utter astonishment and was filled with an unexpected sense of pride, before slowly bowing my head in shame.

Before we left for the bus station, Masha, and Dasha presented Katya with a handmade illustration of a flag that was half American and half Ukrainian and completely surrounded by a heart. It was captioned: "To Katya: Good luck in America!"

Katya hugged them both. Tanya then gave both me and then Katya a big hug.

We headed outside, where a shirtless Andrei was waiting for us in his car. For a brief moment, I feared he was completely naked. Almost—he had nothing but a Speedo on. He planned on taking a dip in the Black Sea after dropping us off.

We headed for the bus terminal, clouds of black smoke emitting from both ends of the vehicle. Since the air conditioning did not work, our open windows were an open invitation for the smoke to come in.

When we arrived, Andrei helped us unload our bags from the trunk of the car, which barely fit due to the enormous case of vodka lodged in there.

Andrei then hugged me and whispered into my ear in English: "Climb high. Climb, Bobby."

"Thank you," I replied, as Andrei pulled me closer to his almost-naked body, before kissing me on both cheeks. Being hugged and kissed by a man in a Speedo could now be crossed off my bucket list.

Andrei then turned to hug Katya, saying something long and presumably profound to her, which caused her to tear up.

Katya explained how Andrei had told her that he was not sure whether he would be able to make it to our upcoming engagement party. He was mixed up in dirty politics and "legal matters" that often put his life in jeopardy. She didn't elaborate beyond that.

Andrei got back into his car, which sputtered and smoked toward the beach, before disappearing into a cloud of smoke.

Tired and sweaty, we were thankful to see that passengers were already boarding the bus to Dnipropetrovsk. We handed our bus tickets to the driver and went to look for our seats. The driver called us back.

"*Podazde!*" ("Wait!") he said sternly. "These tickets are not valid."

"What do you mean they're not valid?" Katya asked.

"Not valid," he repeated.

"But we bought them at the station," Katya replied.

"These seats are already taken," the driver said.

"How can they already be taken? We purchased these at the station in Dnipropetrovsk."

"That's Dnipropetrovsk. This is Gaspra. You need to buy tickets here."

"No. We already paid for our tickets," Katya insisted, refusing to back down.

"They are invalid. You cannot ride"

"Are there other seats?"

"No. Bus is full," the driver said, taking a ticket from the person next in line.

"I don't understand," I said, confused. "We have tickets!"

"It's a scam," Katya said, explaining how the bus station clerks in Dnipropetrovsk most likely had an arrangement with the clerks in Gaspra to oversell tickets (i.e., selling multiple tickets for the same seats) and pocket the extra money. The clerks in Gaspra would benefit since the duplication of tickets created a bidding war amongst desperate passengers. Seats go to the highest bidder.

Katya continued arguing with the bus driver, but he simply ignored us. At that moment, something inside me snapped. Maybe it was the wine?

Or the mountain air? Or just Ukraine? Regardless, I tore the bus driver a new asshole—in English:

"What the fuck is wrong with you people? I'm sick of getting fucked up the ass by the insanity of this motherfucking country! We have tickets, so you'd better let us the fuck on! Now!"

Even though the driver didn't understand English, I'm sure he understood tone. And I'm pretty sure he was familiar with the word "fuck."

My tantrum actually (sort of) worked—probably due to the simple fact that Ukrainians usually just accept the fact that this is how things are, mostly out of fear of retribution. I figured I had nothing to lose.

Now that this crazy foreigner had everyone's attention, the bus driver finally demonstrated some compassion by offering us a spot on the floor— for $200 U.S. dollars.

"You've got to be fucking kidding me," I said.

"If you don't like, then wait for next bus," the driver said. "Or walk."

Katya decided to take matters into her own hands and we headed inside the bus station, where she threatened to call the police. I was also pretty sure that I heard her invoke Sergei's name, but she later denied it. This threat must have struck a chord because a clerk accompanied us to the bus and demanded that we be let on board. We were shown to our seats, which were different than the seat numbers printed on our tickets. The seats were also located on opposite ends of the bus, which I'm sure was the bus driver's way of snatching at least some semblance of victory from the jaws of defeat since his superior had forced him to let us on.

As proud as we were that we had beaten the system, I couldn't help but think that all we had really done was screw over someone else who had rightfully purchased tickets for the seats we were now occupying. It's sad that so many Ukrainians are conditioned to passively accept what they're told. Nobody fights back. Nobody makes a stink. Because even if they did, the system would still find a way to get them in the end. It's how things were before the Soviet Union, during the Soviet Union, and now after the Soviet Union. And how things probably will always be—reminding me just how much we take for granted in the U.S.

And so we began our long journey back to Dnipropetrovsk. I'd had enough of Crimea. In fact, I'd had enough traveling period. Dnipropetrovsk felt safe, familiar, and inviting. It's amazing how quickly a strange place begins to feel like home.

As it turned out, the young, attractive girl sitting next to me could speak English and therefore understood everything I said during my rant. She explained that she had paid a bribe to get on the bus, never purchasing a ticket at all!

And with that, I drifted off to sleep. Our engagement party was fast approaching, and I needed all the rest I could get.

38

PSEUDO WEDDING, UKRAINIAN STYLE

The pinnacle of my second trip to Ukraine finally arrived—our engagement party, which was sort of a quasi-wedding for Katya's family who would be unable to attend our actual wedding in the U.S. So our engagement party was the next best thing. All that mattered to our guests were the two—yes, *two*—full days of celebration, which was typical of Ukrainian weddings. And this naturally meant lots of vodka.

Becoming officially married in Ukraine wasn't an option, due to the terms of Katya's visa. And sadly, only Sergei would be able to attend our real wedding, since the U.S. government rarely issued a visa to the spouse of a visitor from Ukraine, for fear that the visiting couple would try to stay past the length of their visa, or simply disappear.

Hours before the party, the apartment was bustling with out-of-town guests who treated me more like a curious novelty than an unwelcome foreigner as I had grown accustomed to with many of the strangers I had encountered in Ukraine.

While Katya and I finished getting dressed for the celebration, the guests headed outside into a light drizzle and piled into a private route van that Sergei had arranged through another of his endless connections.

I was waiting alone for Katya in the living room when she emerged in a gorgeous maroon dress and her hair professionally curled in ringlets—a portrait of exquisite beauty.

"You look so beautiful," I remarked as I stood up alongside her. With her high heels on, my head was literally level with her chest.

Meanwhile, Sergei—resplendent in a blue suit and bowtie—led us outside and toward a shiny, red Mercedes that he had somehow procured. Sergei and Elena drove separately in their car.

The light drizzle had turned into a steady downpour. "Too bad about the weather," I remarked.

"No, it's good," Katya said. "Rain on a wedding day is good luck."

"Sounds like something that was made up to make brides and grooms feel better about the fact that it is raining on their wedding day," I remarked.

"Yeah, probably so," Katya said, as it began to rain harder.

Minutes later, we arrived at the "hall," which was actually the kindergarten where Elena used to work as a doctor. It had been converted into a banquet hall for the occasion. The exterior was adorned with balloons and a giant banner that read, in handwritten Cyrillic:

Поздравляю, Бобби и Катя!
(Congratulations, Bobby & Katya!)

Uniformed police officers stood guard outside the entrance.

"Are they here because of us?" I asked.

"Yes, of course," Katya said.

"Let me guess. Connections?" I asked.

"Right," Katya said.

"But why?" I asked.

"For our security," Katya responded.

"Against who? Paparazzi?" I said sarcastically.

"Uninvited guests," Katya replied.

Meanwhile, about fifty of our *invited* guests stood outside the building, applauding our arrival. There were several unrecognizable faces—including a dapper gentleman who looked just like the Monopoly Man, complete with tux, top hat, and cane—but most people I recognized: the Champion, Kostya, Uncle Vladimir, Aunt Nina, and Karina. Maxim was there to provide "special service." And I was pleased to see Andrei, Tanya, Masha, and Dasha.

"So glad you could come!" I said to Andrei. He was *almost* fully dressed for the occasion, save for a few tufts of wild chest hair that popped out from his half unbuttoned dress shirt.

"Bobby ... never underestimate the power of the bribe," Andrei said with bravado. I didn't ask for clarification, but did find myself wondering if Andrei's "situation" had anything to do with the police presence.

The rest of the guests were distant relatives, friends of Katya, and friends and colleagues of Sergei and Elena. For the most part, everyone was in dressy casual fashion—men in short sleeved dress shirts and ties and women in sundresses or skirts. An attractive young lady in her early twenties was wearing a tutu. The scene reminded me of the grand finale of a romantic comedy.

After we were escorted out of the car by two of Sergei's attendants, Katya took me by the arm and we headed into the building. Each guest then individually showered us with congratulatory greetings, words of advice, hugs, kisses, unwrapped presents, and massive bouquets of flowers. Apparently, a gift table wasn't available.

We waited in the lobby as our guests were seated before we were formally introduced by the emcee. Formal Ukrainian celebrations typically include an emcee, who dictates when we should be eating, toasting, or dancing (or sometimes, all three at once). This particular emcee hired for our party was a blonde cougar of a woman in tight leather pants with a shrill voice.

Following a prolonged preamble, we were finally introduced, and welcomed with thunderous applause and a standing ovation. We headed to our seats at the head of the U-shaped banquet table, which was filled with numerous platters of roast beast. It reminded me of the final scene of "How the Grinch Stole Christmas."

After we took our seats, the emcee invited Sergei to present his opening remarks. Sergei took the mic, welcoming everyone and thanking them for being there for this special occasion. He ended his welcoming address with a toast—the first of nearly fifty toasts heard that evening—since Ukrainian custom requires each guest to provide one. Wisely, I decided to stick to champagne—but even that would turn out to be a mistake—not of the wandering variety, but rather of the porcelain god kind.

After the toast, the emcee invited us all to begin eating. Everyone eagerly tucked into their food, while I scavenged for anything I could stomach—which was sadly, and later, regretfully very little. My meal essentially consisted of bread and pickles. The widely-popular fish-floating-in-gelatin just wasn't going to cut it for me. As I continued my vain search for nourishment, the crowd began to chant in unison:

"*Gorko! Gorko! Gorko!*"

"What's going on?" I asked.

"*Gorko.* It means bitter," explained Katya, smiling.

"*Gorko! Gorko! Gorko! Gorko!*"

"I don't understand," I said.

"It means they want us to kiss to chase the bitterness of life away. Now kiss me, before you disappoint our guests."

I gave Katya a peck on the cheek, but the guests began chanting for more. I looked around the room, then at Katya.

"More," she pleaded.

"So I kissed her again, this time lightly on the mouth. But the crowd still wanted more. So I gave them what they wanted by kissing her with all my passion. As we kissed, the guests began to count each passing second. I stopped at eight. When I pulled away, my face was smeared in lipstick. Everyone laughed and cheered. This "gorko" business would happen a dozen or so more times before the night was over. And by then, the guests were counting to over thirty seconds.

After the first round of "gorko," the guests resumed eating. Standing along the wall around the perimeter of the room were students hired by Sergei to ensure that no shot glass or champagne glass remained empty for more than a few seconds.

After fifteen minutes or so, the emcee invited the first guest to give a toast. It was Katya's beloved Godmother—Tatiana—who, as Katya's English tutor, was indirectly responsible for bringing us together. She was one of the kindest, most genuine people I had encountered during my time in Ukraine. It also helped that she spoke fluent English. Tatiana first spoke in Russian:

"Dearest Katya. From the moment of your very first English lesson, I knew you were destined to one day leave us all behind. And I couldn't be more happy ... or sad. Happy, because I know you will soar to greatness. Sad, because we will have to witness your greatness from afar. We are all rooting for you. And we hope you will always hear our cheers no matter where you are."

She then switched over to English: "I will conclude with a quote from one of my favorite pieces of literature—*Romeo & Juliet*, which is fitting considering the occasion, but with a happier ending. 'Parting is such sweet sorrow, that I shall say good night till it be morrow.'"

Tatiana lifted up her glass, before adding "God bless you both."

As the evening wore on, we were treated to a variety of toasts, ranging from humorous to deeply profound and poetic. Some of our guests even recited poetry specially composed for the occasion. Take this poem by Uncle Vladimir, for instance:

They're always the same.
When we part.
Time turns memories into dreams.
When we part.

Bright joy turns to burning tears.
When we part.
No matter how many times we face it.
When we part.
It's always like the first time.
When we part.
Piercing the heart.
Goodbye.

By the time he got to the end of the poem, there wasn't a dry eye in the room. It was shortly after Uncle Vladimir finished his toast that I noticed he was drinking vodka from a spoon.

"Why is your Uncle drinking from a spoon?" I asked Katya.

"His doctor said he needs to limit his drinking because of his heart," Katya explained. "He thinks if he drinks from a spoon, then he's drinking less."

As the celebration progressed, I watched as Uncle Vladimir continued to drink spoonful after spoonful of vodka until his entire bottle was gone.

The next toast, quite possibly my favorite, was from a female colleague of Sergei:

"Katya, we wish you to have a mink on your neck, a Jaguar in your garage, a tiger in your bed … and a jackass who pays for it!"

The next "toast" belonged to the young lady in the tutu, the daughter of a family friend.

"So why exactly is she in a tutu?" I asked Katya.

"Because that's her talent," Katya replied, leaving me even more confused, and secretly hoping that there might be a fire-eater in the crowd.

Rather than actually saying anything, she had decided to perform a ballet number from *The Nutcracker*. When she was finished, the guests applauded wildly.

The emcee then invited Katya and me onto the dance floor for our first dance. The song was called *Tam De Ty Ye* ("There Where You Are") by Ukrainian popstar Ani Lorak. As we danced, I had to try at all costs to avoid burying my face into Katya's bosom, which was at my eye level.

"I feel like a midget," I said.

"You are a midget!" Katya replied. "*My midget.* We're what Ukrainians refer to as an Italian couple."

"Then it's a good thing I'm actually Italian!" I remarked.

"Well, only half," Katya said, as though I had somehow forgotten.

When the song was over, the guests were then invited out to the dance floor to join us for Sergei's favorite song, "Sharmanka." Everyone formed a circle around us, singing and dancing without a care in the world. And when I say everyone, literally *every* guest of every age came out to dance. Several more songs were played, including Russian pop and Ukrainian folk music (of course, Verka Serduchka drove everyone into a frenzy!).

Taking a break from dancing, Katya headed to the restroom. One of Katya's cousins approached me.

"Bobby. Hello," he said—a nervous, jittery man in his mid-twenties. "I want to practice English … to you, please."

"Sure," I replied.

"My English is not … as good."

"No. It's fine!" I said, urging him to continue.

"You like Jim Belushi, Hollywood actor?" he asked, reminding me of our bus ride to Yalta.

"I'm more of a John Belushi fan myself," I replied.

"I know not of this man. He is relation?"

"Yes," I replied. "They're brothers."

"Ah! Brothers. Brothers!" he repeated. He proceeded to slap me five, before walking away laughing.

Before I was able to process what had just transpired, Kostya—the Champion's son—approached me.

"So. Have you learned Russian yet?" he asked in a cocky, aggressive tone.

"I've picked up a few more words and phrases, but that's about it," I replied, trying my utmost to be cordial.

"Well don't you think it would be fair to your wife that you learn to speak her language?" Kostya responded.

Katya, returning from the restroom, scolded him in Russian.

"I want to learn," I explained. "But with school, I have not had the chance."

"Well, I suggest you find the chance," Kostya said, before walking away.

"Just ignore him," Katya said, leading me back to the dance floor.

I claimed his jealousy another victory.

A few minutes later, the emcee directed us all back to our seats for another round of toasts, followed by more eating and drinking.

The emcee then presented us with an apple filled with toothpicks.

"This is the apple of dispute," the emcee explained. "The reason for all evil. With this, you each take turns removing one of the toothpicks until all the toothpicks—or evil—are removed. However, it's not as simple as just removing the toothpick. After each toothpick is pulled, you must say something romantic to one another. And whoever ends up with the longest toothpick will be the one who wears the pants in the family."

"You go first," I said to Katya, who removed the first toothpick.

"*Ya lyublyu tebya*," she said.

I then removed a toothpick, before saying "*Ya lyublyu tebya, tozhe.*"

"Forever," Katya continued.

"And ever," I said.

And on and on this went until all twenty or so toothpicks had been removed. We then sorted through our pulled toothpicks to determine who pulled the longest one. As it turned out, I wouldn't be needing pants.

After another round of toasts and dancing, the emcee brought out a pair of baby pajamas. One leg had a blue ribbon wrapped around it and the other leg had a pink one. She proceeded to pass the pajamas around to each guest to put money down either leg. Katya explained that whichever leg ended up with the most money determined the gender of our first baby.

"What's if it's a tie?" I asked.

"Twins!" Katya replied.

"Do we get to keep the money?" I asked.

"Yes, of course," Katya said, laughing.

After the money was tallied up, it was announced that our first child would be a boy.

More toasts, dancing, and games followed. At one point, the guests had to pass a rolling pin from one person to the next using only their legs. Nothing like a bunch of drunk, elderly Ukrainians sporting giant rolling pin woodies! I was also forced to drink champagne out of Katya's shoe—a Russian wedding ritual. And just when I thought things couldn't get any stranger, the DJ played a swing version of "O' Little Town of Bethlehem." It took me a few seconds to realize what I was hearing, mostly because it was so out of context.

"Are they really playing this?" I asked.

"Playing what?" Katya asked.

"This song," I said.

"I asked the DJ to play jazz for you," Katya said.

"Then why is he playing Christmas music?" I asked.

"Is it not jazz?" Katya asked, puzzled.

"Well, it's *Christmas jazz*, so yeah ...," I replied with a wry smile.

"The guests don't know any better," Katya said as our guests became the first people in the world to slow dance to "O' Little Town of Bethlehem." Katya and I joined them. Sergei leaned over while dancing with Elena and said, enthusiastically:

"Bobby, jazz, da?"

"Da!" I said in reply. "'tis the season!"

When the song was over, we headed back to the table, where the emcee announced:

"And now, Bobby will entertain us on the saxophone!"

Everyone cheered.

"Wait! What?" I said. Surely this was a joke. But if the young lady in the tutu taught me anything, it was: prepare to show off your talent if you have one.

When Sergei presented me with an old, tarnished saxophone, I knew it wasn't a joke.

"Saxophone! Bobby!" Sergei said enthusiastically, imitating a jamming saxophonist.

"I can't do this here," I pleaded.

The guests began clapping in unison for me to perform.

"I don't really think you have much of a choice," Katya replied, smiling.

I looked around the room and realized that I truly did not have any choice. So I assembled the mildew-infested sax and started to jam, trying not to think about the dirty, used mouthpiece and cracked reed in my mouth. Having no sheet music, I was forced to improvise, playing the few riffs I knew: "The Star Spangled Banner," "When the Saints go Marching In," and even "Mary Had a Little Lamb." As I began to feel more comfortable, I started to really tear it up, showboating to our guests, walking right up to them and practically playing in their faces as I let loose a free-form jazz solo—perhaps the greatest of my musical "career."

It was shortly after my sax solo that I felt the beginnings of what would become a crippling headache. While the guests danced, we returned to the table. I began rubbing my temples, but I knew it was no use.

"It's because you haven't eaten much," Katya said. "You need to eat."

Katya convinced me to eat some cold chicken—despite my justified fear of eating any meat in Ukraine whose origin was unknown. For good measure, I nibbled on another piece of bread, but nothing helped alleviate my headache, nor the throbbing pain in my stomach, which began to feel like something repeatedly stabbing me from the inside. These symptoms would ultimately continue to worsen over the next three weeks. Upon my return home, I would experience the most excessive vomiting of my life, which helped contribute to a nearly twenty-pound weight loss, which landed me in the ER, before finally being diagnosed with a bacterial infection. So much for alcohol fighting off the germs. Perhaps I should have had more? Of course, Katya was concerned she was marrying a sickly person, just as her babushka warned her the previous summer.

"Let's go outside and get some fresh air," Katya suggested.

We headed out into the cool, spring night under a full moon, tipsy from champagne. I nodded at the two police offers standing guard outside the door of the school, but they chose to completely ignore me, as though on strict orders.

We climbed into a metal jungle gym and sat inside.

"Hearing all these toasts ... it just really hit me," Katya said, beginning to cry. "I'm leaving all these people who love me so much."

"You'll be back. It's not forever," I said, comforting her.

"Yes, but it will never be the same. It can't be. From now on, I'll only be a visitor."

"This will always be your home," I promised her.

I searched for something else to say, but all I could do was hold her, feeling her warm tears against my face.

"Can I ask you a question?" Katya asked.

"Of course."

"I know I asked you this before, but if it were really the other way around, would you leave everything you knew for me?"

"Of course I would," I said. "You know that."

She hugged me tightly and at that point, the magnitude of what was to become of our lives began to really hit home. And I couldn't help but feel like the Big Bad Wolf coming to steal a little girl from everything and everybody she knew and loved.

Sergei appeared, poking his head into the jungle gym.

"Everything okay?" he asked.

"*Da*, papa," Katya said, quickly wiping away her tears.

"It's almost time to say your goodbye toasts," Sergei replied.

"*Spasibo*, papa," said Katya.

Katya leaned over and hugged her dad.

"Take a minute," Sergei said, before heading back inside.

"We need to go in. The guests are waiting for our goodbye toast," Katya said.

"*Our* as in both of us?" I asked, nervously.

"Yes, that's generally what 'our' means," Katya replied. "Don't worry. I'll do most the talking. How's your headache?"

"*Bivaet huzhe*," I replied ("Things could be worse.").

Katya laughed through the remnants of her tears, as we headed back inside for the final round of toasts, leading up to our goodbye toast. Of course, a handful of goodbye "*gorkos*" were thrown in for good measure.

The final toast of the evening was given by Nastya, speaking on behalf of Sergei and Elena, who by that point were too emotional to take the mic. Nastya had to fight through tears to get her words out:

"Katya ... even after all of these years, you are still my little sister. That will never change. It seems like just yesterday, I was holding you in my arms when you were a small baby. Now, you are a grown woman about to leave your nest behind for good.

"Imagining a life without you around seems impossible. Yet, here we all are about to face that reality. We will never be the same. *Ukraine* will never be the same. We are all very happy for you. But because we—and especially I—love you so much, I am more sad than happy. At least right now in this moment. And I'm certain for several moments beyond this day. We know you will miss us, too."

Katya nodded in agreement, with tears brimming in her eyes.

"So I'll take comfort in knowing that I am not alone. And comfort in knowing that you are truly happy overall. That is the most important thing."

Nastya turned toward me.

"And Bobby. I know Katya is lucky to have you. But we hope you realize just how lucky you are to have Katya."

I nodded in agreement.

Nastya continued: "And we also hope you realize how much we'll miss Katya every moment that she's away."

Nastya turned back to face Katya.

"Katya … I know I have never said it often enough, but I will now: I love you so, so much. I hope you realize that. And remember, I will always be here for you."

Katya approached her sister and they shared a tearful embrace. Dimitri reached over and gave me a playful noogie, totally shattering the solemnity and spirit of the moment.

The emcee announced: "Now that everyone has had their say, we must prepare for the moment we all dread—the end of a party. The goodbye."

The emcee handed the mic over to Katya, who thanked everyone for coming, told them how much they would be missed, and promised that we would be back again soon. Next thing I knew, the mic was in my hand and somehow, the same muse who grabbed a hold of me during my jazz solo, inspired me to rattle off the following speech, made slightly awkward due to the fact that it had to be translated by Katya:

"I honestly don't know what I have done to deserve any of this—and most of all—Katya. I can't help but feel guilty knowing that I'm taking her away from all of you. Trust me, I know what it's like to miss her. And I haven't known her all her life like most of you have. I also know that most of you have not yet had the chance to get to know me, but I can promise you this …," I said, choking back tears, "she is in good hands."

"When I look around this room, all I see is how much all of you love Katya and how much of an obligation I have to provide her with as much love as you have provided her, plus more. I promise with every ounce of my heart to take good care of Katya. Whenever you miss her, please remember that as our love proves, love knows no boundaries. From the bottom of my heart, thank you."

The room remained silent for several long, excruciating moments, accompanied by the occasional sniffle. Finally, the crowd erupted into wild applause, leading to a long line of congratulatory hugs, kisses, handshakes, and well wishes.

"Please take good care of Katya," pleaded Katya's childhood friend, Yuliya. "We love her so much," she said with tears in her eyes.

"I promise," I said in reply, my headache throbbing more than ever.

Maxim approached us next. He shook my hand, looked me directly into the eye and said "special service for special people." The Champion and Kostya (aka Champion, Jr.) each gave me a handshake that came close to cracking bone. Champion, Jr.—in my estimation—gave Katya a few too many pecks on the cheek, seemingly catching the corners of her mouth. He knew it was his last shot.

Finally, Uncle Vladimir presented us with vodka in a clear, unlabeled bottle (which Sergei confiscated from us the next day for reasons not really clear to me, other than that it was "for our own good").

Our guests headed out boisterously into the rainy night, wandering off in various directions down the street in their drunken stupors. The young lady in the tutu did pirouettes around the corner. The Monopoly Man passed go. Several guests piled into route vans. Not a single person got into a personal vehicle; not a single person was sober.

And just like that, the party was over.

It was just us.

As we stepped outside, I realized I had left my camera on the table. I went back inside, where I decided to take one last picture. I took one final look around—shaking my throbbing head in astonishment at this whole surreal experience—before heading back outside. The two police officers who had guarded the front doors drove us back to the apartment. Once we arrived, my primary concern was to make sure that Sergei didn't catch wind of my inebriated condition and force me to do another death march. The only thing I had going for me was the fact that I had avoided vodka the entire evening.

Fortunately, the apartment was filled with too many guests scrambling for spots to sleep to allow for Sergei to take notice of my worsening condition. Katya handed me a couple of pills that she assured me worked miracles for headaches and stomachaches. She couldn't tell me exactly what they were, but I reluctantly took her word for it.

Once in her room, Katya quickly fell asleep. I lay awake, amazed at both my headache's—and stomachache's—continuing ability to grow worse. I began to wonder if the pills Katya gave me were making matters worse. They certainly weren't *helping*. I felt as though somebody had put my head into a vice, and was tightening it ever so slowly. Finally, I was forced out of bed and headed straight to the bathroom, where I preceded to puke my guts out. It was mostly champagne, with a few morsels of soggy bread, along with a smorgasbord of other miscellaneous food items that I had been forced to try. I even saw a few things that I was pretty sure I had not sampled!

As I hauled myself out of the bathroom, I noticed Sergei, limping down the hallway, his leg dripping with blood.

"What happened?" I asked in English.

"*Sobaka!*" Sergei replied, imitating a dog biting into something.

"Are you okay?" I asked.

Sergei nodded. Realizing that we reached the limits of our bilingual ability, we bid goodnight and headed our separate ways. I found out the next morning that Sergei was walking back from parking the car in his garage when a mutt—quite possibly the same one who had growled at us on my previous trip—guarding her puppies had sprung at him.

The next day—despite my massive hangover—the celebration continued with the guests who had spent the night, along with a few others who stopped by. Our meal consisted of cold leftovers from the night before, and once again, I didn't eat much. It was probably a wise decision; most of the food was also left sitting out overnight because it didn't fit in the fridge.

By late afternoon, all of our guests had left. And in their place was the growing realization that Katya had just two days to finish packing for her future and to say goodbye to life as she knew it.

39

KIEV

As excited as I was to bring Katya home with me, our final two days in Ukraine were two of the gloomiest days I have ever experienced, as I truly began to realize the magnitude of what both Katya and her parents were going through. I rationalized this guilt by reminding myself that this was the life they dreamed of for their daughter. Yet by the same token, I couldn't help but wish life in Ukraine didn't necessitate that desire in the first place.

Deep down, I'm sure they would have done anything to keep their daughter with them in Ukraine. It was truly an ultimate sacrifice on their part. And here I was, the American thief coming to steal what was rightfully theirs. As eager as Katya was to start her new life with me, preparing to say goodbye to her parents was the hardest thing she ever had to do in her life. I certainly didn't consider myself worthy enough of such a sacrifice. Somehow, Katya did. I almost felt compelled to call the whole thing off, to free myself from the guilt. But I loved Katya too much to do that. As a result, I was determined to do everything in my power to return the favor to Sergei and Elena by being the best possible husband for their daughter.

The night before our departure, Katya and I, along with Sergei, Elena, and Nastya gathered for our last supper. As would be expected, Sergei stood up to give a toast. Only, instead of vodka, his glass consisted of mineral water. In fact, he didn't even offer me a shot. This was the first time he had not taken a shot of vodka during a meal since my arrival. It was as though he didn't want to blur the memory of this final night with his little girl. Or maybe he was worried it would make him too melancholy?

Before he could utter a single word, he broke down in tears. He lowered himself to his seat, wiping away his tears with both hands completely concealing his face. Elena comforted him, remaining stoic with her usual demeanor. Her sadness went beyond tears. Sergei attempted to stand back up, but Elena silently urged him to remain seated.

"Let your tears be the toast," she said. He finally relented, realizing his wife was right.

In the spirit of Sergei's melancholy toast, we ate in silence. Words were simply not necessary. Sometimes, the best way to handle occasions such as this is with reserved silence. We were all sharing the same thoughts. Expressing them verbally only would have made things even more painful. As much as I wanted to say something to soothe their sadness, I knew there was simply no point.

It is no coincidence that it is Ukrainian custom to not give toasts at funeral wakes, nor to even speak at all. Our last supper certainly had the feel of a funeral, so it was only fitting we followed suit.

While we ate in our shared silence, I fully realized that despite my general criticisms of Ukrainian customs and the perceived rudeness of Ukrainians in general, the love and generosity I experienced from both Katya and her family was the *true* Ukraine—the one lying just beneath the deceptively blunt exterior.

When we were done eating, the mood lifted slightly when we presented Sergei and Elena with a CD player we had bought earlier in the day from a hot, stuffy appliance store—from a salesman with noxious body odor pouring out of his short-sleeved shirt. Nothing spells customer satisfaction like a stinky Ukrainian salesman. This gift was a small token of appreciation for everything they had done.

After we had finished eating, Sergei tested out his new toy by playing the handful of CDs we bought him. This seemed to lighten the mood— if only for a moment. The brief moment of levity came to an end when "Sharmanka" came on, reducing everyone to tears—first Sergei, then Katya, Natasha, Elena, and, finally, myself.

Elena composed herself and headed into the kitchen to fix tea, which she served with a sponge cake she picked up at nearby bakery. It was here where I learned not to assume that silver-colored decorative beads were candy. They were actually made of metal (and hopefully not lead), which I learned by attempting to bite into several of them at once, nearly cracking my teeth. Fortunately, I caught my mistake early enough and didn't swallow them, spitting them out into a napkin. At least, everyone got a laugh out of it before we headed off to bed, though I doubt anybody got much sleep. I certainly didn't. I lay there for an eternity trying to imagine what Katya and her parents were thinking.

The next morning, following breakfast, the time had finally come for Katya to say goodbye. She was about to start a new life in a whole new culture and country. Of course, my life would be changing as well—just not nearly as drastically as Katya's. My friends and family would still be close by. My customs and culture would still be the same. I would still be speaking my native language. For Katya, everything was about to change. And there was no turning back.

Nastya was the first to say goodbye. She was unable to join us on the drive to Kiev due to work. Katya and Nastya's goodbye was heartbreaking to watch. They simply hugged one another tightly, crying so hard, their bodies shook. I could only imagine what they were feeling on the inside—probably similar to the feeling I had when I left Ukraine and Katya on my last trip. However, as painful as my goodbye had been, this one was a lot more permanent. No matter how hard I tried, I couldn't fathom what it would be like to leave my family and move to an entirely different country and culture. I know people do it all the time, but I didn't even leave home for college.

Katya, Nastya, Sergei, and Elena sat in Katya's bedroom and embraced, through tears and Russian that needed no translation. Even Fernando joined in the family's goodbye, perched upon Katya's shoulder. I stood in the hallway, respecting their privacy.

After Katya kissed Fernando goodbye and put him back into his cage, we headed outside with our first load of luggage. Waiting for us in a van was Ivan—yet another driver who owed Sergei some sort of favor. Ivan was a fifty-something overweight schlub with an old-fashioned curly-cue moustache—the anti-Maxim. He wore an overly-tight, stained tank top, which allowed his massive, hairy potbelly to protrude above a pair of ragged Adidas warm-up pants. He drove an old rusted out van, littered with empty chip bags and cigarette butts. Somehow, this van was expected to transport us on our six-hour drive to Kiev. I wasn't sure what was most likely to break down first: Ivan, or the van?

Ivan was accompanied by a haggard-looking woman with a bad dye job, who I naturally assumed was his wife. I found out later that she was a "friend" who coming along for a free night of romance in Kiev. She looked as though she could well have been picked up in front of the Hotel Dnipropetrovsk en route to Katya's apartment.

We settled into the van (including Nastya, whose work-place was on our route). After we dropped Nastya off, she ran alongside the van, waving at Katya with tears in her eyes until she disappeared from view. Not another word was spoken until Dnipropetrovsk was behind us for good.

Six hours later, we arrived in Kiev. Our lodging for the evening was a dormitory room at the Taras Shevchenko National University of Kiev.

It was a small, cramped room, barely spacious enough for two people, let alone four. There was literally only enough floor space for two beds, which were put together in a L-formation. And of course, the shower left much to be desired—it didn't work at all. After dropping us off, we didn't see Ivan and his "friend" again until the next morning when we headed off to the airport.

After freshening up, we headed out into the Kiev evening. We all seemed to be in a subdued daze—a combination of exhaustion and resignation to the fact that we were in a purgatory between two worlds —our past and our future; the white space between chapters. With the sad weight of this awareness on our minds, nobody had much to say, as our new tomorrow awaited.

Compared to the other parts of Ukraine, I was rather impressed with what Kiev had to offer. For starters, it had a much more western European feel to it. It also seemed a lot cleaner. The architecture was more modern. And perhaps most impressive, there was actual English signage and more spoken English. For once, Katya didn't have to warn me to stop speaking "the English." Somehow, I stumbled into an alternate universe Ukraine. The people seemed more open to foreigners, which really came as no surprise considering Kiev clearly has more foreigners than most other cities in Ukraine. Beneath the main square of the city was a huge, modern shopping mall filled with countless American brand-name stores.

Meanwhile, my stomach issues had returned, so we headed into a McDonald's to use the restroom. What would bladders and bowels across the world do without the convenience of McDonald's restrooms? However, this was Ukraine, so nothing was as easy as it should be. A keypad passcode was required in order to enter the restroom and the only way to obtain the passcode was by making a purchase, which was the last thing my aching stomach desired. Expecting a menu full of Ukrainian-centric items such as *McBorscht* or *Filet-O-Gelatin-Fish*, I was surprised that the offerings were *exactly* as they were back in the U.S. There was *one* exception, however; the Quarter Pounder was dubbed the Royale with Cheese. I couldn't help but chuckle to myself, as I thought of Samuel L. Jackson in one of my all-time favorite movies: *Pulp Fiction*.

I ended up buying Katya a cherry pie, obtained the password, and took care of my business. At least I didn't have to pay directly. And at least it was a McDonald's, rather than a Ukrainian outhouse. I did notice that the employees in this McDonald's were surprisingly upbeat and cheerful—one of the few places in Ukraine where I had encountered such friendly and courteous staff. In place of glares ... smiles. In place of snarls ..."thank yous". When I mentioned this to Katya, she told me that McDonald's workers in Ukraine have to be trained in American friendliness and are literally expected to be smiling at all times. This had to be one of the hardest jobs in all of Ukraine.

On my way out of the restroom, I had an unexpected moment of serendipity when I ran into the very same missionaries I had spoken to at the airport in Detroit, almost three weeks prior. What were the odds that I would not only run into these same people again, but that they would be leaving on the same day? They told me that their trip had been nothing short of an amazing learning experience. They didn't have a single criticism about Ukraine whatsoever. Nothing negative to say. They truly had a wonderful time and all hoped to return someday. I suppose it's really all a matter of perspective.

On the way back to the dormitory, we stopped at a deli for some bread and lunchmeat. At the deli counter stood the first black person I had seen in Ukraine who wasn't wearing face paint and tribal gear. Once again, I was reminded that at least *part* of Ukraine was up to speed, waiting for the rest of the country to catch up.

After arriving back at the dormitory and having eaten our sandwiches, Elena produced tea and cookies from her purse for dessert.

It was then time to sleep before our world would once again change forever.

40

COMING TO AMERICA

morning arrived and we headed off to the airport, bracing for the inevitable: separation. No matter how excited we were for our future, the pangs of separation outweighed these feelings. This was a feeling I remembered all too well from the previous summer. Once again, I couldn't imagine how Katya and her parents felt at that moment. Tearful goodbyes at airports would become a fixture in all our lives and something nobody would ever become accustomed to.

Prior to our expected separation there was a totally unexpected one.

While struggling with my suitcase through the throngs of people in the crowded airport terminal, I lost sight of Katya and her parents. At first, I assumed that I would quickly find them. However, there were too many people for me to be able to see them in the moving crowd. Perhaps things would have been easier if they had realized that I had been separated from the pack right away. But by the time they figured it out, I was completely out of view. I tried not to panic, assuming that it was only a matter of time before they would find me.

When I finally realized just how far I had drifted from where I first became separated, I turned around, going upstream against traffic, hoping that I would somehow cross paths with Katya and her parents. But there was no sign of them. Now, I really began to panic, praying that I wouldn't be singled out, kidnapped, and sold into sex slavery. I kept circling around a relatively small area, like those scuba divers I encountered in the Black Sea. And each time around, my panic deepened.

Almost thirty minutes after we first became separated, I heard my name mentioned in a thick accent over the PA system in the middle of a message spoken in Russian. However, I had no idea what the announcer had said and therefore didn't know what to do, but I felt comforted by the fact that I now knew for sure that they knew I was lost. In the meantime, I continued walking around in circles. A few moments later, the announcer repeated the message—just in case I didn't hear it the first time, or perhaps learned Russian in a span of a few seconds. At that point, I decided simply to sit against a column and pray that I would be found.

Minutes later, I looked up and saw Katya running towards me, in tears. Her parents were right behind her. Katya hugged me like a runaway puppy that had been found.

"We thought you had been kidnapped!" she exclaimed, legitimizing my concerns. "Where were you?"

"I thought I was going to be kidnapped. Where were you?" I replied.

"We thought you were behind us. How could you be so irresponsible?" Katya added.

"You lost me! How am I irresponsible?" I said, flummoxed.

"I'm going to need to get you a leash!" Katya retorted.

Sergei and Elena approached.

"We're so glad that you're okay," Elena said.

"We better get going," Sergei said, glancing at his watch, clearly annoyed by my disappearing act. Fortunately, we had arrived at the airport early enough to make up for lost time.

Katya took me tightly by the hand. "Do-not-let-me-go," she warned, as though she was speaking to a small child. We headed toward the security line.

Sergei and Elena remained with us until the last possible moment. They hugged and kissed both of us goodbye, holding on to their daughter tightly, in full awareness of the fact that they had no idea when they would see her again. I stepped aside as Sergei and Elena continued to shower their daughter with hugs and kisses and parting words, for which no translation was expected, or even necessary.

"Bobby ... remember your promise to us," Sergei reminded me, glassy-eyed, referring to the promise I made that they would see their daughter at least once a year.

"I will," I said, fully hoping I would be able to live up to this promise. The reality was, I didn't know how often we would be able to afford for Katya to fly back. At that point, I didn't even have a job lined up. And it would be months before Katya could legally work. We would have to cross that bridge when we came to it.

And with that, it was time to go.

After passing through security, we waved goodbye until Sergei and Elena were out of sight.

And then it was just us. And the future that lay ahead.

As we headed toward our gate, Katya began to sob. I simply held her, and told her over and over that everything was going to be okay, flooded with a painful reminder of the feeling of loss and separation I had encountered on the plane on my previous trip. At least this time I wasn't alone. But in that exact moment, I was keenly aware that Kayta and her parents could not have felt any more lonely.

By the time we boarded our plane, Katya seemed more composed. But as we took off, she broke down in tears again, as she stared out of the tiny aircraft window and literally watched her country grow smaller and further away. I held Katya's hand with one hand and my crucifix with the other, reminding her once again of how much I loved her and how everything was going to be fine, despite the wide-open road that was our new life together.

After a brief, two-hour flight, we arrived in Amsterdam for an eight-hour layover. Katya's sadness seemed to have dissipated—at least for the time being. The soul-sucking nature of airports and layovers have that effect. They eventually turn us numb, no matter the circumstance.

We passed the time by watching the player piano in the lounge that I remembered so clearly from a few weeks prior. Just as we sat down, the phantom player started playing "Fly Me to the Moon," one of the songs I had put on a mix tape that I sent to Katya shortly after we had first met. We then drifted through what was essentially a shopping mall disguised as an airport.

Nothing felt real anymore. We quickly lost count of how many times we asked one another "Is this really happening?" thinking that by asking, we would both wake up from what was surely a dream in separate beds, in separate parts of the world.

In the meantime, our layover dragged on and it started to feel as though our life together in the U.S. was going to remain in eternal airport purgatory. The only thing that would have made things more excruciating would be if our flight was delayed. Fortunately, it was not.

Our flight from Amsterdam to Detroit was highlighted by a horrific stench coming from what I assumed was the restroom, close to where we were seated. Our apologetic flight attendant informed us that we were actually smelling sheep testicles that a passenger had brought aboard on a previous flight—for reasons perhaps not even known to God. A fitting end to my Ukrainian adventure!

Almost twenty four hours after leaving Dnipropetrovsk, we arrived in Detroit. Despite some paranoid apprehension on both our parts, Katya passed through customs without incident.

We loaded our luggage onto a cart and—with a deep breath—headed through the opaque sliding glass doors, adorned with the words:

"WELCOME TO MICHIGAN"

... taking our first steps into our future.

49097119R00158

Made in the USA
Charleston, SC
16 November 2015